Ame
Recipes

A 1990 HOMETOWN COLLECTION

America's Best Recipes

ISBN: 0-8487-1009-6
ISSN: 0898-9982

Manufactured in the United States of America
First Printing 1990

Executive Editor: Ann H. Harvey
Production Manager: Jerry Higdon
Associate Production Manager: Rick Litton
Art Director: Bob Nance
Production Assistant: Theresa L. Beste

America's Best Recipes: A 1990 Hometown Collection

Editor: Janice L. Krahn
Copy Editor: Mary Ann Laurens
Editorial Assistants: Kay Hicks, Kelly E. Hooper
Director, Test Kitchen: Vanessa Taylor Johnson
Assistant Director, Test Kitchen: Gayle Hays Sadler
Test Kitchen Home Economists: Angie Neskaug,
   Christina A. Pieroni, Kathleen Royal, Jan A. Smith
Senior Photographer: Jim Bathie
Photo Stylist: Kay E. Clarke
Senior Designer: Cynthia R. Cooper
Designer: Melissa Jones Clark

Project Consultants: Meryle Evans, Audrey P. Stehle

Illustrations by Dana Moore

Cover: *America's favorite flavor is celebrated with Wonderful
Hot Chocolate (page 16), Chocolate Chip Cookies (page 27),
Fudge Truffle Cake (page 26), French Double Chocolate Pie
(page 43), and English Toffee (page 34).*

Frontispiece: *Farm and fields in Crawford County, Iowa*

Oxmoor House, Inc., is also the publisher of *Cooking
Light* books. For subscription information for *Cooking
Light* magazine, write to *Cooking Light*®, P.O. Box C-549,
Birmingham, Alabama 35283.

Contents

Introduction

The very best recipes from treasured community cookbooks are now celebrated in one volume, *America's Best Recipes - A 1990 Hometown Collection*. We collected recipes from across the country to discover the delicious fare responsible for the reputation for excellence that American cuisine possesses. Our experienced food writers chose recipes that were "must tries"—those on the cutting edge of current food trends as well as those that simply represented good home cooking. In addition, we asked cookbook committee chairpersons to nominate recipes that they considered to be noteworthy. Over six hundred recipes were rigorously tested, judged, and rated on a scale of one to three (three being outstanding) by our staff of home economists to ensure that each recipe met our high standards. Only those select recipes that received the highest ratings were included in this volume.

The result is *America's Best Recipes*—a collection of over four hundred outstanding regional recipes from across America. Here you'll find recipes for the way you like to cook, whether you need to use up an abundant supply of garden vegetables or need an eye-catching, extra-special dessert for a festive occasion. We focused special attention upon the luscious world of chocolate! Whether you are a bittersweet, semisweet, milk, or white chocolate lover, you'll be sure to find your favorite among our collection of scrumptious chocolate recipes.

This cookbook salutes the volunteers who have successfully raised the funds critical to meeting the needs of their communities. Each cookbook featured was a labor of love—an accomplishment each organization can be proud of. We invite you to review the Acknowledgments beginning on page 324, and order other cookbooks that may be of interest to you. The successes of the organizations responsible for creating the fascinating community cookbooks featured in *America's Best Recipes - A 1990 Hometown Collection* depend upon your support.

The Editors

In Celebration of Chocolate

A street lamp in the shape of a milk chocolate kiss lights the corner of Cocoa and E. Chocolate avenues in Hershey, Pennsylvania, founded in 1903 by Milton Hershey. Mr. Hershey's personal beliefs regarding the obligations of wealth and the importance of the quality of life in his community led him to establish the Milton Hershey School in 1909 to provide a home and an education for needy orphan boys.

All About Chocolate

Whether one prefers bittersweet, semisweet, milk, or white chocolate, it seems that almost everyone is a chocolate lover. The unique, creamy texture and rich taste of chocolate have made it one of the world's favorite flavors.

The essence of chocolate, the cacao bean, is derived from evergreen trees of the genus Theobroma cacao, "the food of the gods." It took Cortez (while conquering Mexico for Spain in the early 16th century) to appreciate the importance of *chocolatl* ("choco" meaning cocoa, and "latl" meaning water) when he observed the Aztec Emperor Montezuma sipping the thick, frothy beverage from a golden goblet. The Aztec chocolatl was a spicy, bitter-tasting beverage that included chile peppers, black pepper, annatto, and corn flour. Cortez returned to Spain laden with cacao beans. Spanish monks followed the Aztec's recipe for chocolatl, but added cane sugar to the mixture.

Eventually the beverage's popularity spread to Italy, France, Holland, and England. In England, drinking chocolate became so popular that chocolate houses were created where people in the highest social circles gathered to enjoy the exotic, elite beverage. Cacao beans came to the shores of America around 1760 when a group of fishermen from Massachusetts accepted the beans in exchange for fish. Several years later, the first American chocolate factory was established in Dorchester, Massachusetts, by Doctor James Baker (chocolate was thought to have medicinal properties), and America's love affair with chocolate began.

We invite you to sample the following collection of outstanding chocolate recipes and enjoy the unique richness of chocolate in all of its forms (recipes begin on page 16).

Types of Chocolate

To understand the differences between types of chocolate, it helps to start at the beginning of the chocolate-making process. All chocolate begins with cacao beans which are dried, partially fermented, roasted, and ground before being turned into the various forms of chocolate that reach the marketplace.

Cacao (cocoa) beans are harvested from the fruit pods of the cacao tree which grows in a limited climate, 20 degrees north and south of the Equator, and mainly in West Africa and Latin America. The hard pods grow directly on the tree branches to a length of 6 to 12 inches and a width of 3 to 4 inches. Each pod contains 20 to 40 cacao beans, 1 to 1½ inches long. The beans are cleaned and roasted to bring out their full flavor; then the outer shells are removed.

Cacao nibs, which contain more than 50 percent cocoa butter, are the inside "meat" of the cacao beans.

Cocoa butter is the vegetable fat contained in the cacao nib. The nibs are ground by a process that produces enough heat and pressure to liquefy and extract the cocoa butter.

Chocolate liquor is the liquid essence of chocolate that remains after the cocoa butter has been extracted from the cacao nibs. Chocolate liquor is the ingredient that makes all real chocolate products truly chocolate.

American-process cocoa is the powder ground from the chocolate liquor after most of the cocoa butter has been extracted. (Cocoa powder can contain 8 to 24 percent cocoa butter.) Cocoa powder has the lowest fat content of any chocolate product derived from the cacao bean.

Dutch-process cocoa powder, a darker cocoa powder with a milder flavor than that of American-process cocoa powder, is produced when chocolate liquor is treated with an alkali agent.

Unsweetened chocolate, commonly called bitter, baking, or cooking chocolate, is chocolate liquor that has been cooled and molded. Unsweetened chocolate is the basis of most other types of chocolate and is sold in 8-ounce packages or in 1-ounce molded blocks.

Bittersweet chocolate is unsweetened chocolate that has been sweetened slightly with sugar. Bittersweet chocolate must contain at least 35 percent chocolate liquor and may contain as much as 60 percent.

Semisweet chocolate is unsweetened chocolate that has been sweetened with sugar and has extra cocoa butter and flavorings added to soften it and give it a satiny gloss. To be called semisweet chocolate, the product must contain at least 35 percent chocolate liquor. It is molded into 1-ounce blocks and sold in 8-ounce packages or formed into chocolate chips that are lightly glazed so that they will retain their shape during baking.

Sweet baking chocolate, often called German sweet chocolate or sweet dark chocolate, is sweetened bitter chocolate that lacks the extra cocoa butter of semisweet chocolate and is therefore darker and more brittle. Sweet baking chocolate contains more sugar than semisweet chocolate, and it must contain at least 15 percent chocolate liquor.

Milk chocolate is semisweet chocolate that has milk or cream added to it and must contain at least 10 percent chocolate liquor. Milk chocolate is sold in various shapes, bars, and chips.

White chocolate is made with cocoa butter, sugar, milk, and vanilla and has a very sweet, subtle flavor and creamy texture. White chocolate contains no chocolate liquor. In lower grades of white chocolate, most of the cocoa butter has been removed and is replaced by vegetable fat. Read ingredient labels carefully before purchasing.

Almond bark is an artificial chocolate made with colorings, flavorings, and vegetable fat instead of cocoa butter. It is sold in 1½-pound packages or in blocks or disks.

Chocolate flavor is the label applied to products that get their flavor from cocoa and/or chocolate liquor, but do not contain enough of these ingredients to meet the government's labeling standards for a true chocolate product.

Artificial chocolate is a product of food technology and the laboratory. Artificial chocolate products do not contain any components derived from the cacao bean.

Carob is the powder of the dried locust bean. Carob has a sweet flavor that is somewhat similar to the flavor of chocolate. Carob does not contain any caffeine.

Chocolate Substitutions

1 (1-ounce) square unsweetened chocolate = 3 tablespoons cocoa powder plus 1 tablespoon vegetable shortening

1 (1-ounce) square semisweet chocolate = 3 tablespoons semi-sweet chocolate morsels or 1 (1-ounce) square unsweetened chocolate plus 1 tablespoon sugar

1 (6-ounce) package semisweet chocolate morsels = 6 (1-ounce) squares semisweet chocolate or 6 tablespoons cocoa powder plus 7 tablespoons sugar and ¼ cup vegetable shortening

1 (4-ounce) bar sweet baking chocolate = ¼ cup cocoa powder plus ⅓ cup sugar and 3 tablespoons vegetable shortening

1 envelope premelted unsweetened chocolate = 3 tablespoons cocoa powder plus 1 tablespoon vegetable oil or melted vegetable shortening

Storing Chocolate

The ideal storage temperature for chocolate is 78°F. Chocolate can be stored for well over a year without any significant change in flavor or texture if stored tightly wrapped or covered in a cool, dry place (65° to 70°F).

When chocolate is exposed to temperature changes, "cocoa butter bloom" (the grayish coating that sometimes appears on chocolate) may occur. This phenomenon is merely the cocoa butter rising to the surface of the chocolate. Blooming is harmless and will not alter the chocolate's flavor, but it may make the chocolate crumbly in texture.

If sweetened chocolate is not stored tightly wrapped, condensation may form, causing the sugar to dissolve and rise to the surface of the chocolate as "sugar bloom." Sugar bloom does not affect the flavor of chocolate and, once melted, the chocolate will regain its original color.

Melting Chocolate

Chocolate may be melted in a double boiler, over direct heat, or in the microwave oven. Whichever method you prefer, use a gentle heat to prevent scorching, and be sure your utensils are completely dry. Just one drop of moisture will cause the chocolate to "tighten up" and become lumpy and stiff. If this should occur, stir in one teaspoon of shortening for each ounce of chocolate. Unsweetened chocolate liquefies when melted, but semisweet and sweet baking chocolate will retain their molded shapes until they are stirred. To melt chocolate more quickly, cut it or chop it into small pieces.

Double Boiler

The double boiler is really the safest method to use when melting chocolate to prevent scorching. Simply place chocolate in the top of a double boiler over hot, not boiling, water.

Direct Heat

Placing chocolate in a pan over direct heat is a riskier method to use when it comes to melting chocolate. Caution and attention must be exercised to prevent scorching when using this method. If you choose the direct heat method, be sure you use a heavy saucepan, very low heat, and stir the chocolate constantly.

Microwave Oven

The microwave oven is an easy, fast, and neat way to melt chocolate. To melt unsweetened chocolate and semisweet chocolate, unwrap the desired number of squares and break them in half. Place the chocolate in a measuring cup or bowl, and microwave at HIGH for the minimum time listed below; stir the chocolate and allow it to stand several minutes to complete the melting process.

1 (1-ounce) square chocolate = 1 to 1½ minutes at HIGH
2 (1-ounce) squares chocolate = 1½ to 2 minutes at HIGH
3 (1-ounce) squares chocolate = 2 to 2½ minutes at HIGH
4 (1-ounce) squares chocolate = 2½ to 3 minutes at HIGH
6 ounces semisweet chocolate chips = 1 to 1½ minutes at HIGH

Garnishing with Chocolate

Grated Chocolate

Grated chocolate is perhaps the simplest chocolate garnish. To grate chocolate, rub the chocolate across the grater, catching the grated chocolate on a piece of wax paper. Any size grating surface can be used, depending upon the dish you are garnishing and the look you are trying to achieve.

Chocolate Curls

Chocolate curls come in a variety of shapes and sizes with a personality all their own. Whether you want curls that are diminutive and delicate or large and dramatic, the key to success is to work with the chocolate at the proper temperature. The chocolate should be slightly warm to the touch but still firm.

The easiest way to create chocolate curls is to draw a vegetable peeler along the underside of the chocolate, using a steady even pressure. Use a toothpick to lift the chocolate curl onto a wax paper-lined tray, then chill until firm enough to handle. When firm, chocolate curls can be transferred to an airtight container and stored almost indefinitely in the refrigerator. Use squares or larger blocks or chunks of chocolate, depending upon what size curl you want.

For larger, more dramatic curls, melt 4 (1-ounce) squares semisweet chocolate, and pour the melted chocolate out onto a wax paper-lined baking sheet. Spread the chocolate with a spatula into a smooth, even 3-inch-wide strip. Place the baking sheet in the refrigerator to chill the chocolate until it feels slightly tacky but not firm. (If the chocolate becomes too hard, the curls will break, and if it is too soft, the chocolate will not curl.) When the chocolate is the correct consistency, gently draw the edge of a knife across the chocolate strips to form curls. Transfer curls to a tray, using a wooden pick, and chill until firm.

Chocolate Leaves

Chocolate leaves are an elegant, impressive garnish. Choose leaves that have distinctive veins on the underside, which is where you will be spreading the chocolate, as this will create a more interesting pattern. Rose, mint, and lemon leaves work well, though most leaves are safe to use, providing they have been thoroughly washed to remove all traces of sprays or insecticides.

Make sure the leaves are dry. Melt semisweet, milk, or white chocolate. Using a small, soft-bristled pastry brush, paint the melted chocolate on the underside of each leaf. Be careful not to let the chocolate go over the edge of the leaf, as it will make separation of the leaf from the chocolate difficult. Place the coated leaves on a wax paper-lined tray, chocolate side up, and chill until the chocolate is firm. To remove the leaf from the chocolate, grasp the leaf at the stem end, and carefully peel the leaf away from the chocolate. Return the chocolate leaves to the tray, then cover and chill until they are needed.

Chocolate Silhouettes/Designs

Any design or outline can be traced with chocolate to form unique garnishes of your own creation. Simply place the desired pattern on a tray, and cover with a piece of wax paper. Then, melt semisweet or milk chocolate; let cool slightly. Spoon the melted chocolate into a pastry bag fitted with a small writing tip. Pipe chocolate with steady pressure onto a wax paper-lined tray, tracing over the desired pattern. Chill the chocolate patterns on the tray until the chocolate is firm, then carefully peel the wax paper away from the chocolate. Cover and chill the patterns until ready to use.

Chocolate Cups

Chocolate cups are a popular way to present an elegant dessert. For chocolate cups, melt 2 cups semisweet chocolate chips along with 2 teaspoons shortening; let cool slightly. Place 12 (2¾-inch) paper baking cups in muffin pans. Miniature (1¾-inch) paper baking cups can also be used. Using a narrow, soft-bristled pastry brush, thickly and evenly coat the sides and bottom of each cup. Chill cups 10 minutes or until firm; then apply another coating of melted chocolate to any thin spots. Cover and chill until very firm (about 1 hour). Carefully peel paper from each cup. Cover and chill at least 1 hour. Fill chilled cups with ice cream, chocolate mousse, or almost any filling you desire.

Wonderful Hot Chocolate

2½ (1-ounce) squares
  unsweetened chocolate
½ cup water
¾ cup sugar
Dash of salt

½ cup whipping cream,
  whipped
1 gallon plus 3 cups hot milk
Additional whipped cream

Combine chocolate and water in top of a double boiler; bring water in bottom of double boiler to a boil. Reduce heat to low; cook until chocolate melts, stirring occasionally. Add sugar and salt; cook over medium heat, stirring occasionally, 4 minutes or until sugar dissolves.

Remove from heat; let chocolate mixture cool to room temperature. Fold in whipped cream.

To serve, place 2 tablespoons chocolate mixture in a cup. Add 1 cup hot milk, and stir well. Garnish with additional whipped cream. Yield: 1 gallon plus 3 cups.

The Kentucky Derby Museum Cookbook
The Kentucky Derby Museum
Louisville, Kentucky

Chocolate Syrup

¾ cup cocoa
½ cup sugar
1¼ cups light corn syrup

½ cup hot water
1 tablespoon butter
1 teaspoon vanilla extract

Combine cocoa and sugar in a small saucepan; add corn syrup and hot water, stirring well. Cook over medium heat until mixture comes to a boil, stirring occasionally; cook 3 minutes.

Remove from heat. Add butter and vanilla, stirring until butter melts and mixture is smooth. Serve warm or cool over ice cream or pound cake, or stir into cold milk. Store in an airtight container in the refrigerator. Yield: 2⅓ cups.   Alice Kniskern

The True Essentials of a Feast
The Library of Congress/LC Cooking Club
Washington, DC

Chocolate Pancakes

1½ cups all-purpose flour
1 teaspoon baking soda
½ teaspoon salt
¼ cup sugar
¼ cup cocoa

2 eggs, lightly beaten
1 cup milk
¼ cup butter or margarine, melted
½ cup milk chocolate morsels

Sift together first 5 ingredients in a large bowl. Combine eggs and milk; add to flour mixture, stirring just until dry ingredients are moistened. Add melted butter and chocolate morsels, stirring just until combined.

For each pancake, pour about 2 tablespoons batter onto a hot, lightly greased griddle. Turn pancakes when tops are covered with bubbles and edges look cooked. Yield: 18 (4-inch) pancakes.

The Delaware Heritage Cookbook
The Delaware Heritage Commission
Wilmington, Delaware

Mocha Nut Bread

2 cups all-purpose flour
½ teaspoon baking soda
¼ teaspoon salt
1 cup sugar
½ cup cocoa
¼ cup instant coffee granules
1¼ cups sour cream

2 eggs, lightly beaten
⅓ cup butter, melted
1 (6-ounce) package semisweet chocolate morsels
½ cup chopped pecans or walnuts (optional)

Combine first 6 ingredients in a medium bowl; stir well. Combine sour cream, eggs, and butter in a large bowl; stir well. Add flour mixture to sour cream mixture, stirring until blended. Stir in chocolate morsels and, if desired, pecans. Pour batter into a greased and floured 9- x 5- x 3-inch loafpan. Bake at 350° for 50 to 55 minutes or until top appears glazed and sides pull away from pan. Let cool in pan 10 minutes; remove from pan, and let cool completely on a wire rack. Yield: 1 loaf.   Elizabeth A. Ennis

Cookin' with the Lion
The Penn State Alumni Association
University Park, Pennsylvania

Chocolate Chip Coffee Cake

½ cup butter or margarine,
  softened
1 cup sugar
2 eggs
2 cups all-purpose flour
1½ teaspoons baking powder
1 teaspoon baking soda

1 cup sour cream
1 teaspoon vanilla extract
1 (12-ounce) package
  semisweet chocolate
  morsels
½ cup sugar
½ teaspoon ground cinnamon

Cream butter; gradually add 1 cup sugar, beating well at medium speed of an electric mixer. Add eggs, one at a time, beating well after each addition.

Combine flour, baking powder, and soda; add to creamed mixture alternately with sour cream, beginning and ending with flour mixture. Mix after each addition. Stir in vanilla.

Spread half of batter in a greased and floured 13- x 9- x 2-inch pan. Sprinkle with chocolate morsels. Combine ½ cup sugar and cinnamon. Sprinkle half of cinnamon-sugar over morsels. Top with remaining batter; sprinkle with remaining cinnamon-sugar. Bake at 350° for 30 minutes or until a wooden pick inserted in center comes out clean. Yield: 15 servings.   Judy Toth

Favorite Recipes from Friends
The Town Hill School
Lakeville, Connecticut

Chocolate Sour Cream Pound Cake

1 cup butter
2 cups sugar
1 cup firmly packed brown
  sugar
6 eggs
¼ teaspoon baking soda

1 cup sour cream
2½ cups all-purpose flour
½ cup cocoa
½ teaspoon salt
2 teaspoons vanilla extract
Powdered sugar (optional)

Cream butter; gradually add 2 cups sugar and brown sugar, beating well at medium speed of an electric mixer. Add eggs, one at a time, beating after each addition.

Combine soda and sour cream. Sift together flour, cocoa, and salt. Add to creamed mixture, alternately with sour cream mixture, beginning and ending with flour mixture. Mix just until blended after each addition. Stir in vanilla.

Pour batter into a greased and floured 10-inch tube pan. Bake at 325° for 1 hour and 20 minutes or until a wooden pick inserted in center comes out clean. Let cool in pan 15 minutes. Remove from pan; let cool completely on a wire rack. Sift powdered sugar over top of cake, if desired. Yield: one 10-inch cake.   Phyllis Parrish

. . . More Than Cookies!
The Northwest Georgia Girl Scout Council, Inc.
Atlanta, Georgia

Chocolate Sheath Cake

2 cups all-purpose flour	½ cup buttermilk
2 cups sugar	2 eggs
1 cup water	1 teaspoon baking soda
1 cup butter or margarine	1 teaspoon vanilla extract
¼ cup cocoa	Frosting (recipe follows)

Combine flour and sugar; stir well. Combine water, butter, and cocoa in a saucepan; bring to a boil, stirring until butter melts. Gradually add to flour mixture, beating well. Combine buttermilk, eggs, soda, and vanilla; mix well. Add to chocolate mixture; mix well. Pour batter into a greased 13- x 9- x 2-inch baking pan. Bake at 400° for 25 to 30 minutes or until a wooden pick inserted in center comes out clean. Let cool 10 minutes. Spread frosting over warm cake. Let cool completely on a wire rack. Yield: 15 servings.

Frosting

½ cup butter or margarine	¼ cup plus 2 tablespoons
¼ cup cocoa	milk
1 (16-ounce) package	1 cup chopped pecans or
powdered sugar, sifted	walnuts

Combine butter and cocoa in a saucepan; bring to a boil, stirring constantly. Add sugar and milk; stir until smooth (frosting will be thin). Stir in pecans. Yield: 2½ cups.   Edith Carlile

Central Texas Style
The Junior Service League of Killeen, Texas

Devil's Food Cake

½ cup cocoa
1½ teaspoons baking soda
½ cup water
⅔ cup butter or margarine,
  softened
1¾ cups sugar

2 eggs
¾ cup buttermilk
1 teaspoon vanilla extract
2½ cups sifted cake flour
½ teaspoon salt
Frosting (recipe follows)

Combine first 3 ingredients in a small bowl; stir well, and set aside. Cream butter; gradually add sugar, beating well at medium speed of an electric mixer. Add eggs, one at a time, beating well after each addition. Add cocoa mixture, beating until blended.

Combine buttermilk and vanilla in a small bowl. Combine flour and salt in a medium bowl; add flour mixture to creamed mixture alternately with buttermilk mixture, beginning and ending with flour mixture. Mix after each addition.

Pour batter into 2 greased and floured 9-inch round cakepans. Bake at 350° for 30 to 35 minutes or until a wooden pick inserted in center comes out clean. Let cool in pans 10 minutes; remove from pans, and let cool completely on wire racks.

Spread frosting between layers and on top and sides of cake. Yield: one 2-layer cake.

Frosting

1 cup firmly packed brown
  sugar
½ cup water
3 tablespoons butter or
  margarine
3 (1-ounce) squares semisweet
  chocolate

½ teaspoon salt
5 cups sifted powdered sugar
1 teaspoon vanilla extract
1 cup chopped pecans or
  walnuts

Combine brown sugar, water, butter, semisweet chocolate, and salt in a heavy saucepan. Bring mixture to a boil over medium heat, and cook 3 minutes. Remove from heat, and let cool slightly. Gradually add powdered sugar, beating at low speed of an electric mixer until mixture is smooth. Stir in vanilla and chopped pecans. Yield: 3½ cups.   Leila Brazell

The Florida Cooking Adventure
The Florida Federation of Women's Clubs
Lakeland, Florida

German's Sweet Chocolate Cake

1 (4-ounce) package sweet
  baking chocolate
½ cup water
1 cup butter or margarine,
  softened
2 cups sugar
4 eggs, separated

1 teaspoon vanilla extract
2½ cups all-purpose flour
1 teaspoon baking soda
½ teaspoon salt
1 cup buttermilk
Coconut-Pecan Frosting

Grease three 8-inch round cakepans, and line with wax paper; grease wax paper. Set aside.

Combine chocolate and water in top of a double boiler; bring water in bottom of double boiler to a boil. Reduce heat to low; cook until chocolate melts, stirring occasionally. Set aside to cool.

Cream butter; gradually add sugar, beating well at medium speed of an electric mixer. Add egg yolks, one at a time, beating well after each addition. Add chocolate mixture and vanilla to creamed mixture, beating until blended. Combine flour, soda, and salt; add to creamed mixture alternately with buttermilk, beginning and ending with flour mixture. Mix after each addition.

Beat egg whites (at room temperature) at high speed of electric mixer until stiff peaks form. Gently fold beaten egg whites into batter. Pour batter into prepared pans. Bake at 350° for 30 to 40 minutes or until a wooden pick inserted in center comes out clean. Let cool in pans 10 minutes; remove from pans, and let cool completely on wire racks. Spread Coconut-Pecan Frosting between layers and on top of cake. Yield: one 3-layer cake.

Coconut-Pecan Frosting

1 cup sugar
1 cup evaporated milk
½ cup butter or margarine
3 egg yolks

1 teaspoon vanilla extract
1⅓ cups flaked coconut
1 cup chopped pecans

Combine first 5 ingredients in a medium saucepan. Cook over medium heat 12 minutes or until mixture thickens, stirring constantly. Remove from heat. Add coconut and pecans; stir until frosting cools and reaches spreading consistency. Yield: 2¾ cups.

Breaking Bread Together
The Circle of Serbian Sisters
Columbus, Ohio

Black Forest Cherry Cake

2 (1-ounce) squares
  unsweetened chocolate
¼ cup water
⅔ cup butter, softened
1½ cups sugar
3 eggs
2 cups sifted cake flour
½ teaspoon baking soda
1 cup sour cream
1 teaspoon vanilla extract
½ cup sugar

¾ cup water
⅓ to ½ cup kirsch
3 cups whipping cream
½ cup sifted powdered sugar
¼ cup kirsch
1 cup maraschino cherries,
  chopped
Chocolate curls (optional)
6 to 12 maraschino cherries
  with stems (optional)

Grease and flour two 9-inch round cakepans, and line with wax paper; grease wax paper. Set aside.

Combine chocolate squares and ¼ cup water in top of a double boiler; bring water in bottom of double boiler to a boil. Reduce heat to low; cook until chocolate melts, stirring occasionally. Let cool.

Cream butter; gradually add 1½ cups sugar, beating well. Add eggs, one at a time, beating well after each addition.

Combine flour and soda; stir well. Add to creamed mixture, alternately with sour cream, beginning and ending with flour mixture. Mix after each addition. Stir in melted chocolate and vanilla.

Pour batter into prepared pans. Bake at 350° for 30 to 35 minutes or until a wooden pick inserted in center comes out clean. Let cool in pans 10 minutes. Remove from pans; cool completely on wire racks.

Combine ½ cup sugar and ¾ cup water in a small saucepan; bring to a boil, reduce heat, and simmer 5 minutes. Remove from heat, and let cool. Stir in ⅓ to ½ cup kirsch.

Prick surface of cake layers at 1-inch intervals with a wooden pick; pour syrup over layers. Cover and let stand overnight.

Beat whipping cream in a large mixing bowl at high speed of an electric mixer until foamy; gradually add powdered sugar and ¼ cup kirsch, beating until stiff peaks form. Spread 2 cups frosting on one cake layer; sprinkle with half of chopped cherries. Place second cake layer on top of cherries, and repeat procedure, using 1¾ cups frosting and remaining chopped cherries. Spread top and sides of cake with remaining 3½ cups frosting. If desired, garnish with chocolate curls and stemmed cherries. Yield: one 2-layer cake.

Savannah Style
The Junior League of Savannah, Georgia

White Chocolate Cake

4 ounces white chocolate,
  broken into pieces
½ cup water
1 cup butter, softened
2 cups sugar
4 eggs, separated

1 teaspoon vanilla extract
2½ cups sifted cake flour
1 teaspoon baking soda
½ teaspoon salt
1 cup buttermilk
White Chocolate Frosting

Combine white chocolate pieces and water in top of a double boiler; bring water in bottom of double boiler to a boil. Reduce heat to low; cook until chocolate melts, stirring frequently. Set aside, and let cool.

Cream butter; gradually add sugar, beating well at medium speed of an electric mixer. Add egg yolks, one at a time, beating well after each addition. Add chocolate mixture and vanilla, beating until blended.

Combine flour, soda, and salt; add to creamed mixture alternately with buttermilk, beginning and ending with flour mixture. Mix after each addition. Beat egg whites (at room temperature) at high speed of electric mixer until stiff peaks form. Gently fold beaten egg whites into batter.

Pour batter into 3 greased and floured 9-inch round cakepans. Bake at 350° for 30 to 35 minutes or until a wooden pick inserted in center comes out clean. Let cool in pans 10 minutes; remove from pans, and let cool completely on wire racks.

Spread White Chocolate Frosting between layers and on top and sides of cake. Yield: one 3-layer cake.

White Chocolate Frosting

3 egg yolks, beaten
1 cup sweetened condensed
  milk
1 cup sugar

½ cup butter, melted
4 ounces white chocolate,
  grated
1 cup pecans, chopped

Combine first 4 ingredients in top of a double boiler; bring water to a boil. Reduce heat to low; cook until thickened, stirring constantly. Add chocolate, stirring until chocolate melts and mixture is smooth. Stir in pecans. Yield: 2⅔ cups.   Sherry Taylor

Land of Cotton
John T. Morgan Academy
Selma, Alabama

Jessica's Chocolate Brownie Cheesecake

1 cup chocolate wafer crumbs
3 tablespoons butter, melted
1 (12-ounce) package semisweet chocolate morsels
3 (8-ounce) packages cream cheese, softened
1 cup sugar
3 eggs
1 (8-ounce) carton sour cream
1 teaspoon vanilla extract
⅛ teaspoon salt
1½ cups commercial brownies, cut into 1-inch cubes
Whipped cream (optional)

Combine crumbs and butter, stirring well. Firmly press crumb mixture evenly on bottom of a 9-inch springform pan. Set aside.

Place chocolate morsels in top of a double boiler; bring water to a boil. Reduce heat to low; cook until chocolate melts, stirring occasionally. Remove from heat, and set aside.

Beat cream cheese in a large bowl at high speed of an electric mixer until light and fluffy. Gradually add sugar, beating well. Add eggs, one at a time, beating well after each addition. Add sour cream, vanilla, and salt; mix well. Add melted chocolate; mix well. Fold in brownie cubes. Pour batter into prepared pan. Bake at 350° for 55 to 60 minutes or until cheesecake is set. Let cool to room temperature on a wire rack; chill at least 8 hours. To serve, carefully remove sides of springform pan. Garnish with whipped cream, if desired. Yield: 10 to 12 servings.

The Mystic Seaport All Seasons Cookbook
Mystic Seaport Museum Stores
Mystic, Connecticut

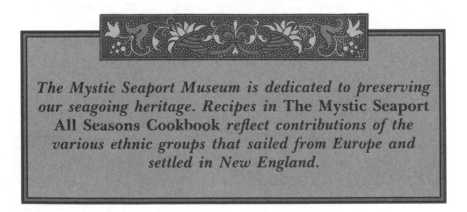

The Mystic Seaport Museum is dedicated to preserving our seagoing heritage. Recipes in The Mystic Seaport All Seasons Cookbook *reflect contributions of the various ethnic groups that sailed from Europe and settled in New England.*

White Chocolate Cheesecake

1½ cups graham cracker
  crumbs
2 tablespoons sugar
¼ cup plus 2 tablespoons
  unsalted butter, melted
10 ounces white chocolate,
  broken into pieces
4 (8-ounce) packages cream
  cheese, softened
½ cup unsalted butter,
  softened

¾ cup sugar, divided
3 tablespoons all-purpose
  flour
4 eggs
1 tablespoon plus 2 teaspoons
  vanilla extract, divided
Pinch of salt
2 cups sour cream
White chocolate curls
  (optional)

Combine graham cracker crumbs, 2 tablespoons sugar, and melted butter in a medium bowl, stirring well. Firmly press crumb mixture evenly on bottom and ½ inch up sides of a 9-inch springform pan. Chill 1 hour.

Place white chocolate pieces in top of a double boiler; bring water to a boil. Reduce heat to low; cook until chocolate melts, stirring frequently. Remove from heat, and stir until chocolate is smooth. Set aside, and let cool.

Combine cream cheese and ½ cup butter; beat well at high speed of an electric mixer until light and fluffy. Combine ½ cup sugar and flour, stirring well; add to creamed mixture, beating well. Add eggs, one at a time, beating well after each addition. Add cooled chocolate, 1½ tablespoons vanilla, and salt; beat until well blended. Pour mixture into prepared pan. Bake at 350° for 50 minutes or until cheesecake is set.

Combine sour cream, remaining ¼ cup sugar, and remaining ½ teaspoon vanilla in a small bowl; stir well. Spread sour cream mixture over cheesecake. Bake at 350° for 10 minutes. Let cheesecake cool to room temperature on a wire rack; chill at least 8 hours.

To serve, carefully remove sides of springform pan. Garnish cheesecake with white chocolate curls, if desired. Yield: 10 to 12 servings.   Ginny Puryear Fleming

Sampler
The Women's Art Guild, Laguna Gloria Art Museum
Austin, Texas

Fudge Truffle Cake

8 (1-ounce) squares semisweet
  chocolate
1 cup sugar
1 cup unsalted butter
4 eggs, beaten
½ cup brewed coffee

1 cup whipping cream
½ teaspoon vanilla extract
¼ cup sifted powdered sugar
Fresh raspberries, strawberries,
  or cherries
Chocolate leaves or curls

Grease a 9-inch springform pan, and line with wax paper; grease wax paper. Set aside.

Combine chocolate squares, 1 cup sugar, and butter in top of a double boiler; bring water to a boil. Reduce heat to low; cook until chocolate and butter melt, stirring occasionally. Set aside, and let mixture cool. Add beaten eggs and coffee, beating well at medium speed of an electric mixer.

Pour batter into prepared pan. Bake at 350° for 35 to 40 minutes or until top forms a crust. (Cake will not test done.) Let cool on a wire rack. Cover and chill at least 8 hours.

Beat whipping cream and vanilla until foamy; gradually add powdered sugar, beating until soft peaks form. To serve, carefully remove sides of springform pan. Garnish with whipped cream, raspberries, and chocolate leaves. Yield: 8 to 10 servings.

Palm Country Cuisine
The Junior League of Greater Lakeland, Florida

Black Bottom Cupcakes

1 (8-ounce) package cream
  cheese, softened
⅓ cup sugar
1 egg, beaten
⅛ teaspoon salt
1 (6-ounce) package
  semisweet chocolate
  morsels
1½ cups all-purpose flour

1 teaspoon baking soda
½ teaspoon salt
1 cup sugar
¼ cup cocoa
1 cup water
⅓ cup vegetable oil
1 teaspoon vinegar
1 teaspoon vanilla extract

Combine cream cheese, ⅓ cup sugar, egg, and ⅛ teaspoon salt in a medium bowl; beat well with a wire whisk. Stir in chocolate morsels, and set aside.

Sift together flour, soda, ½ teaspoon salt, 1 cup sugar, and cocoa. Combine water, oil, vinegar, and vanilla; add to flour mixture. Beat at low speed of an electric mixer until well blended.

Spoon batter into paper-lined miniature (1¾-inch) muffin pans, filling half full. Spoon 1 teaspoon reserved cream cheese mixture into center of each cupcake. Bake at 350° for 25 to 30 minutes. Let cool in pans 10 minutes; remove from pans, and let cupcakes cool completely on wire racks. Yield: 2½ dozen.   Rita Flood

Our Favorite Recipes
St. Edmond's Church
Philadelphia, Pennsylvania

Chocolate Chip Cookies

1 cup shortening
¾ cup sugar
¾ cup firmly packed brown
  sugar
2 eggs
1 teaspoon vanilla extract
1 teaspoon water
2¼ cups all-purpose flour

1 teaspoon baking soda
1 teaspoon salt
1 (12-ounce) package
  semisweet chocolate
  morsels
1 cup chopped pecans
  (optional)

Cream shortening in a large bowl at medium speed of an electric mixer. Gradually add sugars, beating well. Add eggs, vanilla, and water; beat well.

Combine flour, soda, and salt in a medium bowl; add flour mixture to creamed mixture, mixing well. Stir in chocolate morsels and, if desired, chopped pecans.

Drop dough by teaspoonfuls onto greased cookie sheets. Lightly press cookies with a fork to flatten slightly. Bake at 350° for 8 to 10 minutes. Let cool slightly on cookie sheets; transfer cookies to wire racks to cool completely. Yield: 10 dozen.   Wilma Capps

The Scott & White Collection
The Scott and White Memorial Hospital Auxiliary
Temple, Texas

White Chocolate Cookies

1 cup butter, softened
¾ cup sugar
¾ cup firmly packed light
  brown sugar
2 eggs
1 teaspoon vanilla extract
2½ cups all-purpose flour

1 teaspoon baking soda
1 teaspoon salt
12 ounces white chocolate,
  coarsely chopped
1¼ cups golden raisins
¾ cup coarsely chopped
  macadamia nuts

Cream butter; gradually add sugars, beating well at medium speed of an electric mixer. Add eggs, one at a time, beating well after each addition. Add vanilla; mix well.

Combine flour, soda, and salt in a medium bowl; gradually add to creamed mixture, mixing well. Stir in white chocolate, raisins, and chopped macadamia nuts.

Drop dough by rounded teaspoonfuls onto greased cookie sheets. Bake at 350° for 8 to 10 minutes or until golden brown. Let cool slightly on cookie sheets; transfer cookies to wire racks to cool completely. Yield: 6 dozen.

Lasting Impressions
The Saint Joseph's Hospital of Atlanta Auxiliary
Atlanta, Georgia

Rocky Road Fudge Bars

½ cup butter
1 (1-ounce) square
  unsweetened chocolate
2 eggs, beaten
1 cup sugar
1 cup all-purpose flour
1 teaspoon baking powder
1 teaspoon vanilla extract
½ to 1 cup chopped pecans
  or walnuts

Filling (recipe follows)
1 (6-ounce) package
  semisweet chocolate
  morsels (optional)
2 cups miniature
  marshmallows
Frosting (recipe follows)

Place butter and unsweetened chocolate in top of a double boiler; bring water to a boil. Reduce heat to low, and cook until butter and chocolate melt, stirring constantly. Let chocolate mixture cool to room temperature.

Combine chocolate mixture and eggs. Add sugar, beating well at medium speed of an electric mixer until blended.

Combine flour and baking powder; add to chocolate mixture, mixing well. Stir in vanilla and pecans.

Pour batter into a greased and floured 13- x 9- x 2-inch baking pan. Top with filling; if desired, sprinkle with chocolate morsels. Bake at 350° for 25 to 35 minutes or until a wooden pick inserted in center comes out clean. Top with marshmallows, and bake an additional 2 minutes. Remove from oven, and immediately pour frosting over marshmallows; swirl with a knife. Let cool completely; cut into bars. Yield: 3 dozen.

Filling

2 (3-ounce) packages cream cheese, softened
¼ cup butter, softened
1 egg
½ cup sugar
2 tablespoons all-purpose flour
½ teaspoon vanilla extract
¼ cup chopped pecans or walnuts

Combine cream cheese and butter in a medium mixing bowl; beat well at high speed of an electric mixer until smooth. Add egg, and beat well.

Combine sugar and flour; add to creamed mixture, mixing well. Stir in vanilla and pecans. Yield: 1½ cups.

Frosting

¼ cup butter
1 (1-ounce) square unsweetened chocolate
1 (16-ounce) package powdered sugar, sifted
2 ounces cream cheese, softened
¼ cup milk
1 teaspoon vanilla extract

Combine butter and chocolate in top of a double boiler; bring water to a boil. Reduce heat to low; cook until butter and chocolate melt, stirring occasionally.

Add sugar and remaining ingredients to chocolate mixture; stir until smooth. Yield: 2 cups.   Evelyn Whittenton Bingham

Taste of the Town—Second Serving
The Charity League of Lexington, North Carolina

Ultimate Brownie

4 (1-ounce) squares
  unsweetened chocolate
½ cup butter or margarine
1 cup sugar
1 cup firmly packed brown
  sugar
3 eggs, beaten

2 teaspoons vanilla extract
1½ cups all-purpose flour
½ teaspoon salt
1 cup chopped pecans or
  walnuts (optional)
Frosting (recipe follows)

Combine chocolate and butter in top of a double boiler; bring water to a boil. Reduce heat to low; cook until chocolate and butter melt, stirring occasionally. Remove from heat. Add sugars; stir well. Add eggs and vanilla; stir well. Add flour and salt, stirring until blended. Stir in pecans, if desired.

Spread batter in a greased 13- x 9- x 2-inch baking pan. Bake at 325° for 20 to 25 minutes. Let cool completely. Spread frosting over brownies. Cut into bars. Yield: 3 dozen.

Frosting

2 (1-ounce) squares
  unsweetened chocolate
2 tablespoons butter or
  margarine

⅓ cup half-and-half or
  evaporated milk
2½ cups sifted powdered
  sugar

Combine chocolate and butter in top of a double boiler; bring water to a boil. Reduce heat to low; cook until chocolate and butter melt, stirring occasionally. Remove from heat; stir in half-and-half. Add powdered sugar; beat at medium speed of an electric mixer until smooth. Yield: 1¼ cups.   Amy Grant

Angel Fare
St. Michael and All Angels Episcopal Church
Portland, Oregon

White Confetti Fudge

1½ pounds white chocolate,
  coarsely chopped
1 (14-ounce) can sweetened
  condensed milk

1 cup chopped candied
  cherries
1 teaspoon vanilla extract
⅛ teaspoon salt

Combine chocolate and milk in top of a double boiler; bring water to a boil. Reduce heat to low; cook until chocolate melts, stirring occasionally. Remove from heat, and stir until smooth. Stir in candied cherries, vanilla, and salt.

Spread mixture evenly in a wax paper-lined 8-inch square pan. Chill 2 to 3 hours or until mixture is firm. Invert pan, and peel off wax paper. Cut fudge into squares. Store in the refrigerator. Yield: 2½ pounds.   Lola Binford

Secret Recipes II
4450th Tactical Group, Nellis Air Force Base
Las Vegas, Nevada

Two-Tone Fudge

2 cups firmly packed brown sugar
1 cup sugar
1 cup evaporated milk
½ cup butter
1 (7-ounce) jar marshmallow cream
1 teaspoon vanilla extract

1 (6-ounce) package peanut butter morsels
1 cup coarsely chopped walnuts, divided
1 (6-ounce) package semisweet chocolate morsels

Combine brown sugar, sugar, evaporated milk, and butter in a medium saucepan. Cook over medium heat, stirring constantly, until mixture comes to a boil; cook 10 minutes, stirring occasionally. Remove from heat. Add marshmallow cream and vanilla; stir until mixture is smooth. Transfer 2 cups marshmallow cream mixture to a bowl; add peanut butter morsels and ½ cup chopped walnuts, stirring until morsels melt.

Spread peanut butter mixture evenly in a lightly buttered 13- x 9- x 2-inch baking pan. Add chocolate morsels and remaining ½ cup chopped walnuts to remaining marshmallow cream mixture, stirring until chocolate morsels melt. Spread chocolate mixture evenly over peanut butter mixture. Let candy cool completely, and cut into squares. Yield: 3 pounds.   Karen Kuhns

Recipes to Cherish
WMSC, Harrisonburg Mennonite Church
Harrisonburg, Virginia

Mamie's Fudge

4½ cups sugar
1 (12-ounce) can evaporated
milk
9 (1.65-ounce) milk chocolate
candy bars
1 (12-ounce) package
semisweet chocolate
morsels
1 (7-ounce) jar marshmallow
cream
1 cup chopped pecans or
walnuts
2 teaspoons vanilla extract
Pinch of salt (optional)

Combine sugar and evaporated milk in a large saucepan. Cook over medium heat until mixture comes to a boil, stirring occasionally. Boil milk mixture 5 minutes without stirring. Remove from heat, and set aside.

Combine milk chocolate bars, chocolate morsels, and marshmallow cream in top of a double boiler; bring water to a boil. Reduce heat to low; cook until chocolate melts, stirring occasionally. Combine milk mixture and chocolate mixture, beating with a wooden spoon until mixture thickens and begins to lose its gloss. Add pecans, vanilla, and, if desired, salt, and stir well. Pour into a lightly buttered 13- x 9- x 2-inch baking dish. Chill until firm. Cut fudge into squares. Yield: 4½ pounds.   Dee Enrico-Janik

Movers & Shakers Cookbook
Lake County Public Library
Merrillville, Indiana

Chocolate Truffles

7 ounces semisweet chocolate,
coarsely chopped
½ cup whipping cream
2 tablespoons butter
¾ cup sifted powdered sugar
2 egg yolks, beaten
1 to 2 tablespoons Grand
Marnier or other
orange-flavored liqueur
Cocoa, chopped nuts, or
sifted powdered sugar

Combine chocolate, whipping cream, and butter in top of a double boiler; bring water to a boil. Reduce heat to low; cook until chocolate and butter melt. Add ¾ cup powdered sugar and egg yolks; stir with a wire whisk until mixture is smooth. Remove from heat, and stir in liqueur.

Pour mixture into a shallow dish. Cover and chill 2 to 3 hours or until firm.

Shape mixture into 1-inch balls. Roll in cocoa, chopped nuts, or powdered sugar. Place in paper candy cups, and chill at least 8 hours or until firm. Yield: 3 dozen.

Biscayne Bights and Breezes
The Villagers, Inc.
Coral Gables, Florida

Truffles Framboise

1½ pounds white chocolate, broken into pieces and divided
¼ cup whipping cream
2 teaspoons Chambord or other raspberry-flavored liqueur

Sifted powdered sugar
Fresh raspberries or candied violets

Position knife blade in food processor bowl; add ½ pound white chocolate. Process until finely chopped.

Heat whipping cream thoroughly in a small saucepan (do not boil). Add liqueur, stirring well. Pour cream mixture through food chute with processor running; process until smooth, scraping sides of processor bowl occasionally. Pour mixture into a bowl; cover and freeze 30 minutes.

Shape mixture into 1-inch balls; roll lightly in powdered sugar. Place on a wax paper-lined baking sheet; freeze.

Place remaining 1 pound chocolate in top of a double boiler; bring water to a boil. Reduce heat to low; cook until chocolate melts, stirring frequently. Remove from heat, and stir until smooth.

Working quickly, dip each ball in melted chocolate. Place on wax paper-lined baking sheet, and let cool slightly. Garnish each truffle with a fresh raspberry or candied violet. Chill 2 hours or until firm. Place truffles in paper candy cups. Store in the refrigerator. Yield: 20 truffles.

Gourmet LA
The Junior League of Los Angeles, California

English Toffee

2 cups sugar
2 cups butter
1½ cups chopped blanched
  almonds, divided

¼ cup plus 1 tablespoon
  water
2⅔ cups semisweet chocolate
  morsels

Combine sugar, butter, 1 cup almonds, and water in a large heavy saucepan. Cook over low heat, stirring gently, until sugar dissolves. Cover and cook over medium heat 2 to 3 minutes to wash down sugar crystals from sides of pan. Uncover and cook to hard crack stage (300°), stirring constantly. Pour into a greased 15- x 10- x 1-inch jellyroll pan, spreading to edges of pan.

Sprinkle chocolate morsels over toffee; let stand 1 minute or until chocolate begins to melt. Spread chocolate over entire candy layer; sprinkle with remaining ½ cup almonds. Let stand until set. Break into pieces. Store in an airtight container in the refrigerator. Yield: about 2½ pounds.

Treasured Recipes from Camargo to Indian Hill
The Indian Hill Historical Society
Cincinnati, Ohio

Triple Chocolate Peanut Clusters

2 pounds white chocolate
1 (12-ounce) package
  semisweet chocolate
  morsels

1 (11½-ounce) package milk
  chocolate morsels
1 (16-ounce) jar unsalted dry
  roasted peanuts

Combine first 3 ingredients in top of a double boiler; bring water to a boil. Reduce heat to low; cook until chocolate melts, stirring occasionally. Remove from heat, and stir until smooth. Let cool 5 minutes. Stir in peanuts. Drop by tablespoonfuls onto wax paper. Let cool completely. Store in an airtight container in the refrigerator. Yield: 6½ dozen.

Second Round, Tea-Time at the Masters®
The Junior League of Augusta, Georgia

Haystacks

1 pound white chocolate,
  coarsely chopped
2 cups pretzel sticks, broken
  into small pieces

1 cup unsalted peanuts

Place chocolate in top of a double boiler; bring water to a boil. Reduce heat to low; cook until chocolate melts, stirring occasionally. Remove from heat, and stir until chocolate is smooth. Add pretzels and peanuts to melted chocolate, and stir until well coated with chocolate.

Pour into a buttered 15- x 10- x 1-inch jellyroll pan, spreading to edges of pan. Chill 20 minutes or until firm. Break into pieces. Store in an airtight container. Yield: 1½ pounds.   Jan Showalter

Recipes to Cherish
WMSC, Harrisonburg Mennonite Church
Harrisonburg, Virginia

Homemade Chocolate Ice Cream

6 eggs
¾ cup sugar
4 cups chocolate syrup
2½ tablespoons vanilla
  extract

¾ teaspoon salt
6 cups whipping cream
6 cups milk

Beat eggs in a large bowl at medium speed of an electric mixer until frothy; add sugar, beating well. Stir in chocolate syrup, vanilla, and salt.

Pour into freezer can of a 1½-gallon hand-turned or electric ice cream freezer. Add whipping cream and milk, stirring well. Freeze according to manufacturer's instructions. Let ice cream ripen 1 hour before serving. Yield: 1½ gallons.   Shirley R. French

The Belle Grove Plantation Cookbook
Belle Grove, Inc.
Middletown, Virginia

White Chocolate Ice Cream

1 cup water
¾ cup sugar
6 egg yolks
1 tablespoon light rum

12 ounces white chocolate,
 melted
2 cups whipping cream

Combine water and sugar in a heavy saucepan. Cook over low heat, stirring until sugar dissolves. Cook over medium heat until mixture comes to a boil, stirring occasionally; cook 5 minutes.

Combine egg yolks and rum in a large bowl; beat at high speed of an electric mixer 8 minutes or until thick and lemon colored. Pour hot sugar mixture in a thin, steady stream over egg yolk mixture; beat until thickened and cooled (about 12 minutes). Gradually add melted white chocolate, and beat 8 minutes. Stir in cream. Cover and freeze 8 hours or until firm. Yield: 1 quart.

Bound to Please
The Junior League of Boise, Idaho

Chocolate Nut Bombe

1 cup chopped walnuts,
 divided
1 quart coffee ice cream,
 softened
1 quart chocolate ice cream,
 softened
1 tablespoon brandy

1 pint vanilla ice cream,
 softened
2 (1-ounce) squares
 unsweetened chocolate
¼ cup light corn syrup
1 egg

Line a 2-quart bowl with aluminum foil. Stir ½ cup walnuts into coffee ice cream. Spoon into bowl; press ice cream mixture firmly on bottom and up sides of bowl. Freeze until firm.

Spoon chocolate ice cream over coffee ice cream layer; spread over bottom and up sides of bowl, pressing firmly. Freeze until firm.

Stir brandy into vanilla ice cream. Press mixture firmly into center of bowl over chocolate ice cream layer. Freeze 3 to 4 hours. Turn bombe out onto a cold tray. Remove aluminum foil, and return dessert to freezer.

Place chocolate in top of a double boiler; bring water to a boil. Reduce heat to low; cook until chocolate melts, stirring occasionally.

Remove from heat; let cool. Combine melted chocolate, corn syrup, and egg in a small bowl. Beat at medium speed of an electric mixer 3 to 4 minutes. Working quickly, frost bombe with chocolate mixture. Sprinkle with remaining ½ cup walnuts. Freeze at least 8 hours before serving. Yield: 10 to 12 servings.

Simply Sensational
TWIGS, The Auxiliary of the Children's Medical Center
Dayton, Ohio

Chocolate Ice Cream Torte

1 cup chocolate wafer crumbs
3 tablespoons butter, melted
½ gallon chocolate ice cream, softened

½ gallon coffee ice cream
½ cup chopped English toffee-flavored candy bars
Chocolate Rum Sauce

Combine crumbs and butter in a small bowl; stir well. Press firmly on bottom of a 9-inch springform pan. Bake at 350° for 10 minutes. Let cool completely. Spread chocolate ice cream evenly over cooled crust. Freeze until ice cream is firm.

To serve, carefully remove sides of springform pan. Top chocolate ice cream with scoops of coffee ice cream. Sprinkle with chopped candy, and drizzle with warm Chocolate Rum Sauce. Serve immediately. Yield: 8 to 10 servings.

Chocolate Rum Sauce

¼ cup sugar
½ cup unsalted butter
½ cup cocoa
3 (1-ounce) squares unsweetened chocolate

⅛ teaspoon salt
1 cup whipping cream
2 tablespoons dark rum

Combine first 5 ingredients in a medium saucepan. Cook over low heat until butter and chocolate melt, stirring constantly. Gradually add whipping cream; stir until mixture is smooth. Stir in rum. Yield: 2 cups.   Meegie Glass

Pegasus Presents
Pegasus of Germantown, Tennessee

Ice Cream Clad in Chocolate

4 cups chocolate wafer
   crumbs, divided
1 cup butter, melted
1 quart vanilla ice cream,
   softened
1 quart pistachio ice cream,
   softened
1 quart chocolate ice cream,
   softened
Chocolate Sauce

Combine 3⅓ cups chocolate wafer crumbs and melted butter in a medium bowl, and stir well. Press crumb mixture evenly on bottom and 2 inches up sides of a 10-inch springform pan. Freeze until crust is firm.

Spread vanilla ice cream over bottom of frozen crust. Sprinkle with ⅓ cup crumbs; freeze until firm. Repeat procedure with pistachio ice cream and remaining ⅓ cup crumbs; freeze until firm. Spread chocolate ice cream over crumbs. Cover dessert with aluminum foil, and freeze at least 8 hours.

To serve, remove foil, and carefully remove sides of springform pan. Slice dessert, and serve with Chocolate Sauce. Yield: 12 to 14 servings.

Chocolate Sauce

3 (1-ounce) squares
   unsweetened chocolate
½ cup water
¾ cup sugar
¼ teaspoon salt
¼ cup plus ½ tablespoon
   butter
¾ teaspoon vanilla extract

Combine unsweetened chocolate and water in top of a double boiler; bring water in bottom of double boiler to a boil. Reduce heat to low; cook until chocolate melts, stirring occasionally. Add sugar and salt, and cook, stirring constantly, 5 minutes or until sugar dissolves and mixture thickens. Remove from heat. Add butter and vanilla to melted chocolate mixture, stirring until butter melts. Let cool. Yield: 1½ cups.   Pat Bonham

Knollwood Cooks II
Christian Women's Guild, Knollwood United Methodist Church
Granada Hills, California

Jean's Delicious Chocolate Pudding

2 (1-ounce) squares
  unsweetened chocolate
½ cup sugar
3 tablespoons cornstarch

¼ teaspoon salt
2¼ cups milk
1 teaspoon vanilla extract

Place chocolate in top of a double boiler; bring water to a boil. Reduce heat to low; cook until chocolate melts, stirring occasionally. Set aside.

Combine sugar, cornstarch, and salt in a medium saucepan; gradually stir in milk.

Add melted chocolate to milk mixture, and cook over medium heat, stirring constantly, until mixture is smooth and thickened. Remove from heat; stir in vanilla.

Spoon chocolate pudding evenly into individual dessert dishes. Cover each dish with plastic wrap, gently pressing plastic wrap directly on pudding. Chill pudding thoroughly before serving. Yield: 4 servings.   Jean Keys

We, The Women of Hawaii Cookbook
We, The Women of Hawaii
Waialua, Oahu

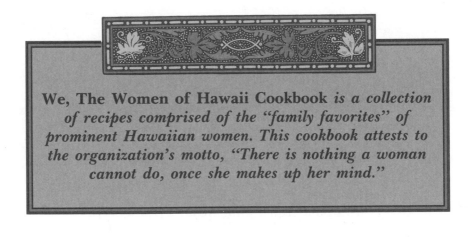

We, The Women of Hawaii Cookbook *is a collection of recipes comprised of the "family favorites" of prominent Hawaiian women. This cookbook attests to the organization's motto, "There is nothing a woman cannot do, once she makes up her mind."*

Pots de Crème

⅔ cup milk
1 (6-ounce) package
  semisweet chocolate
  morsels
1 egg

2 tablespoons sugar
1 teaspoon vanilla extract
Pinch of salt
Whipped cream

Place milk in a small saucepan. Cook over medium heat until thoroughly heated (do not boil).

Combine chocolate morsels and next 4 ingredients in container of an electric blender; blend at high speed 1 minute or until thickened. Add warm milk; blend 1 minute or until smooth. Spoon mixture into small cordial glasses or pots de crème cups. Chill thoroughly. Garnish with whipped cream. Yield: 6 servings.   Mary Strickler

What's Cooking in Philadelphia
The Rotary Club of Philadelphia, Pennsylvania

Chocolate Mousse

8 (1-ounce) squares semisweet
  chocolate
6 eggs, separated
3 tablespoons water
½ cup amaretto, Grand
  Marnier, or other liqueur

2 cups whipping cream
¼ cup plus 2 tablespoons
  sugar, divided
1 cup whipping cream,
  whipped
Grated chocolate

Place semisweet chocolate in top of a double boiler; bring water to a boil. Reduce heat to low; cook until chocolate melts, stirring occasionally. Remove from heat, and let cool.

Combine egg yolks and water in a heavy saucepan; stir well. Cook over low heat, beating constantly with a wire whisk, until mixture thickens. Add liqueur, and cook, beating constantly, until mixture heavily coats a spoon. Remove from heat. Stir in melted chocolate; pour chocolate mixture into a large bowl.

Beat 2 cups whipping cream until foamy; gradually add 2 tablespoons sugar, beating until soft peaks form. Fold sweetened whipped cream into chocolate mixture.

Beat egg whites (at room temperature) until foamy. Gradually add ¼ cup sugar, 1 tablespoon at a time, beating until stiff peaks form and sugar dissolves (2 to 4 minutes).

Fold beaten egg whites into chocolate mixture. Spoon mousse into a large serving bowl; chill at least 8 hours. Garnish mousse with whipped cream and grated chocolate before serving. Yield: 16 to 20 servings.   Mary Katherine Welhausen Borchers

Cook 'em Horns: The Quickbook
The Ex-Students Association of the University of Texas
Austin, Texas

Divine Chocolate Soufflé

⅔ cup crème de cacao
½ cup water
2 envelopes unflavored gelatin
1¼ cups firmly packed light brown sugar, divided
1 (12-ounce) package semisweet chocolate morsels
8 eggs, separated
½ teaspoon salt
2 cups whipping cream, whipped
½ cup slivered blanched almonds, toasted
Additional whipped cream
Grated chocolate

Combine crème de cacao and water in a medium saucepan. Sprinkle gelatin and ½ cup sugar over liquid in saucepan, and let stand 1 minute. Cook gelatin mixture over low heat, stirring constantly, until gelatin and sugar dissolve. Add chocolate morsels, and stir until chocolate melts. Remove from heat; let mixture cool slightly. Add egg yolks, one at a time, beating after each addition. Let cool completely.

Beat egg whites (at room temperature) and salt at high speed of an electric mixer until foamy. Gradually add remaining ¾ cup sugar, 1 tablespoon at a time, beating until stiff peaks form and sugar dissolves (2 to 4 minutes). Fold beaten egg whites into gelatin mixture. Fold in whipped cream.

Pour mixture into a 3-quart soufflé dish, and chill at least 8 hours. Sprinkle top with toasted almonds. Spoon or pipe additional whipped cream around edge of soufflé. Garnish with grated chocolate. Yield: 16 servings.   Marian Hill Jackson

A Grand Heritage
The Heritage Academy
Columbus, Mississippi

Triple Chocolate Silk

1 envelope unflavored gelatin
¼ cup cold water
5 egg yolks
½ cup sugar
1 cup half-and-half
3 ounces white chocolate, grated
3 ounces milk chocolate, grated
3 (1-ounce) squares semisweet chocolate, grated
1¾ cups whipping cream, whipped
Vegetable cooking spray
Bittersweet Chocolate Sauce

Sprinkle gelatin over cold water in a medium saucepan; let stand 1 minute.

Combine egg yolks and sugar in a medium bowl. Beat with a wire whisk until mixture is thick and lemon colored. Add half-and-half, beating well with wire whisk. Add yolk mixture to gelatin mixture in saucepan; cook over medium-low heat, stirring constantly, 10 to 12 minutes or until mixture coats a wooden spoon (do not boil). Remove from heat.

Place one-third of yolk mixture in each of 3 small bowls. Quickly add white chocolate to mixture in first bowl, milk chocolate to mixture in second bowl, and semisweet chocolate to mixture in third bowl, whisking each until chocolate melts. Cover and chill until each mixture reaches the consistency of unbeaten egg whites.

Fold one-third of whipped cream into white chocolate mixture, and pour into a 6-cup soufflé dish lightly coated with cooking spray. Freeze 10 to 12 minutes or until firm.

Repeat procedure with remaining 2 bowls of chocolate and whipped cream, freezing 10 to 12 minutes between layers. Chill at least 4 hours or until firm.

Unmold onto a lightly oiled serving platter. To serve, place Bittersweet Chocolate Sauce on individual dessert plates; top with a slice of Triple Chocolate Silk. Yield: 8 to 10 servings.

Bittersweet Chocolate Sauce

1 cup water
½ cup sugar
8 (1-ounce) squares semisweet chocolate
¼ cup butter
1 tablespoon cognac or other brandy

Combine water and sugar in a small saucepan. Bring to a boil; cover, reduce heat, and simmer 5 minutes or until sugar dissolves.

Remove from heat, and let sugar mixture cool slightly. Combine semisweet chocolate and butter in top of a double boiler; bring water to a boil. Reduce heat to low, and cook until chocolate and butter melt, stirring occasionally. Remove from heat, and stir in cooled sugar mixture and cognac. Serve sauce at room temperature. Yield: 2 cups.

Stir Crazy!
The Junior Welfare League of Florence, South Carolina

French Double Chocolate Pie

3 cups chocolate wafer
   crumbs
½ cup plus 2 tablespoons
   unsalted butter, softened
1 teaspoon ground cinnamon
12 (1-ounce) squares
   semisweet chocolate
5 eggs, separated

1 egg
¼ cup dark rum
Dash of salt
1½ cups whipping cream,
   divided
Mandarin orange sections
   (optional)
Fresh mint sprigs (optional)

Combine crumbs, butter, and cinnamon, stirring well. Firmly press crumb mixture evenly on bottom and up sides of a 10-inch pieplate. Bake at 350° for 3 minutes. Let cool on a wire rack.

Place chocolate in top of a double boiler; bring water to a boil. Reduce heat to low; cook until chocolate melts, stirring occasionally. Let cool.

Beat 5 egg yolks and one egg at medium speed of an electric mixer until thick and lemon colored. Stir in melted chocolate, rum, and salt. Beat 5 egg whites in a medium bowl until soft peaks form; gently fold into chocolate mixture. Beat 1 cup whipping cream in a small bowl until stiff peaks form; fold into chocolate mixture until well blended. Gently spoon mixture into prepared crust. Chill until filling is set.

Beat remaining ½ cup whipping cream in a small bowl until stiff peaks form. Spoon or pipe whipped cream over top of pie. If desired, garnish with mandarin orange sections and fresh mint sprigs. Yield: one 10-inch pie.   Kent Conrad

Heritage Cookbook
The Catholic Diocese of Fargo, North Dakota

Chocolate Cream Pie

3 cups milk
1 cup sugar
½ cup all-purpose flour
½ cup cocoa
¼ teaspoon salt
3 eggs, separated

2 tablespoons butter
1 teaspoon vanilla extract
1 baked 9-inch pastry shell
½ teaspoon cream of tartar
¼ cup plus 2 tablespoons
  sugar

Combine first 5 ingredients in top of a double boiler; bring water to a boil. Reduce heat to low; cook 15 minutes or until thickened, stirring constantly.

Beat egg yolks with a wire whisk. Gradually stir about one-fourth of hot mixture into yolks; add to remaining hot mixture, stirring constantly. Cook 3 minutes. Remove from heat; add butter and vanilla, stirring until butter melts. Spoon mixture into pastry shell.

Beat egg whites (at room temperature) and cream of tartar at high speed of an electric mixer until foamy. Gradually add ¼ cup plus 2 tablespoons sugar, 1 tablespoon at a time, beating until stiff peaks form and sugar dissolves (2 to 4 minutes). Spread meringue over hot filling, sealing to edge of pastry. Bake at 425° for 4 minutes or until golden brown. Yield: one 9-inch pie.   Gilda Shapiro

A Rainbow of Kosher Cuisine
The Baltimore Chapter of Hadassah
Baltimore, Maryland

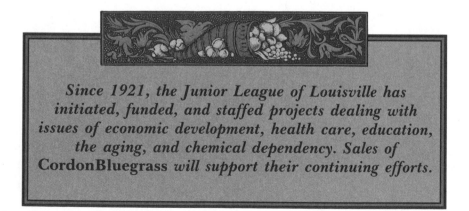

Since 1921, the Junior League of Louisville has initiated, funded, and staffed projects dealing with issues of economic development, health care, education, the aging, and chemical dependency. Sales of **CordonBluegrass** *will support their continuing efforts.*

French Silk Pie

1½ (1-ounce) squares unsweetened chocolate
¾ cup butter
1 cup sugar
1 teaspoon vanilla extract
3 eggs
1 (9-inch) graham cracker crust
1 cup whipping cream
1 tablespoon bourbon
Chocolate curls

Place unsweetened chocolate in top of a double boiler; bring water to a boil. Reduce heat to low; cook until chocolate melts, stirring occasionally. Set aside.

Cream butter; gradually add sugar, beating at medium speed of an electric mixer until light and fluffy. Add melted chocolate and vanilla; beat well. Add eggs, one at a time, beating 2 minutes after each addition. Beat an additional 10 minutes. Pour chocolate mixture into graham cracker crust. Chill 8 hours.

Beat whipping cream at high speed of electric mixer until foamy; add bourbon, beating until stiff peaks form. Spoon or pipe whipped cream on top of pie, and garnish with chocolate curls. Yield: one 9-inch pie.

CordonBluegrass
The Junior League of Louisville, Kentucky

Chocolate Pecan Pie

1 cup sugar
¾ cup light corn syrup
¼ cup butter or margarine, melted
3 eggs, beaten
1 teaspoon vanilla extract
½ cup semisweet chocolate morsels
½ cup chopped pecans
1 unbaked 9-inch pastry shell
1 cup pecan halves (optional)
Whipped cream (optional)

Combine first 5 ingredients in a large bowl; stir well. Add chocolate morsels and chopped pecans, stirring well. Pour mixture into pastry shell, and, if desired, top with pecan halves. Bake at 350° for 45 to 50 minutes or until set. Cool completely. Garnish with whipped cream, if desired. Yield: one 9-inch pie.   Sarah Howell

Southern Secrets
SouthTrust Corporation
Birmingham, Alabama

Milwaukee Million Dollar Pie

2 cups chocolate wafer
  crumbs
½ cup butter, melted
4 (1-ounce) squares
  unsweetened chocolate
1¼ cups butter, softened
1⅓ cups sugar

6 eggs
3 tablespoons cognac
2 cups finely chopped pecans
2 cups whipping cream,
  whipped
Chocolate curls

Combine chocolate wafer crumbs and ½ cup melted butter; stir well. Press mixture firmly on bottom and ½ inch up sides of a 10-inch springform pan. Bake at 350° for 10 minutes. Set crust aside, and let cool.

Place unsweetened chocolate in top of a double boiler; bring water to a boil. Reduce heat to low; cook until chocolate melts, stirring occasionally. Set aside, and let cool.

Cream 1¼ cups softened butter; gradually add sugar, beating well at medium speed of an electric mixer. Add melted chocolate; blend well. Add eggs, one at a time, beating 3 minutes after each addition. Add cognac and pecans, stirring gently to combine. Pour mixture into prepared pan. Chill 3 hours.

To serve, carefully remove sides of springform pan. Garnish with whipped cream and chocolate curls. Yield: 10 to 12 servings.

Gatherings
The Junior League of Milwaukee, Wisconsin

Appetizers & Beverages

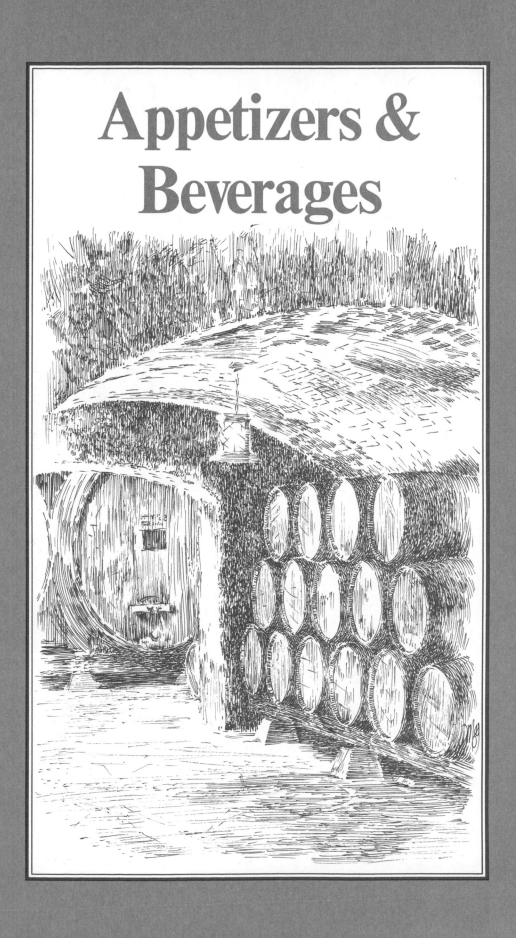

A stone wine-aging cellar containing large oak casks located in Buena Vista is part of California's wine heritage that began in the eighteenth century when Spanish missionaries planted the first vineyards. Today California produces over seventy percent of the wine consumed in the United States.

Moroccan Eggplant Spread

2 teaspoons olive oil
1 medium eggplant, cut into
    ½-inch cubes
½ cup tomato sauce
¼ cup red wine vinegar
1 small green pepper, finely
    chopped

1 clove garlic, minced
1 teaspoon ground cumin
1 teaspoon salt
1 teaspoon sugar
Pinch of ground red pepper
2 tablespoons minced fresh
    cilantro

Heat olive oil in a large skillet. Place eggplant and next 8 ingredients in skillet; stir well. Bring to a boil; cover, reduce heat, and simmer 20 minutes. Remove cover, and cook over medium-high heat, stirring frequently, 10 to 15 minutes or until liquid is reduced by one-fourth. Chill at least 2 hours. Stir in cilantro. Serve with pita bread or cracker bread. Yield: 1⅔ cups.

The Less Fat Cookbook
The Cancer Education and Prevention Center
Oakland, California

Spinach Dip

1 (10-ounce) package frozen
    chopped spinach, thawed
    and drained
1 (8-ounce) carton sour cream
1 cup mayonnaise
1 (6-ounce) can water
    chestnuts, drained and
    chopped

4 to 5 green onions, chopped
1 (1⅝-ounce) package
    vegetable soup mix
1 (1-pound) round loaf
    Hawaiian bread

Combine spinach, sour cream, mayonnaise, water chestnuts, green onions, and soup mix in a medium mixing bowl, stirring well. Cover and chill at least 6 hours.

Using a gentle sawing motion, cut vertically to, but not through, bottom of loaf, ½ inch from edge. Lift out center of loaf; cut bread into 1-inch cubes, and set aside. Fill hollowed bread loaf with dip; serve with bread cubes. Yield: 3 cups.   Peggy H. Shoaf

Elvis Fans Cookbook, Volume 3
The Elvis Presley Memorial Trauma Center
Memphis, Tennessee

Spinach Dipping Sauce

2 to 3 jalapeño peppers
1 medium onion, chopped
2 tablespoons vegetable oil
1 (4-ounce) can chopped
  green chiles, drained
2 medium tomatoes, peeled,
  seeded, and chopped
1 (10-ounce) package frozen
  chopped spinach, thawed
2½ cups (10 ounces)
  shredded Monterey Jack
  cheese

1 (8-ounce) package cream
  cheese, softened
1 cup half-and-half
1½ tablespoons red wine
  vinegar
½ teaspoon salt
⅛ teaspoon pepper
Paprika

Seed and chop jalapeño peppers, reserving ⅛ teaspoon seeds. Sauté chopped jalapeño pepper, ⅛ teaspoon seeds, and onion in oil in a large skillet until pepper and onion are soft. Add green chiles and tomatoes. Cook 2 minutes, stirring constantly. Remove from heat; transfer chile mixture to a large bowl.

Press spinach between layers of paper towels, squeezing until barely moist. Add spinach, Monterey Jack cheese, cream cheese, half-and-half, vinegar, salt, and pepper to chile mixture; stir well. Pour into a greased 10-inch round baking dish. Sprinkle with paprika. Bake at 400° for 20 to 25 minutes or until hot and bubbly. Serve with tortilla chips. Yield: 6 cups.

Second Round, Tea-Time at the Masters®
The Junior League of Augusta, Georgia

Jenny's Liver Pâté

1 pound braunschweiger or
  liverwurst, softened
1 (8-ounce) package cream
  cheese, softened and
  divided
½ cup (2 ounces) finely
  shredded Cheddar
  cheese

1 tablespoon Worcestershire
  sauce
1 tablespoon Dijon mustard
⅛ teaspoon salt
⅛ teaspoon pepper
3 tablespoons chopped fresh
  chives
Fresh parsley sprigs

Combine braunschweiger, 3 ounces cream cheese, and next 5 ingredients in a large mixing bowl. Beat at medium speed of an electric mixer until well blended and smooth. Shape into a ball; cover and chill until firm.

Combine remaining 5 ounces cream cheese and chives in a small bowl, and stir well. Spread cream cheese mixture over pâté, and chill until ready to serve. Place pâté on a serving plate, and garnish with fresh parsley sprigs. Serve pâté with assorted crackers. Yield: one 5½-inch ball.   Mona Howell

A Cook's Book of Recipes from the Pacific Northwest
The Rosehill Community Center
Mukilteo, Washington

Wonderful Cheese and Apples

1 cup (4 ounces) shredded
  Swiss cheese, softened
4 ounces Camembert cheese,
  softened
1 (4-ounce) package blue
  cheese, crumbled
3 (8-ounce) packages cream
  cheese, softened and
  divided

2 tablespoons milk
2 tablespoons sour cream
1¼ cups chopped pecans
Chopped fresh parsley
6 to 8 Granny Smith apples,
  cored and sliced

Combine first 3 ingredients and 2 (8-ounce) packages cream cheese in a large mixing bowl. Beat at medium speed of an electric mixer until smooth; set aside.

Line a 9-inch pieplate with aluminum foil. Combine remaining 8-ounce package cream cheese, milk, and sour cream; mix well. Spread sour cream mixture in prepared pieplate. Sprinkle with pecans, and lightly press pecans into sour cream mixture.

Spoon cheese mixture evenly over pecans. Cover and chill 2 to 3 days. To serve, unmold onto a serving platter, and carefully remove foil. Sprinkle cheese with chopped parsley. Serve with apple slices. Yield: 12 to 16 appetizer servings.   Wanda Witt

Critics' Choice
The Corinth Theatre Arts Guild
Corinth, Mississippi

Tower of Cheese

8 ounces port wine Cheddar
  cheese, softened
1 cup chopped pecans
8 ounces Havarti cheese,
  softened
2 tablespoons half-and-half

½ cup chopped fresh parsley
2 cups (8 ounces) shredded
  sharp Cheddar cheese
Fresh parsley sprigs
Pecan halves

Line a 7-cup crown mold with plastic wrap. Press port wine cheese firmly into bottom of mold. Sprinkle evenly with chopped pecans, pressing firmly into port wine layer.

Combine Havarti cheese and half-and-half; press mixture firmly over pecan layer. Sprinkle with chopped parsley. Firmly press shredded Cheddar cheese over parsley layer. Cover and chill at least 8 hours.

To serve, unmold cheese onto a serving platter, and remove plastic wrap. Garnish cheese mold with parsley sprigs and pecan halves. Serve with water crackers. Yield: 24 appetizer servings.

Palm Country Cuisine
The Junior League of Greater Lakeland, Florida

Danish Cheese Ball

8 ounces Danish blue cheese
  or other blue cheese,
  crumbled
½ cup butter, softened
1 (3-ounce) package cream
  cheese, softened

1 tablespoon cognac
1 teaspoon grated onion
¾ cup chopped pecans,
  toasted

Combine blue cheese, butter, cream cheese, cognac, and grated onion in a medium mixing bowl; beat at medium speed of an electric mixer until smooth. Shape cheese mixture into a ball. Roll in chopped pecans.

Wrap cheese ball in wax paper, and chill at least 1 hour. Yield: one 4-inch cheese ball.
                                                              Glenis Ellis

The Heart of Adirondack Cooking
Women's Fellowship
Warrensburg, New York

Confetti Cheddar Log

2 cups (8 ounces) shredded
  Cheddar cheese
1 (3-ounce) package cream
  cheese, softened
2 tablespoons diced pimiento
¼ cup chopped ripe olives

2 tablespoons chopped green
  pepper
1 teaspoon Worcestershire
  sauce
⅓ cup slivered blanched
  almonds, chopped

Combine cheeses in a medium mixing bowl; beat at medium speed of an electric mixer until smooth. Press pimiento between paper towels to remove excess moisture. Add pimiento, olives, green pepper, and Worcestershire sauce to cheese mixture; mix well. Shape into a log, and roll in chopped almonds. Cover and chill at least 2 hours. Let cheese log stand at room temperature 30 minutes before serving. Serve with assorted crackers. Yield: one 8-inch cheese log.   Elva Shapiro

The Second Helping of the Happy Cooker
Tifereth Israel Sisterhood
New Castle, Pennsylvania

Smoked Salmon-Cream Cheese Balls

2 (8-ounce) packages cream
  cheese, softened
8 ounces smoked salmon,
  finely chopped
3 green onions, finely chopped
¼ cup sour cream
1 teaspoon Worcestershire
  sauce

½ teaspoon prepared
  horseradish
¼ teaspoon garlic powder
¼ teaspoon pepper
¾ cup finely chopped
  walnuts
¼ cup chopped fresh parsley

Combine first 8 ingredients in a medium bowl; stir well. Cover and chill at least 1 hour. Shape salmon mixture into 3 balls. Combine chopped walnuts and chopped parsley; roll balls in walnut mixture. Cover and chill at least 4 hours. Serve with assorted crackers. Yield: three 3-inch cheese balls.   Barbara Thompson

More Memoirs of a Galley Slave
Kodiak Fishermen's Wives Association
Kodiak, Alaska

Golden Cheese Wheel

1 package dry yeast
⅔ cup warm water (105° to 115°)
2 cups all-purpose flour, divided
2 tablespoons vegetable oil
¾ teaspoon sugar
½ teaspoon salt
1 egg, beaten

3 cups (12 ounces) shredded Muenster cheese
½ cup chopped fresh parsley
½ teaspoon garlic salt
⅛ teaspoon pepper
1 egg, beaten
1 tablespoon water
1½ teaspoons sesame seeds
¾ teaspoon sugar

Dissolve yeast in warm water in a large mixing bowl, and let stand 5 minutes. Add 1 cup flour, vegetable oil, ¾ teaspoon sugar, and salt to yeast mixture; beat at medium speed of an electric mixer until mixture is well blended. Gradually stir in enough remaining flour to make a soft dough.

Turn dough out onto a well-floured surface, and knead until smooth and elastic (about 5 to 8 minutes). Place in a well-greased bowl, turning to grease top. Cover and let rise in a warm place (85°), free from drafts, 1 hour or until doubled in bulk.

Punch dough down, and divide in half. Cover each half of dough, and let rest 10 minutes. Turn one half of dough out onto a well-floured surface, and roll to a 13-inch circle. Transfer dough to a greased 12-inch pizza pan.

Combine 1 beaten egg, cheese, parsley, garlic salt, and pepper in a large bowl, stirring well. Spread cheese mixture evenly over dough in pan.

Roll remaining half of dough to a 13-inch circle. Place over filling; fold edges under, and pinch to form crust. Bake at 400° for 20 minutes. Remove from oven.

Combine 1 beaten egg and 1 tablespoon water in a small bowl, stirring well. Brush egg mixture over top crust. Sprinkle top crust evenly with sesame seeds and ¾ teaspoon sugar. Bake pastry an additional 12 to 15 minutes or until crust is golden brown. Cut cheese wheel into narrow wedges, and serve immediately. Yield: 16 appetizer servings.   Ann Erickson Dungan

Chestnut Hill Cookbook
The Chestnut Hill Senior Services Center
Philadelphia, Pennsylvania

Cocktail Biscuits

4¾ cups unbleached flour
3 tablespoons baking powder
1 teaspoon salt
1¾ cups unsalted butter,
  divided
¼ cup plus 2 tablespoons
  shortening
1½ cups milk
3 cups minced fresh
  mushrooms

6 shallots, minced
1¾ cups finely chopped
  smoked ham
7 green onions, finely
  chopped
½ teaspoon salt
¼ teaspoon freshly ground
  pepper
Fresh Herb Cream Cheese

Combine flour, baking powder, and 1 teaspoon salt; cut in 1½ cups butter and shortening with a pastry blender until mixture resembles coarse meal. Add milk, stirring until mixture forms a dough. Cover with plastic wrap, and chill 8 hours.

Place remaining ¼ cup butter in a large skillet. Cook over medium heat until butter melts. Sauté mushrooms and shallots in butter until tender. Add ham, green onions, ½ teaspoon salt, and pepper; cook over medium heat 4 minutes or until onions are tender.

Combine dough and mushroom mixture, kneading until well blended. Shape dough into 1-inch balls, and place on lightly greased baking sheets. Press thumb into each biscuit, leaving an indentation. Bake at 450° for 12 to 14 minutes or until golden brown. Let cool on wire racks. Spoon 1 teaspoon Fresh Herb Cream Cheese into each indentation. Yield: 8 dozen.

Fresh Herb Cream Cheese

2 (8-ounce) packages cream
  cheese, softened
3 tablespoons half-and-half
¼ cup chopped fresh dillweed
3 cloves garlic, minced
1½ teaspoons chopped fresh
  chives

¼ teaspoon hot sauce
¼ teaspoon freshly ground
  pepper
¼ teaspoon dried whole
  chervil (optional)

Combine cream cheese and half-and-half in a medium bowl, stirring well. Add dillweed and next 4 ingredients, stirring well. Add chervil, if desired; stir well. Cover and chill 8 hours. Yield: 2 cups.

Gourmet LA
The Junior League of Los Angeles, California

Little Feta Cheesecakes

½ cup fine, dry breadcrumbs
½ cup ground pecans
¼ cup butter or margarine, melted
1 (8-ounce) package cream cheese, softened
4 ounces feta cheese, crumbled

1 egg
2 tablespoons milk
⅛ teaspoon hot sauce
Herbed Tomato Sauce
Sliced ripe olives (optional)
Fresh parsley sprigs (optional)

Combine first 3 ingredients in a small bowl; stir well. Press 1 teaspoon pecan mixture into paper-lined miniature (1¾-inch) muffin pans.

Beat cream cheese at medium speed of an electric mixer until fluffy; add crumbled feta cheese and egg, beating well. Stir in milk and hot sauce.

Spoon cheese mixture evenly into prepared miniature muffin pans. Bake at 350° for 10 to 12 minutes or until cheesecakes are set. Let cool; cover and chill 2 hours.

To serve, remove cheesecakes from pans, and remove paper liners from cheesecakes. Spoon Herbed Tomato Sauce evenly over cheesecakes. If desired, garnish with sliced ripe olives and fresh parsley sprigs. Yield: 4 dozen.

Herbed Tomato Sauce

½ cup tomato sauce
1 tablespoon minced onion
2 tablespoons tomato paste
¼ teaspoon dried whole basil

¼ teaspoon dried whole oregano
⅛ teaspoon pepper
1 small clove garlic, minced

Combine all ingredients in a small saucepan, and stir well. Cook over medium heat, stirring occasionally, 5 minutes or until mixture thickens. Let sauce cool. Cover tightly, and chill at least 2 hours. Yield: ⅔ cup.

Nancy Lynch

A Collection of Recipes
Worcester Country School Development Office
Berlin, Maryland

Clam Puffs

1 (8-ounce) package cream
  cheese, softened
1 (6½-ounce) can minced
  clams, drained
1 tablespoon grated onion
1 tablespoon Worcestershire
  sauce

2 teaspoons lemon juice
¼ teaspoon salt
1 egg white
36 toast rounds

Combine first 6 ingredients in a medium bowl, stirring well to combine. Beat egg white (at room temperature) at high speed of an electric mixer until stiff peaks form. Gently fold beaten egg white into clam mixture. Spread mixture on toast rounds, and place on baking sheets. Bake at 450° for 3 minutes or until slightly puffed and lightly browned. Yield: 3 dozen. Gail Kittenplan

The Spence Collection
The Spence School
New York, New York

Cranberry Cocktail Meatballs

2 pounds ground chuck
1 cup corn flakes cereal
  crumbs
2 eggs
⅓ cup minced fresh parsley
⅓ cup catsup
2 tablespoons minced green
  onions

2 tablespoons soy sauce
1 clove garlic, pressed
¼ teaspoon pepper
1 (16-ounce) can whole
  cranberry sauce
1 (12-ounce) bottle chili sauce
1 tablespoon brown sugar
1 tablespoon lemon juice

Combine first 9 ingredients in a large bowl; stir well. Shape meat mixture into 1-inch balls. Place in an ungreased 15- x 10- x 1-inch jellyroll pan. Bake, uncovered, at 500° for 8 to 10 minutes. Drain meatballs; transfer to a chafing dish, and keep warm. Combine cranberry sauce and remaining ingredients in a saucepan. Cook over medium heat until bubbly, stirring occasionally; pour over meatballs. Serve warm. Yield: 5 dozen. Josephine Ross

La Salette's Favorite Recipes
The La Salette Shrine
Attleboro, Massachusetts

Danish Meatballs

1½ pounds ground beef
½ cup Italian-seasoned
  breadcrumbs
¼ cup minced onion
¼ cup half-and-half
1 egg, lightly beaten
1 teaspoon salt
¼ teaspoon pepper

¼ cup butter or margarine
¼ cup all-purpose flour
2 cups canned diluted
  chicken broth
1 (8-ounce) carton sour cream
1 tablespoon dried whole
  dillweed
¼ teaspoon salt

Combine first 7 ingredients in a large bowl; stir well. Shape meat mixture into 1-inch balls. Place in a 13- x 9- x 2-inch baking dish. Bake at 375° for 30 minutes. Drain meatballs; transfer to a chafing dish, and keep warm.

Melt butter in a heavy saucepan over low heat; add flour, stirring until smooth. Cook 1 minute, stirring constantly. Gradually stir in broth with a wire whisk; cook over medium heat, stirring constantly, until mixture is thickened and bubbly. Remove from heat. Stir in sour cream, dillweed, and ¼ teaspoon salt. Pour sauce over meatballs, and serve warm. Yield: 4 dozen.

Gourmet by the Bay
The Dolphin Circle of the King's Daughters and Sons
Virginia Beach, Virginia

Glazed Salami

1 (1-pound) hard salami
¼ cup orange marmalade
2 tablespoons brown sugar

1 tablespoon prepared
  mustard

Slice salami into ¼-inch slices, cutting to, but not through, bottom of salami. Combine marmalade, brown sugar, and mustard in a small bowl, stirring well. Spread marmalade mixture over top of salami and between each slice; wrap in aluminum foil. Place on a baking sheet, and bake at 350° for 35 minutes. Uncover and bake an additional 10 minutes. Serve with bread rounds. Yield: 16 appetizer servings.
                                                            Esther Pollack

What's Cooking?
The Sisterhood of Temple Shalom
Succasunna, New Jersey

Phyllis's Pickled Shrimp

6 cups water
2 pounds unpeeled
medium-size fresh shrimp
1 medium onion, sliced and
separated into rings
1 (2¼-ounce) jar capers,
undrained
3 bay leaves

1 cup vegetable oil
1 cup vinegar
¾ cup water
¼ cup fresh lemon juice
2½ teaspoons celery seeds
1½ teaspoons salt
1 teaspoon sugar
Dash of hot sauce

Bring water to a boil in a large saucepan; add shrimp, and cook 3 to 5 minutes. Drain well; rinse shrimp with cold water. Chill. Peel and devein shrimp.

Place half of shrimp in a large bowl. Cover shrimp with half of onion rings and half of capers. Repeat layers with remaining shrimp, onion rings, and capers. Top with bay leaves.

Combine vegetable oil and remaining ingredients in a large bowl, beating well with a wire whisk. Pour marinade mixture over layered shrimp mixture. Cover tightly, and marinate in refrigerator at least 8 hours.

To serve, drain well, and remove and discard bay leaves. Yield: 12 appetizer servings.

Phyllis Royster Rivers

Georgia on My Menu
The Junior League of Cobb-Marietta, Georgia

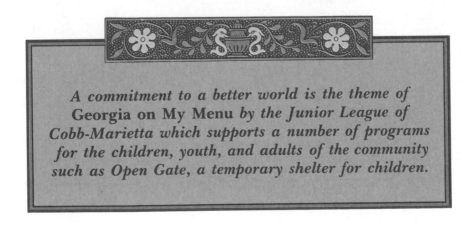

A commitment to a better world is the theme of **Georgia on My Menu** *by the Junior League of Cobb-Marietta which supports a number of programs for the children, youth, and adults of the community such as Open Gate, a temporary shelter for children.*

Bacon-Stuffed Cherry Tomatoes

24 cherry tomatoes
1 pound bacon, cooked and
  crumbled
½ cup finely chopped green
  onions

½ cup mayonnaise
Fresh parsley sprigs
  (optional)

Cut top off each tomato; carefully scoop out pulp, reserving for other uses. Invert tomatoes on paper towels, and let drain 30 minutes.

Combine crumbled bacon, green onions, and mayonnaise; stir well. Spoon 1 teaspoon bacon mixture into each tomato shell. Garnish each tomato with a fresh parsley sprig, if desired. Chill thoroughly. Yield: 2 dozen.   Nancy Gittins

Favorite Recipes from St. Paul's
St. Paul's Episcopal Church
Millis, Massachusetts

Tortilla Pinwheels

1 (8-ounce) package cream
  cheese, softened
2 (4-ounce) cans chopped
  green chiles, drained
1 (4¼-ounce) can chopped
  ripe olives, drained

½ teaspoon garlic powder
¼ teaspoon hot sauce
6 (8-inch) flour tortillas
2 (2½-ounce) packages thinly
  sliced chicken

Combine cream cheese, green chiles, olives, garlic powder, and hot sauce in a small bowl, stirring well.

Spread ¼ cup cream cheese mixture over each tortilla. Arrange 3 slices chicken over cream cheese mixture on each tortilla. Roll up tortillas, jellyroll fashion. Wrap tightly in plastic wrap, and chill at least 2 hours. To serve, slice chilled tortilla rolls into 1-inch rounds. Yield: 3 dozen.

Seasoned with Sun
The Junior League of El Paso, Texas

Frosty Fruit Punch

1 (12-ounce) can frozen
orange juice concentrate,
thawed
1 (6-ounce) can frozen
pineapple juice concentrate,
thawed
1 (6-ounce) can frozen
lemonade concentrate,
thawed

1 quart pineapple sherbet
1 quart lime sherbet
1½ quarts ginger ale or
lemon-lime carbonated
beverage, chilled
Fresh mint sprigs

Prepare orange juice and pineapple juice according to package directions. Prepare lemonade, using 3 cans water. Combine juices; chill at least 2 hours.

When ready to serve, pour juice mixture into a punch bowl. Add sherbets to juice mixture in small scoops. Add ginger ale, stirring gently to combine. Garnish with fresh mint sprigs. Serve immediately. Yield: about 1¼ gallons.

License to Cook New Mexico Style
New Mexico Federation of Business and Professional Women
Albuquerque, New Mexico

Coffee Punch

2 quarts strong brewed
coffee, cooled
2 cups milk
½ cup sugar
1 tablespoon vanilla extract

½ gallon vanilla ice cream,
softened
2 cups whipping cream,
whipped
Ground nutmeg

Combine coffee, milk, sugar, and vanilla; stir well. Chill thoroughly. Place ice cream in a large punch bowl. Pour coffee mixture over ice cream, stirring gently. Top with dollops of whipped cream; sprinkle with nutmeg. Yield: 1¼ gallons.

The Farmer's Daughters
The National Multiple Sclerosis Society
St. Charles, Arkansas

Celebrate the Season Eggnog

8 eggs, separated
2½ cups sugar
2 cups bourbon

5 cups whipping cream, divided
2 cups milk
¼ cup rum

Beat egg yolks at medium speed of an electric mixer. Add sugar; beat until thick and lemon colored. Add bourbon, beating until blended. Add 1 cup cream; beat until smooth. Add milk; beat well. Add remaining 4 cups cream, beating until smooth. Stir in rum. Beat egg whites (at room temperature) until stiff; fold into eggnog. Chill 2 hours. Yield: 1¼ gallons.   Michelle Zimmerlee

Shamrock Specialties
The Trinity High School Foundation
Louisville, Kentucky

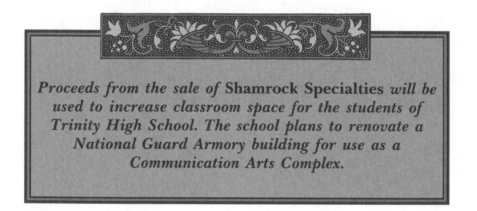

Proceeds from the sale of Shamrock Specialties *will be used to increase classroom space for the students of Trinity High School. The school plans to renovate a National Guard Armory building for use as a Communication Arts Complex.*

White Sangría

1 (750-milliliter) bottle
  Chablis or other dry white
  wine
½ cup Triple Sec or other
  orange-flavored liqueur
¼ cup sugar

1 orange, thinly sliced
1 lemon, thinly sliced
1 lime, thinly sliced
5 large strawberries, sliced
1 (10-ounce) bottle club soda,
  chilled

Combine first 3 ingredients in a pitcher, stirring until sugar dissolves. Add orange, lemon, lime, and strawberry slices; cover and chill at least 1 hour. Just before serving, add club soda, stirring gently. Serve over ice. Yield: 7 cups.   Dottie Reehling

From the Grapevine
The Crossroads Guild of Indianapolis, Indiana

Cool Breeze

1½ cups light rum
¾ cup apricot brandy
⅓ cup Triple Sec or other
   orange-flavored liqueur
12 ice cubes

3 cups orange juice, chilled
3 cups pineapple juice,
   chilled
2 tablespoons grenadine
   syrup

Combine first 4 ingredients in container of an electric blender; blend until smooth.

Combine orange juice and pineapple juice in a large pitcher. Add rum mixture and grenadine syrup; stir well. Serve immediately. Yield: 2½ quarts.

Simply Sensational
TWIGS, The Auxiliary of the Children's Medical Center
Dayton, Ohio

Fresh Virgin Marys

7½ pounds tomatoes, coarsely
   chopped
2 cups chopped onion
1 cup chopped celery
1 clove garlic, minced
3 tablespoons fresh lemon
   juice

2 tablespoons sugar
1 tablespoon salt
1 teaspoon prepared
   horseradish
1 teaspoon Worcestershire
   sauce
½ teaspoon pepper

Combine tomatoes, onion, celery, and garlic in a large Dutch oven. Bring to a boil over medium-high heat; reduce heat, and simmer, uncovered, 20 minutes, stirring occasionally. Press mixture through a food mill or sieve, reserving tomato juice; discard pulp and seeds. Stir in lemon juice and remaining ingredients. Cover and chill thoroughly. Yield: 3 quarts.

Gatherings
The Junior League of Milwaukee, Wisconsin

Hot Fruit Drink

2 cups water
½ cup firmly packed brown
  sugar
6 (3-inch) sticks cinnamon

6 whole cloves
2 cups pineapple juice
2 cups orange juice
½ cup lemon juice

Combine water, brown sugar, cinnamon sticks, and cloves in a large Dutch oven. Bring to a boil; cover, reduce heat, and simmer 10 minutes. Strain mixture, discarding cinnamon sticks and whole cloves. Add pineapple, orange, and lemon juices to sugar mixture in Dutch oven. Cook over medium heat until mixture is thoroughly heated. Serve hot. Yield: 6 cups.   Heather Johnson

Recipes and Remembrances
The Upsala Area Historical Society
Upsala, Minnesota

Amaretto Coffee

2⅔ cups hot brewed coffee
¼ cup amaretto

Whipped cream
Ground cinnamon

Combine coffee and amaretto; stir well. Top each serving with a dollop of whipped cream; sprinkle with cinnamon. Serve immediately. Yield: about 3 cups.

Steeped in Tradition
The Junior Service League of DeLand, Florida

Breads

A tranquil mill pond in South Gouldsboro, Maine, serves as a reminder of the past when grinding and mixing flour from grain grown on individual farms was an essential part of the breadmaking process.

Cranberry Fruit-Nut Bread

2 cups all-purpose flour
1½ teaspoons baking powder
½ teaspoon baking soda
1 teaspoon salt
1 cup sugar
¼ teaspoon ground nutmeg
   (optional)
¼ cup shortening

1 to 2 teaspoons grated
   orange rind
¾ cup orange juice
1 egg, beaten
1 cup fresh cranberries,
   coarsely chopped
½ cup chopped pecans or
   walnuts

Combine first 5 ingredients and, if desired, nutmeg in a large bowl; cut in shortening with a pastry blender until mixture resembles coarse meal. Combine orange rind, orange juice, and egg; stir well. Add to dry ingredients, stirring just until dry ingredients are moistened. Fold in cranberries and pecans.

Pour batter into a greased 9- x 5- x 3-inch loafpan. Bake at 350° for 1 hour or until a wooden pick inserted in center comes out clean. Let cool in pan 15 minutes; remove from pan, and let cool completely on a wire rack. Yield: 1 loaf.   Elsie Kahlden

Columbus Collection
Magnolia Homes Tour
Columbus, Texas

Coconut Plantation Bread

3 cups all-purpose flour
1 tablespoon baking powder
½ teaspoon salt
1 cup sugar

1 cup shredded coconut
1 cup milk
1 egg, beaten
1 teaspoon vanilla extract

Combine first 5 ingredients; stir well. Combine milk, egg, and vanilla; stir well. Stir into flour mixture. Cover and let stand 20 minutes. Pour batter into a greased 9- x 5- x 3-inch loafpan. Bake at 325° for 60 to 70 minutes or until a wooden pick inserted in center comes out clean. Let cool in pan 10 minutes; remove from pan, and let cool on a wire rack. Yield: 1 loaf.

Biscayne Bights and Breezes
The Villagers, Inc.
Coral Gables, Florida

Pumpkin Bread

1½ cups sugar
2 eggs, beaten
1 cup cooked, mashed
  pumpkin
½ cup vegetable oil
¼ cup water
1⅔ cups all-purpose flour

1 teaspoon baking soda
¼ teaspoon baking powder
¾ teaspoon salt
½ teaspoon ground cinnamon
½ teaspoon ground cloves
½ cup chopped pecans or
  walnuts (optional)

Combine sugar and eggs in a large bowl; beat at medium speed of an electric mixer until well blended. Add pumpkin, oil, and water, mixing well.

Combine flour and next 5 ingredients; stir well. Add to pumpkin mixture, mixing well. Add chopped pecans, if desired, stirring well.

Pour batter into a greased 9- x 5- x 3-inch loafpan. Bake at 350° for 1 hour and 10 minutes or until a wooden pick inserted in center comes out clean. Let cool in pan 10 minutes; remove from pan, and let cool completely on a wire rack. Yield: 1 loaf.

The Golden Apple Collection
White Plains Auxiliary of the White Plains Hospital Center
White Plains, New York

Zucchini Bread

2 cups sugar
1 cup vegetable oil
3 eggs
2 teaspoons vanilla extract
2 cups shredded zucchini
½ cup applesauce
¼ cup plus 1 tablespoon
  orange juice
3 cups all-purpose flour

2 teaspoons baking soda
¼ teaspoon baking powder
1 teaspoon salt
1½ teaspoons ground
  cinnamon
¾ teaspoon ground nutmeg
1 cup chopped pecans or
  walnuts

Combine sugar, oil, eggs, and vanilla in a large bowl; beat at medium speed of an electric mixer until well blended. Add zucchini, applesauce, and orange juice; stir well.

Combine flour and next 5 ingredients; add to zucchini mixture, stirring well. Add chopped pecans, stirring gently to combine.

Pour batter into two greased and floured 9- x 5- x 3-inch loafpans. Bake at 350° for 1 hour to 1 hour and 10 minutes or until a wooden pick inserted in center of loaves comes out clean. Let cool in pans 10 minutes; remove from pans, and let loaves cool completely on wire racks. Yield: 2 loaves.   Mary Nell Bryant

The True Essentials of a Feast
The Library of Congress/LC Cooking Club
Washington, DC

Apple Muffins

1 cup unbleached flour	½ cup buttermilk
½ cup whole wheat flour	1 cup peeled, chopped
2 teaspoons baking powder	cooking apple
1 teaspoon baking soda	½ cup chopped walnuts
⅓ cup sugar	½ cup unbleached flour
2 teaspoons ground cinnamon	⅓ cup firmly packed brown
½ teaspoon ground cloves	sugar
2 eggs, lightly beaten	1 teaspoon ground cinnamon
½ cup margarine, melted	¼ cup margarine

Combine 1 cup unbleached flour, whole wheat flour, baking powder, soda, ⅓ cup sugar, 2 teaspoons cinnamon, and cloves in a large bowl; make a well in center of mixture.

Combine eggs, ½ cup melted margarine, and buttermilk in a small bowl; add to flour mixture, stirring just until dry ingredients are moistened. Add apple and walnuts, stirring well.

Spoon batter into greased muffin pans, filling two-thirds full. Combine ½ cup unbleached flour, brown sugar, and 1 teaspoon cinnamon in a medium bowl; cut in ¼ cup margarine with a pastry blender until mixture resembles coarse meal. Sprinkle over batter. Bake at 400° for 15 to 20 minutes or until muffins are lightly browned. Remove from pans immediately. Let cool completely on wire racks. Yield: 1 dozen.   Bonnie Marecki

West Central Vegetarian Cookbook
The West Central Seventh Day Adventist Church
Oak Park, Illinois

Banana Bran Muffins

¾ cup all-purpose flour
¾ cup whole wheat flour
½ cup unprocessed oat bran, uncooked
2 teaspoons baking powder
½ teaspoon baking soda
¼ teaspoon salt
1 teaspoon ground cinnamon

1 egg
¾ cup firmly packed brown sugar
1⅓ cups mashed ripe bananas
½ cup raisins or chopped walnuts
⅓ cup vegetable oil
1 teaspoon vanilla extract

Combine first 7 ingredients in a large bowl; make a well in center of mixture. Set aside.

Combine egg and brown sugar in a medium bowl; beat at medium speed of an electric mixer until smooth. Add bananas, raisins, oil, and vanilla; beat well. Add to flour mixture, stirring just until dry ingredients are moistened.

Spoon batter into greased muffin pans, filling two-thirds full. Bake at 375° for 20 to 25 minutes. Remove from pans immediately. Let cool on wire racks. Yield: 1 dozen.   Mark May

Cooking with the Skins
The National Multiple Sclerosis Society/National Capital Chapter
Washington, DC

Cheese-Studded Caraway Rye Muffins

1 cup rye flour
⅔ cup all-purpose flour
¼ cup plus 2 tablespoons chopped walnuts
1½ teaspoons baking powder
½ teaspoon baking soda
½ teaspoon salt
½ teaspoon caraway seeds
½ teaspoon poppy seeds

1 cup buttermilk
2 eggs, lightly beaten
¼ cup vegetable oil
2 tablespoons honey
4½ ounces Monterey Jack, Muenster, Swiss, or cream cheese, cut into twelve ¾-inch cubes

Combine first 8 ingredients in a large bowl; make a well in center of mixture. Combine buttermilk, eggs, oil, and honey; add to dry ingredients, stirring just until dry ingredients are moistened.

Spoon batter into greased muffin pans, filling two-thirds full. Press a cheese cube into center of each muffin. Bake at 400° for 18 to

20 minutes. Remove muffins from pans immediately, and serve warm. Yield: 1 dozen.

Jackson Hole à la Carte
The Jackson Hole Alliance for Responsible Planning
Jackson, Wyoming

Best-Ever Homemade Pancakes

1½ cups all-purpose flour   1 cup milk
1¾ teaspoons baking powder   2 eggs, lightly beaten
1 teaspoon salt   3 tablespoons butter, melted
3 tablespoons sugar

Combine first 4 ingredients in a large bowl; stir well. Combine milk, eggs, and butter in a small bowl; stir well. Add to dry ingredients, stirring just until blended. For each pancake, pour about ¼ cup batter onto a hot, lightly greased griddle. Turn pancakes when tops are covered with bubbles and edges look cooked. Yield: 12 (4-inch) pancakes.   Nancy Miller Johnson

Diamonds in the Desert
The Woman's League of Ozona, Texas

Buttermilk Pancakes

1¼ cups all-purpose flour   1 tablespoon sugar
2 teaspoons baking powder   1 egg, beaten
½ teaspoon baking soda   1 cup buttermilk
½ teaspoon salt   2 tablespoons vegetable oil

Combine first 5 ingredients in a large bowl; stir well. Combine egg, buttermilk, and oil; stir well. Add to dry ingredients, stirring just until moistened. (Batter will be lumpy.) For each pancake, pour about ¼ cup batter onto a hot, lightly greased griddle. Turn pancakes when tops are covered with bubbles and edges look cooked. Yield: 12 (4-inch) pancakes.   Laura M. Benedickt

Woman to Woman Cookbook
The Zonta Club of the Black Hills
Rapid City, South Dakota

Waffles

1¼ cups all-purpose flour
1 tablespoon baking powder
1 teaspoon salt
2 tablespoons sugar

2 eggs, separated
1 cup milk
2 tablespoons vegetable oil
½ teaspoon vanilla extract

Combine first 4 ingredients; stir well. Combine egg yolks, milk, oil, and vanilla; stir well. Add to dry ingredients; stir until moistened. Beat egg whites (at room temperature) at high speed of an electric mixer until stiff; fold into batter. Bake in preheated oiled waffle iron. Yield: four 8-inch waffles.   Jo Beth Grubbs

Gingerbread . . . and all the trimmings
The Junior Service League of Waxahachie, Texas

The goal of Cook 'em Horns: The Quickbook *is to share recipes that reflect the relaxed lifestyles of Texans. Proceeds from the book will support the University of Texas scholarship fund.*

Corn Waffles

1½ cups cornmeal
⅓ cup all-purpose flour
1 teaspoon baking soda
½ teaspoon salt

2 tablespoons sugar
2 cups buttermilk
¼ cup vegetable oil
1 egg, lightly beaten

Combine first 5 ingredients in a large bowl; stir well, and set aside. Combine buttermilk, oil, and egg; stir well. Add to dry ingredients, stirring until blended. Bake in preheated oiled waffle iron. Yield: four 8-inch waffles.   Joe and Eugenia Nash Belden

Cook 'em Horns: The Quickbook
The Ex-Students Association of the University of Texas
Austin, Texas

Overnight Yeast Waffles
with Cinnamon-Blueberry Sauce

2 cups all-purpose flour
1 package dry yeast
¼ teaspoon ground
 cardamom
2 cups milk
2 tablespoons butter or
 margarine

1 teaspoon sugar
1 teaspoon salt
2 eggs, separated
Cinnamon-Blueberry Sauce

Combine flour, yeast, and cardamom in a large bowl; stir well. Set mixture aside.

Combine milk and next 3 ingredients in a medium saucepan. Cook over medium heat, stirring constantly, just until butter melts. Let cool to 120° to 130°. Add to flour mixture, beating at medium speed of an electric mixer 2 minutes. Cover and chill at least 8 hours.

Beat egg yolks at medium speed 4 minutes or until thick and lemon colored. Stir beaten egg yolks into batter.

Beat egg whites (at room temperature) at high speed until stiff peaks form. Fold one-third of egg whites into batter; carefully fold in remaining egg whites. Bake in preheated oiled waffle iron. Serve with Cinnamon-Blueberry Sauce. Yield: six 8-inch waffles.

Cinnamon-Blueberry Sauce

½ cup sugar
1 tablespoon plus 1 teaspoon
 cornstarch
½ teaspoon grated lemon rind
¼ teaspoon ground cinnamon

1 (10-ounce) package frozen
 unsweetened blueberries,
 thawed and divided
⅔ cup water
1 teaspoon lemon juice

Combine sugar, cornstarch, lemon rind, and cinnamon in a small bowl, and stir well.

Combine ½ cup blueberries and water in a small saucepan; bring to a boil over medium heat. Mash berries in saucepan. Add sugar mixture, and cook, stirring constantly, until sauce thickens. Add remaining blueberries and lemon juice; bring to a boil, and cook 3 to 5 minutes. Yield: 2 cups.

Rave Revues
Lakewood Center Associates, Lakewood Center for the Arts
Lake Oswego, Oregon

Black Bread (Crny Kruh)

2¼ cups water
¼ cup cider vinegar
¼ cup dark molasses
1 (1-ounce) square
  unsweetened chocolate
2 tablespoons caraway seeds
2 teaspoons instant coffee
  granules
2 packages dry yeast
¼ cup warm water (105° to
  115°)

1 tablespoon sugar
1 tablespoon salt
1 cup unprocessed wheat
  bran, uncooked
4 cups rye flour
3½ to 4 cups bread flour
1 egg white, lightly
  beaten

Combine 2¼ cups water, vinegar, molasses, chocolate, caraway seeds, and coffee granules in top of a double boiler; bring water in bottom of double boiler to a boil. Reduce heat to low; cook until chocolate melts and coffee granules dissolve, stirring occasionally. Let cool to 105° to 115°.

Dissolve yeast in ¼ cup warm water in a large mixing bowl; let stand 5 minutes.

Add cooled chocolate mixture, sugar, and salt to yeast mixture; stir well. Add wheat bran and rye flour. Beat at medium speed of an electric mixer until mixture is smooth. Gradually stir in enough bread flour to make a stiff dough.

Turn dough out onto a lightly floured surface, and knead until smooth and elastic (about 10 to 12 minutes). Place in a well-greased bowl, turning to grease top.

Cover dough, and let rise in a warm place (85°), free from drafts, 1½ hours or until doubled in bulk.

Turn dough out onto a lightly floured surface; divide into thirds. Shape each third into a round or oval loaf. Place loaves on a greased baking sheet. Cover and let rise in a warm place, free from drafts, 1½ hours or until doubled in bulk. Bake at 350° for 25 minutes. Brush tops of loaves with egg white. Bake an additional 25 minutes or until loaves sound hollow when tapped. Let cool on wire racks. Yield: 3 loaves.

Spokane Cooks!
The Community Centers Foundation of Spokane, Washington

French Bread

1½ cups warm water (105° to 115°)
1 package dry yeast
1 tablespoon sugar
1 tablespoon shortening
1½ teaspoons salt

4 cups all-purpose flour, divided
1 egg white
1 tablespoon water
Sesame seeds

Combine first 5 ingredients in a large bowl; let stand 5 minutes. Add 2 cups flour; beat at medium speed of an electric mixer until smooth. Gradually stir in enough remaining flour to make a soft dough. Let stand 10 minutes. Stir gently for a few seconds; cover. Repeat gentle stirring at 10-minute intervals for 40 minutes.

Turn dough out onto a lightly floured surface; divide in half. Roll each half to a 15- x 8-inch rectangle. Roll up jellyroll fashion, starting with long side; pinch ends and seam to seal.

Place loaves, seam side down, on a greased baking sheet. Make diagonal slits about ¼-inch deep down the length of loaves, using a razor blade or sharp knife. Combine egg white and 1 tablespoon water in a small bowl; beat with a wire whisk until blended. Brush loaves with egg white mixture, and sprinkle with sesame seeds. Cover and let rise in a warm place (85°), free from drafts, 45 minutes or until doubled in bulk. Bake at 375° for 30 minutes or until loaves sound hollow when tapped. Yield: 2 loaves.   Vickie Frisby

Parker's Blue Ribbon Recipes
The Parker Ward Relief Society
St. Anthony, Idaho

The Spokane Community Centers Foundation offers **Spokane Cooks!** *to benefit community centers in low-income neighborhoods, supporting the idea that those with substantial resources bear a responsibility to help those with less.*

Lemon Cheese Babka

1 package dry yeast
¼ cup warm water (105° to 115°)
¼ cup sugar, divided
3½ to 4 cups all-purpose flour, divided
2 teaspoons grated lemon rind
¾ teaspoon salt
2 eggs, lightly beaten

2 egg yolks, lightly beaten
⅓ cup warm milk (105° to 115°)
½ cup plus 2 tablespoons butter, softened
½ cup raisins
Cheese Filling
Crumb Topping
Sifted powdered sugar

Combine yeast, warm water, and ½ teaspoon sugar in a small bowl; let stand 5 minutes.

Combine 2 cups flour, remaining 3 tablespoons plus 2½ teaspoons sugar, lemon rind, and salt in a large bowl; stir well. Add yeast mixture, eggs, egg yolks, and milk; beat at low speed of an electric mixer until smooth. Gradually add butter, mixing well. Gradually stir in enough remaining flour to make a soft dough.

Turn dough out onto a lightly floured surface, and knead until smooth and elastic (about 10 minutes). Place dough in a well-greased bowl, turning to grease top. Cover and let rise in a warm place (85°), free from drafts, 1½ hours or until doubled in bulk.

Punch dough down; knead in raisins. Divide dough into 4 equal portions. Press 2 portions into bottom and ½ inch up sides of 2 greased 8-inch round cakepans. Spread Cheese Filling over dough in pans. Pat remaining 2 portions of dough to 8-inch circles. Place circles over Cheese Filling in pans; pinch edges, and tuck in to seal.

Sprinkle half of Crumb Topping over each loaf. Cover and let rise in a warm place, free from drafts, 1 hour or until doubled in bulk. Bake at 350° for 40 minutes or until loaves sound hollow when tapped. Remove from pans, and let cool on wire racks. Sprinkle with powdered sugar. Yield: two 8-inch loaves.

Cheese Filling

1 (8-ounce) package cream cheese, softened
½ cup cottage cheese

¼ cup sugar
1 egg yolk
1 teaspoon grated lemon rind

Combine cream cheese and cottage cheese in a medium bowl; beat at medium speed of an electric mixer until smooth. Add sugar and egg yolk, beating well. Stir in lemon rind. Yield: about 2 cups.

Crumb Topping

3 **tablespoons all-purpose flour**
3 **tablespoons sugar**
¼ **teaspoon ground cinnamon**

3 **tablespoons butter**
⅓ **cup chopped pecans or walnuts**

Combine first 3 ingredients in a small bowl; cut in butter with a pastry blender until mixture resembles coarse meal. Stir in pecans. Yield: about ½ cup.   Sonya Petroff

A Book of Favorite Recipes
Sisterhood of SS. Cyril and Methodius Orthodox Church
Terryville, Connecticut

Portuguese Sweet Bread

2 **packages dry yeast**
¼ **cup warm water (105° to115°)**
1 **cup milk**
½ **cup butter**
1 **cup sugar**

1 **teaspoon salt**
6 **cups all-purpose flour, divided**
3 **eggs, beaten**
1 **egg, beaten**

Dissolve yeast in warm water; let stand 5 minutes. Combine milk and butter in a saucepan; cook over medium heat until butter melts, stirring occasionally. Remove from heat; stir in sugar and salt. Let cool to 120° to 130°. Add 2 cups flour; beat at medium speed of an electric mixer until smooth. Add 3 eggs and yeast mixture, beating well. Stir in enough remaining flour to make a soft dough.

Turn dough out onto a lightly floured surface, and knead until smooth and elastic (about 8 to 10 minutes). Place in a well-greased bowl, turning to grease top. Cover and let rise in a warm place (85°), free from drafts, 1 hour or until doubled in bulk. Punch dough down; divide in half. Shape each half into a round, slightly flat loaf. Place in two greased 9-inch pieplates. Cover and let rise in a warm place, free from drafts, 1 hour or until doubled in bulk. Brush with egg. Bake at 350° for 25 minutes or until lightly browned. Remove from pieplates; cool on wire racks. Yield: 2 loaves.

The Mystic Seaport All Seasons Cookbook
Mystic Seaport Museum Stores
Mystic, Connecticut

Apricot Braids

3¼ cups all-purpose flour,
  divided
¼ cup sugar
1 package dry yeast
1 teaspoon salt
⅔ cup milk
2 tablespoons butter

2 eggs
Apricot Filling
2 tablespoons butter,
  melted
Topping (recipe follows)
Glaze (recipe follows)

Combine 2 cups flour, sugar, yeast, and salt in a large mixing bowl; stir well, and set aside.

Combine milk and 2 tablespoons butter in a small saucepan; heat until butter melts, stirring occasionally. Let cool to 120° to 130°. Add milk mixture and eggs to flour mixture, beating at medium speed of an electric mixer 2 minutes. Stir in enough remaining flour to make a stiff dough.

Turn dough out onto a lightly floured surface, and knead until smooth and elastic (about 10 minutes). Place in a well-greased bowl, turning to grease top. Cover and let rise in a warm place (85°), free from drafts, 1½ hours or until doubled in bulk.

Punch dough down, and divide in half. Cover and let rest 30 minutes. Roll each half to a 14- x 8-inch rectangle. Place each rectangle on a greased baking sheet.

Spread half of Apricot Filling lengthwise down center of each rectangle of dough. On each long side, cut 1-inch strips, 2 inches long. Starting at one end, fold strips at an angle across filling, alternating from side to side.

Cover loaves, and let rise in a warm place, free from drafts, 1½ hours or until doubled in bulk.

Brush loaves with melted butter, and sprinkle with topping. Bake at 350° for 20 minutes or until loaves are golden brown. Remove from baking sheets, and let cool on wire racks. Drizzle glaze over loaves. Yield: two 14-inch loaves.

Apricot Filling

1½ cups chopped dried
  apricots
1 cup water

1 cup firmly packed brown
  sugar

Place apricots and water in a medium saucepan. Bring water to a boil; cover, reduce heat, and simmer 20 to 25 minutes or until apricots are tender. Remove from heat. Add brown sugar, stirring until dissolved. Yield: 1 cup.

Topping

⅓ cup all-purpose flour

2 tablespoons sugar

1 teaspoon ground cinnamon

2 tablespoons butter

Combine flour, sugar, and cinnamon in a small bowl; stir well. Cut in butter with a pastry blender until mixture resembles coarse meal. Yield: about ½ cup.

Glaze

⅔ cup sifted powder sugar

1 tablespoon butter, melted

1 tablespoon milk

Combine all ingredients in a small bowl, stirring until mixture is smooth. Yield: ¼ cup.

Very Innovative Parties
The Loma Linda University School of Dentistry Auxiliary
Loma Linda, California

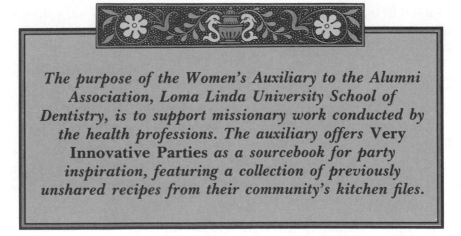

The purpose of the Women's Auxiliary to the Alumni Association, Loma Linda University School of Dentistry, is to support missionary work conducted by the health professions. The auxiliary offers **Very Innovative Parties** *as a sourcebook for party inspiration, featuring a collection of previously unshared recipes from their community's kitchen files.*

Sour Cream Twists

1 package dry yeast
¼ cup warm water (105° to 115°)
3 to 4 cups all-purpose flour, divided
1 cup warm sour cream (105° to 115°)
1 egg

3 tablespoons sugar
2 tablespoons butter, softened
1 teaspoon salt
2 tablespoons butter, melted
⅓ cup firmly packed brown sugar
1 teaspoon ground cinnamon
Creamy Glaze

Dissolve yeast in warm water in a large bowl; let stand 5 minutes. Add 1 cup flour, sour cream, egg, 3 tablespoons sugar, 2 tablespoons softened butter, and salt; beat at medium speed of an electric mixer until mixture is smooth. Gradually stir in enough remaining flour to make a soft dough.

Turn dough out onto a lightly floured surface, and knead until smooth and elastic (about 10 minutes). Place in a well-greased bowl, turning to grease top. Cover and let rise in a warm place (85°), free from drafts, 1 hour and 15 minutes or until doubled in bulk.

Punch dough down, and turn out onto a lightly floured surface. Roll dough to a 24- x 6-inch rectangle, and brush with 2 tablespoons melted butter.

Combine brown sugar and cinnamon in a small bowl; sprinkle lengthwise over half of rectangle. Fold dough in half lengthwise, and cut into 3- x 1-inch strips. Twist each strip twice. Place twists 2 inches apart on greased baking sheets, pressing ends down. Cover and let rise in a warm place, free from drafts, 1 hour or until doubled in bulk. Bake at 375° for 12 to 15 minutes or until rolls are golden brown. Remove to wire racks. Drizzle Creamy Glaze over warm rolls. Yield: 2 dozen.

Creamy Glaze

1½ cups sifted powdered sugar
2 tablespoons butter, softened

1 to 2 tablespoons hot water
1½ teaspoons vanilla extract

Combine all ingredients in a bowl; beat at medium speed of an electric mixer until smooth. Yield: about ½ cup.   Debbie East

Southern Secrets
SouthTrust Corporation
Birmingham, Alabama

Whole Wheat Doughnuts

2 medium potatoes, peeled
  and quartered
3 packages dry yeast
1 cup warm water (105° to
  115°)
3½ cups milk
1 cup vegetable oil
4 eggs, beaten
6½ cups whole wheat flour
1 cup sugar

2 teaspoons baking powder
1 tablespoon plus 1 teaspoon
  salt
1 teaspoon nutmeg
1 teaspoon lemon juice
1 teaspoon vanilla extract
6½ cups all-purpose flour
Vegetable oil
Glaze (recipe follows)

Cook potatoes in boiling water to cover 15 minutes or until tender; drain. Mash potatoes to measure 1 cup; set aside. Reserve any remaining potatoes for other uses. Dissolve yeast in warm water; let stand 5 minutes. Add 1 cup mashed potatoes, milk, and next 9 ingredients; beat at medium speed of an electric mixer 2 minutes or until blended. Stir in all-purpose flour.

Divide dough in half; place each half in a well-greased bowl, turning to grease top. Cover and let rise in a warm place (85°), free from drafts, 1 hour or until doubled in bulk.

Punch dough down; turn dough out onto a well-floured surface, and knead several times. Roll dough to ½-inch thickness, and cut with a 2½-inch doughnut cutter. Place doughnuts on lightly floured baking sheets. Cover and let rise in a warm place, free from drafts, 30 minutes or until doubled in bulk.

Heat 2 to 3 inches of oil to 375° in a large Dutch oven; drop in 4 or 5 doughnuts at a time. Cook about 1 minute or until golden brown on one side; turn and cook other side about 1 minute. Drain well. Dip hot doughnuts into glaze, letting excess glaze drip off. Let glazed doughnuts cool on wire racks. Yield: 5 dozen.

Glaze

4 cups sifted powdered sugar
½ cup milk

1 teaspoon vanilla extract
1 teaspoon lemon juice

Combine all ingredients in a small mixing bowl; stir until smooth. Yield: 2 cups.

Carolyn C. Huffman

Recipes to Cherish
WMSC, Harrisonburg Mennonite Church
Harrisonburg, Virginia

Cinnamon Crispies

2½ to 3½ cups all-purpose
  flour, divided
2 tablespoons sugar
1 package dry yeast
½ teaspoon salt
¾ cup water
½ cup unsalted butter or
  margarine
1 egg

2 tablespoons unsalted butter
  or margarine, softened
1 to 1½ cups sugar
1 tablespoon ground
  cinnamon
¼ cup plus 2 tablespoons
  finely chopped pecans or
  walnuts (optional)

Combine 1 cup flour, 2 tablespoons sugar, yeast, and salt in a large mixing bowl; stir well, and set aside.

Combine water and ½ cup butter in a small saucepan; cook over medium heat until butter melts, stirring constantly. Let cool to 120° to 130°. Add butter mixture and egg to flour mixture; mix at low speed of an electric mixer just until dry ingredients are moistened. Beat at medium speed of electric mixer 3 minutes. Gradually stir in enough remaining flour to make a stiff dough. Cover dough, and chill 2 hours.

Turn dough out onto a lightly floured surface; cover and let rest 20 minutes. Roll dough to an 18- x 10-inch rectangle; spread with 2 tablespoons softened butter. Combine 1 to 1½ cups sugar and cinnamon. Sprinkle ½ cup sugar mixture over dough. Roll up jellyroll fashion, starting at long side. Pinch seam to seal (do not seal ends). Cut into 1-inch slices.

Sprinkle remaining sugar mixture on aluminum foil. Place slices, cut side down and one at a time, on sugar mixture; roll each slice to a 5-inch circle, turning once. Sprinkle one side with chopped pecans, if desired. Place on ungreased baking sheets. Bake at 400° for 8 to 10 minutes or until pastries are golden brown. Let cool on wire racks. Yield: 1½ dozen.   Vivian Hilt

RSVP—Recipes Shared Very Proudly
First Church of Christ
Simsbury, Connecticut

Cakes

*A hand-carved wooden entrance door and graceful curving
set of marble steps once bid guests welcome to the home built
in 1825 by wealthy rice planter William Johnston. The
beaded trim over the windows is typical of the intricately
detailed woodwork of the era. Once located at 173 Rutledge
Avenue in Charleston, South Carolina, the house was razed to
make way for modern apartment buildings.*

Ron's Favorite Applesauce-Date Cake

2 cups all-purpose flour
2 teaspoons baking soda
¼ teaspoon salt
1 teaspoon ground
  cinnamon
½ teaspoon ground
  allspice
½ teaspoon ground nutmeg
¼ teaspoon ground cloves
1 cup firmly packed brown
  sugar

2 cups warm applesauce,
  divided
½ cup butter or margarine,
  softened
2 eggs
¾ cup coarsely chopped
  walnuts
½ cup chopped dates
Cream Cheese Frosting

Combine flour, soda, salt, cinnamon, allspice, nutmeg, and cloves in a large bowl; stir well. Add brown sugar, 1 cup applesauce, butter, and eggs; beat at low speed of an electric mixer 1 minute or until mixture is blended. Beat at medium speed 2 minutes. Add remaining 1 cup applesauce, coarsely chopped walnuts, and chopped dates, and stir well.

Pour batter into a greased and floured 9-inch square baking pan. Bake at 350° for 50 minutes or until a wooden pick inserted in center comes out clean. Let cake cool completely in pan on a wire rack. Spread Cream Cheese Frosting evenly on top of cake. Yield: 9 servings.

Cream Cheese Frosting

1 (3-ounce) package cream
  cheese, softened
1 tablespoon butter or
  margarine, softened

1 teaspoon vanilla extract
2 cups sifted powdered sugar

Combine cream cheese, butter, and vanilla in a small mixing bowl; beat at medium speed of an electric mixer until mixture is light and fluffy. Add powdered sugar, beating until mixture is smooth. Yield: 1 cup.

Con Mucho Gusto
The Desert Club of Mesa, Arizona

Blueberry Cake

½ cup butter, softened
1 cup sugar
2 eggs, separated
2 cups all-purpose flour
2 teaspoons baking powder
½ teaspoon salt
½ teaspoon ground cinnamon
½ teaspoon ground nutmeg

1 cup milk
2 cups fresh or frozen
   blueberries, thawed and
   drained
2 teaspoons all-purpose flour
Butterscotch Rum Sauce
2 cups whipping cream,
   whipped (optional)

Cream butter; gradually add sugar, beating at medium speed of an electric mixer. Add egg yolks, one at a time, beating well after each addition.

Combine 2 cups flour, baking powder, salt, cinnamon, and nutmeg in a medium bowl; add to creamed mixture alternately with milk, beginning and ending with flour mixture. Mix just until blended after each addition.

Beat egg whites (at room temperature) at high speed until stiff peaks form; fold into batter. Dredge blueberries in 2 teaspoons flour, and fold into batter.

Pour batter into a greased 8-inch square baking pan. Bake at 350° for 50 to 55 minutes or until a wooden pick inserted in center comes out clean. Let cool completely in pan; cut into squares. Serve cake with Butterscotch Rum Sauce and, if desired, whipped cream. Yield: 9 servings.

Butterscotch Rum Sauce

1½ cups firmly packed brown
   sugar
⅔ cup light corn syrup
¼ cup half-and-half or
   evaporated milk

¼ cup butter
½ teaspoon rum extract
½ teaspoon vanilla extract

Combine brown sugar, corn syrup, half-and-half, and butter in a medium saucepan; bring mixture to a boil over medium heat, stirring frequently. Reduce heat to low, and cook 20 minutes, stirring sauce occasionally. Add rum and vanilla extracts, stirring well. Yield: 1½ cups.   Mrs. Laurence K. Harper, Jr.

Two and Company
St. Thomas' Church, Garrison Forest
Owings Mills, Maryland

Cranberry Christmas Cake with Butter Sauce

2 cups all-purpose flour	1 cup milk
1 teaspoon baking powder	3 tablespoons butter, softened
¼ teaspoon salt	3 cups fresh cranberries
1 cup sugar	Butter Sauce

Combine first 6 ingredients in a large bowl; beat at medium speed of an electric mixer until blended. Fold in cranberries. Pour batter into a greased 9-inch square baking pan. Bake at 350° for 40 to 45 minutes or until a wooden pick inserted in center comes out clean. Serve immediately with warm Butter Sauce. Yield: 9 servings.

Butter Sauce

1 cup sugar	1 tablespoon all-purpose flour
½ cup butter, melted	1 tablespoon vinegar
½ cup whipping cream	1 teaspoon vanilla extract

Combine all ingredients in a saucepan; cook over high heat until hot and bubbly, beating at low speed of an electric mixer. Remove from heat; stir in vanilla. Yield: 1¾ cups.   Betsy Tepley

Recipes and Remembrances
The Upsala Area Historical Society
Upsala, Minnesota

"Nothing gets our little group down!" reads an excerpt from the minutes of a 1980 meeting of the Upsala Area Historical Society which provides fun, history, and "roots" for citizens of Upsala, Minnesota. The society dedicates Recipes and Remembrances *to all cooks, past and present, and includes Upsala area historical data in the cookbook.*

Christmas Pecan Cake

2 cups butter or margarine, softened
2½ cups firmly packed brown sugar
6 eggs, separated
4 cups all-purpose flour
3 tablespoons lemon extract
3 to 4 cups chopped pecans
½ pound candied cherries, chopped
½ pound candied pineapple, chopped
½ cup rum

Cream butter; gradually add brown sugar, beating at medium speed of an electric mixer until light and fluffy. Add egg yolks, and beat well. Add flour and lemon extract; beat until blended.

Beat egg whites (at room temperature) at high speed until stiff peaks form. Gently fold one-fourth of egg whites into batter. Gently fold in remaining egg whites, pecans, cherries, and pineapple. Pour batter into a greased 10-inch tube pan. Bake at 250° for 2½ to 3 hours or until a wooden pick inserted in center comes out clean. Let cool completely in pan on a wire rack.

Moisten several layers of cheesecloth with rum; cover cake completely with cheesecloth. Wrap with aluminum foil; chill at least 24 hours. Cake can be stored in refrigerator up to 1 week. Yield: one 10-inch cake.

Celebrated Seasons
The Junior League of Minneapolis, Minnesota

Million Dollar Pound Cake

2 cups butter, softened
3 cups sugar
6 eggs
4 cups all-purpose flour
¾ cup milk
1 teaspoon almond extract
1 teaspoon vanilla extract

Cream butter; gradually add sugar, beating well at medium speed of an electric mixer. Add eggs, one at a time, beating after each addition. Add flour to creamed mixture alternately with milk, beginning and ending with flour. Mix just until blended after each addition. Stir in flavorings.

Pour batter into a greased and floured 10-inch tube pan. Bake at 350° for 1 hour and 20 minutes or until a wooden pick inserted in center comes out clean. Let cake cool in pan 10 minutes. Remove from pan, and let cake cool completely on a wire rack. Yield: one 10-inch cake.   Kathleen Plummer

Southern Secrets
SouthTrust Corporation
Birmingham, Alabama

Almond Cake

1 cup butter, softened	½ teaspoon salt
1 cup sugar	2 tablespoons milk
3 eggs	2 tablespoons amaretto
1 (12-ounce) can almond	Almond Glaze
paste	¼ cup sliced almonds,
2¼ cups all-purpose flour	toasted
2 teaspoons baking powder	

Cream butter; gradually add sugar, beating well at medium speed of an electric mixer. Add eggs, one at a time, beating well after each addition. Add almond paste; beat until smooth. Combine flour, baking powder, and salt; stir well. Combine milk and amaretto. Add flour mixture to creamed mixture alternately with milk mixture, beginning and ending with flour mixture. Mix after each addition.

Pour batter into a greased and floured 9-inch tube pan. Bake at 350° for 1 hour and 10 minutes or until a wooden pick inserted in center comes out clean. Let cool in pan 10 minutes; remove from pan, and let cool completely on a wire rack. Spoon Almond Glaze over top of cake, allowing it to drizzle down sides. Sprinkle toasted sliced almonds over top of cake. Yield: one 9-inch cake.

Almond Glaze

1 cup sifted powdered sugar	1 tablespoon amaretto
2 tablespoons half-and-half	¼ teaspoon almond extract

Combine all ingredients in a small bowl; stir until sugar dissolves and mixture is smooth. Yield: ⅓ cup.   Deb Wimler

Korn Brew
The Durham Elementary Parent Organization
Durham, Connecticut

Almond Cake with Raspberry Sauce

½ cup unsalted butter,
  softened
1 (8-ounce) can almond paste
¾ cup sugar
3 eggs
1 tablespoon kirsch or Triple
  Sec

¼ teaspoon almond extract
¼ cup all-purpose flour
½ teaspoon baking powder
Powdered sugar
1 (16-ounce) package frozen
  raspberries, thawed
2 tablespoons sugar

Cream butter and almond paste; gradually add ¾ cup sugar, beating well at medium speed of an electric mixer. Add eggs, kirsch, and almond extract; beat well.

Combine flour and baking powder; add to creamed mixture, beating just until blended. Pour batter into a greased and floured 8-inch round cakepan. Bake at 350° for 40 to 50 minutes or until a wooden pick inserted in center comes out clean. Let cool in pan 10 minutes. Remove from pan, and let cool completely on a wire rack. Sift powdered sugar over cake, and set aside.

Place raspberries and 2 tablespoons sugar in container of an electric blender or food processor; process until pureed. Strain; discard seeds. Spoon sauce onto individual dessert plates, and top with slices of cake. Yield: 8 servings.

Gourmet by the Bay
The Dolphin Circle of the King's Daughters and Sons
Virginia Beach, Virginia

The Dolphin Circle's purposes are to help those who are unable to help themselves, contribute to community needs, and endeavor to develop the spiritual life of the community. To these ends, the Circle will use the funds generated from the sale of Gourmet by the Bay.

Pear-Oatmeal Cake

1 (29-ounce) can pear halves
  in heavy syrup, undrained
1 cup quick-cooking oats,
  uncooked
½ cup butter, softened
1 cup firmly packed brown
  sugar
2 eggs
1 teaspoon vanilla extract

2 cups sifted cake flour
1 teaspoon baking powder
1 teaspoon baking soda
¼ teaspoon salt
1 teaspoon ground cinnamon
¼ teaspoon ground nutmeg
½ cup buttermilk
⅓ cup hazelnuts
½ cup sugar

Drain pears, reserving 1¼ cups syrup. Set pear halves aside. Pour syrup into a small saucepan, and bring to a boil over medium heat. Remove from heat; stir in oats, and let stand 20 minutes.

Cream butter at medium speed of an electric mixer; gradually add brown sugar, beating well at medium speed of electric mixer. Add eggs, one at a time, beating well after each addition. Add vanilla and oatmeal mixture; beat well.

Combine flour, baking powder, soda, salt, cinnamon, and nutmeg in a medium bowl; add to creamed mixture alternately with buttermilk, beginning and ending with flour mixture. Mix after each addition.

Pour batter into a greased and floured 9-inch springform pan. Bake at 350° for 45 to 55 minutes or until a wooden pick inserted in center comes out clean. Let cool in pan 10 minutes; remove from pan, and let cool completely on a wire rack.

Spread hazelnuts in a shallow baking pan. Bake at 350° for 15 minutes, stirring occasionally. Let cool; place hazelnuts between paper towels, and rub briskly to remove skins. Coarsely chop hazelnuts; set aside.

Remove cake to a serving plate. Cut pear halves in half lengthwise, and arrange pear slices on top of cake. Sprinkle with hazelnuts, and set aside.

Place ½ cup sugar in a heavy saucepan; cook over medium heat, stirring constantly, until sugar melts and syrup is light golden brown. Remove from heat, and let cool 5 minutes. Drizzle or spin syrup over top of cake. Yield: one 9-inch cake.   Olga Wrettick

A Book of Favorite Recipes
Sisterhood of SS. Cyril and Methodius Orthodox Church
Terryville, Connecticut

Queen Elizabeth Cake

1 cup boiling water
1 cup chopped dates
1 teaspoon baking soda
¼ cup butter, softened
1 cup sugar
1 egg
1¼ cups all-purpose flour
1 teaspoon baking powder
¼ teaspoon salt

1 teaspoon vanilla extract
⅓ cup chopped pecans
¼ cup plus 1 tablespoon
    firmly packed brown sugar
¼ cup plus 1 tablespoon
    whipping cream
2 tablespoons butter
Pecan halves
Maraschino cherries

Combine water, dates, and soda; stir well. Let stand 15 minutes.

Cream ¼ cup butter; gradually add 1 cup sugar, beating well at medium speed of an electric mixer. Add egg; beat well. Combine flour, baking powder, and salt; add to creamed mixture alternately with date mixture, beginning and ending with flour mixture. Mix after each addition. Stir in vanilla and chopped pecans.

Pour batter into a greased 8½- x 4½- x 3-inch loafpan. Bake at 350° for 55 to 60 minutes. (Cake will not test done.) Let cool in pan 10 minutes. Remove from pan, and place on a serving plate.

Combine brown sugar, cream, and 2 tablespoons butter in a saucepan; stir well. Bring to a boil over medium heat. Reduce heat to low; simmer 3 to 5 minutes or until slightly thickened, stirring constantly. Pour over cake. Let cool completely. Garnish with pecan halves and cherries. Yield: 1 loaf.   Gwen Walker

The Oaks Cookbook
Colonel Timothy Bigelow Chapter, DAR
Worcester, Massachusetts

Self-Frosting Date Cake

1 cup chopped dates
1 teaspoon baking soda
1¼ cups boiling water
¾ cup shortening
1 cup sugar
2 eggs
1⅔ cups all-purpose flour
1 teaspoon baking powder

¾ teaspoon salt
½ cup firmly packed brown
    sugar
½ cup chopped pecans or
    walnuts
1 (6-ounce) package
    semisweet chocolate
    morsels

Stir dates and soda into boiling water; set aside, and let cool.

Cream shortening; gradually add 1 cup sugar, beating well at medium speed of an electric mixer. Add eggs, one at a time, beating well after each addition.

Combine flour, baking powder, and salt; add to creamed mixture alternately with date mixture, beginning and ending with flour mixture. Mix after each addition. Pour batter into a greased and floured 13- x 9- x 2-inch baking pan.

Combine brown sugar, pecans, and chocolate morsels; sprinkle over top of batter. Bake at 350° for 40 minutes or until a wooden pick inserted in center comes out clean. Let cool in pan on a wire rack. Yield: 15 servings.   Lorrie Fischer

Calvary Collections
Calvary Lutheran Church
Kalispell, Montana

Ginger-Raisin Cake

1 cup butter, softened	1 tablespoon ground ginger
1 cup firmly packed dark brown sugar	1½ teaspoons ground cinnamon
1 cup light molasses	1½ teaspoons ground cloves
3 eggs	1 cup boiling water
3 cups all-purpose flour	½ cup chopped crystallized ginger
1 teaspoon baking powder	⅓ cup golden raisins
1 teaspoon baking soda	

Cream butter; gradually add sugar, beating at medium speed of an electric mixer. Add molasses; beat well. Add eggs, one at a time, beating well after each addition.

Combine flour and next 5 ingredients; add to creamed mixture alternately with boiling water, beginning and ending with flour mixture. Mix after each addition. Stir in crystallized ginger and raisins. Pour batter into a greased and floured 13- x 9- x 2-inch baking pan. Bake at 350° for 30 to 40 minutes or until a wooden pick inserted in center comes out clean. Let cool in pan on a wire rack. Yield: 15 servings.

Gourmet LA
The Junior League of Los Angeles, California

Orange Kiss-Me Cake

1 large orange
1 cup raisins
⅓ cup walnuts
½ cup shortening
1⅓ cups sugar, divided
2 eggs

2 cups all-purpose flour
1 teaspoon baking soda
1 teaspoon salt
1 cup milk
¼ cup chopped walnuts
1 teaspoon ground cinnamon

Cut orange in half; remove and discard seeds. Squeeze ⅓ cup juice from orange; set juice aside. Position knife blade in food processor bowl; add orange halves, raisins, and ⅓ cup walnuts. Process until finely chopped; set aside.

Cream shortening; gradually add 1 cup sugar, beating until light and fluffy. Add eggs, one at a time, beating well after each addition. Combine flour, baking soda, and salt; add to creamed mixture alternately with milk, beginning and ending with flour mixture. Mix after each addition. Stir in raisin mixture.

Pour batter into a greased and floured 13- x 9- x 2-inch baking pan. Bake at 350° for 40 to 50 minutes or until a wooden pick inserted in center comes out clean. Let cool in pan 10 minutes. Drizzle reserved orange juice over cake. Combine remaining ⅓ cup sugar, ¼ cup walnuts, and cinnamon; sprinkle over warm cake. Let cool in pan on a wire rack. Yield: 15 servings.

A Pinch of Salt Lake
The Junior League of Salt Lake City, Utah

Rhubarb Cake

½ cup shortening
1½ cups sugar
1 egg
2 cups all-purpose flour
1 teaspoon baking soda
½ teaspoon salt

1 cup buttermilk
3 cups finely chopped
   rhubarb
Additional sugar
Ground cinnamon

Cream shortening; gradually add 1½ cups sugar, beating well. Add egg; beat well. Combine flour, soda, and salt; add to creamed mixture alternately with buttermilk, beginning and ending with flour mixture. Mix after each addition. Stir in rhubarb. Pour batter into a greased and floured 13- x 9- x 2-inch baking pan. Sprinkle sugar and cinnamon over batter. Bake at 350° for 45 minutes or until cake tests done. Let cool in pan on a wire rack. Yield: 15 servings. Rose Marie Fowler

Exclusively Rhubarb Cookbook
The Charity Cookbook Fund
Coventry, Connecticut

Coffee Chiffon Cake

2½ cups sifted cake flour
1 tablespoon baking powder
⅛ teaspoon baking soda
1 teaspoon salt
1 cup sugar
⅓ cup vegetable oil
2 eggs, separated
½ cup milk
½ cup cold coffee
2 teaspoons vanilla extract
½ cup sugar
Fluffy Coffee Frosting

Combine first 5 ingredients; make a well in center of mixture. Add oil, egg yolks, milk, coffee, and vanilla. Beat 5 minutes or until satiny smooth. Beat egg whites (at room temperature) until soft peaks form. Add ½ cup sugar, 2 tablespoons at a time, beating until stiff peaks form. Pour egg yolk mixture in a thin, steady stream over egg whites; fold egg whites into yolk mixture.

Pour batter into 2 greased and floured 8-inch round cakepans. Bake at 350° for 30 to 35 minutes or until cake springs back when lightly touched. Let cool in pans 10 minutes; remove from pans, and let cool completely on wire racks. Split each cake layer in half horizontally. Spread Fluffy Coffee Frosting between layers and on top and sides of cake. Yield: one 4-layer cake.

Fluffy Coffee Frosting

1½ cups shortening
1 cup sugar
½ teaspoon salt
¼ cup cold coffee
1 teaspoon vanilla extract
2 eggs

Combine all ingredients; beat at high speed of an electric mixer 5 minutes or until fluffy. Yield: 4 cups. Rosemary Harris

Land of Cotton
John T. Morgan Academy
Selma, Alabama

Caramel Cake

1 cup butter, softened
2 cups sugar
4 eggs
3 cups sifted cake flour
1 tablespoon baking
 powder

¼ teaspoon salt
1 cup milk
2 teaspoons vanilla extract
Frosting (recipe follows)

Cream butter in a large mixing bowl at medium speed of an electric mixer; gradually add sugar, beating well at medium speed of electric mixer. Add eggs, one at a time, beating well after each addition.

Combine flour, baking powder, and salt; add to creamed mixture alternately with milk, beginning and ending with flour mixture. Mix after each addition. Stir in vanilla.

Pour batter into 4 greased and floured 9-inch round cakepans. Bake at 350° for 25 to 30 minutes or until a wooden pick inserted in center comes out clean.

Let cool in pans 10 minutes. Remove from pans, and let cool completely on wire racks.

Spread frosting between layers and on top and sides of cake. Yield: one 4-layer cake.

Frosting

4 cups sugar, divided   2 cups whipping cream

Sprinkle 1 cup sugar in a large cast-iron skillet; cook over medium heat, stirring constantly, until sugar melts and is light golden brown.

Combine remaining 3 cups sugar and whipping cream in a large saucepan; cook over low heat until sugar melts, stirring occasionally. Gradually add caramelized sugar. (The mixture will tend to lump, becoming smooth with further cooking.) Cook over medium heat, stirring frequently, 20 to 25 minutes or until a candy thermometer registers 238°. Remove from heat, and let cool 5 minutes.

Beat frosting with a wooden spoon to almost spreading consistency (about 5 minutes). Immediately spread frosting on cake. Yield: 3 cups.   Julia Jones

The Share-Cropper
The Central Delta Academy Parent-Teacher Organization
Inverness, Mississippi

Italian Cream Cake

½ cup shortening
½ cup butter or margarine,
  softened
2 cups sugar
5 eggs, separated
2 cups all-purpose flour
1 teaspoon baking soda

1 cup buttermilk
1 cup chopped pecans
1 (3½-ounce) can flaked
  coconut
1 teaspoon vanilla extract
Frosting (recipe follows)
1 cup chopped pecans

Cream shortening and butter; gradually add sugar, beating well at medium speed of an electric mixer. Add egg yolks, one at a time, beating well after each addition.

Combine flour and soda in a small bowl. Add flour mixture to creamed mixture alternately with buttermilk, beginning and ending with flour mixture. Mix after each addition. Stir in 1 cup chopped pecans, coconut, and vanilla.

Beat egg whites (at room temperature) in a medium mixing bowl at high speed of electric mixer until stiff peaks form. Gently fold beaten egg whites into batter.

Pour batter into 3 greased and wax paper-lined 9-inch round cakepans. Bake at 350° for 25 to 30 minutes or until a wooden pick inserted in center comes out clean. Let cool in pans 10 minutes; remove from pans, and let cool completely on wire racks.

Spread frosting between layers and on top and sides of cake. Sprinkle 1 cup chopped pecans evenly over frosting. Yield: one 3-layer cake.

Frosting

1 cup butter or margarine,
  softened
1 (8-ounce) package cream
  cheese, softened

1 (16-ounce) package
  powdered sugar, sifted
1 teaspoon vanilla extract

Combine butter and cream cheese in a large mixing bowl, and beat at medium speed of an electric mixer until well blended. Gradually add powdered sugar, beating until mixture is smooth. Stir in vanilla. Yield: 3⅓ cups.   Shirley Smithson Langston

A Samford Celebration Cookbook
Samford University Auxiliary
Birmingham, Alabama

Blue Ribbon Banana Cake

¾ cup shortening
1½ cups sugar
2 eggs
1 cup mashed banana
2 cups sifted cake flour
1 teaspoon baking
  powder
1 teaspoon baking soda

½ teaspoon salt
½ cup buttermilk
½ cup chopped pecans
1 teaspoon vanilla
  extract
1 cup flaked coconut
Creamy Nut Filling
White Snow Frosting

Cream shortening in a large mixing bowl at medium speed of an electric mixer. Gradually add sugar, beating well at medium speed of electric mixer. Add eggs, one at a time, beating well after each addition. Add banana; beat well.

Combine flour, baking powder, soda, and salt in a medium bowl. Add flour mixture to creamed mixture alternately with buttermilk, beginning and ending with flour mixture. Mix after each addition. Stir in pecans and vanilla.

Pour batter into 2 greased and floured 9-inch round cakepans. Sprinkle ½ cup flaked coconut evenly over batter in each cakepan. Bake at 350° for 30 to 35 minutes or until a wooden pick inserted in center of cake layers comes out clean. Let cake layers cool in pans 10 minutes. Carefully remove cake layers from pans, and let cool completely on wire racks.

Place one cake layer, coconut side down, on a serving plate. Spread top of cake layer with Creamy Nut Filling. Top with remaining layer, coconut side up. Spread White Snow Frosting on sides and 1 inch around top edge of cake, leaving center unfrosted. Yield: one 2-layer cake.

Creamy Nut Filling

½ cup sugar
2 tablespoons all-purpose
  flour
¼ teaspoon salt
½ cup half-and-half

2 tablespoons butter or
  margarine
½ cup chopped pecans
1 teaspoon vanilla extract

Combine sugar, flour, salt, half-and-half, and butter in a small saucepan. Cook over medium heat, stirring constantly, until mixture is thickened.

Remove saucepan from heat, and stir in chopped pecans and vanilla. Let frosting cool completely. Yield: 1 cup.

White Snow Frosting

¼ cup shortening
¼ cup butter or margarine, softened
1 egg white
½ teaspoon coconut extract

½ teaspoon vanilla extract
2 cups sifted powdered sugar

Combine shortening, softened butter, egg white, and coconut and vanilla extracts in a medium mixing bowl. Beat at medium speed of an electric mixer until blended.

Gradually add sifted powdered sugar to creamed mixture, beating at medium speed until frosting reaches spreading consistency. Yield: 1⅓ cups.   St. Mary's, Lakota

Heritage Cookbook
The Catholic Diocese of Fargo, North Dakota

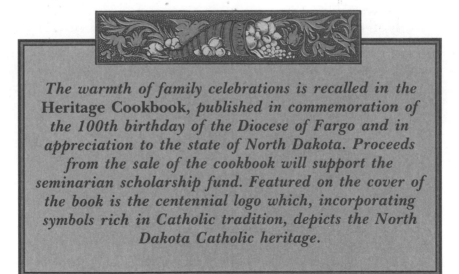

The warmth of family celebrations is recalled in the **Heritage Cookbook,** *published in commemoration of the 100th birthday of the Diocese of Fargo and in appreciation to the state of North Dakota. Proceeds from the sale of the cookbook will support the seminarian scholarship fund. Featured on the cover of the book is the centennial logo which, incorporating symbols rich in Catholic tradition, depicts the North Dakota Catholic heritage.*

Best Carrot Cake

2 cups sugar
¾ cup buttermilk
¾ cup vegetable oil
3 eggs, beaten
2 teaspoons vanilla extract
2 cups all-purpose flour
2 teaspoons baking soda
½ teaspoon salt
2 teaspoons ground cinnamon

2 cups grated carrots
1 cup chopped walnuts
1 (8-ounce) can crushed
   pineapple, drained
1 (3½-ounce) can flaked
   coconut
Buttermilk Glaze
Cream Cheese Frosting

Combine first 5 ingredients; beat well. Combine flour, soda, salt, and cinnamon; add to sugar mixture, stirring well. Add carrot, walnuts, pineapple, and coconut; stir well.

Pour batter into 3 greased and floured 9-inch round cakepans. Bake at 350° for 35 to 40 minutes or until a wooden pick inserted in center comes out clean. Pour Buttermilk Glaze over warm cake layers. Let cool in pans 15 minutes; remove from pans, and let cool completely on wire racks. Spread Cream Cheese Frosting between layers and on top and sides of cake. Yield: one 3-layer cake.

Buttermilk Glaze

1 cup sugar
½ cup buttermilk
½ cup butter

1 tablespoon light corn syrup
½ teaspoon baking soda
1 teaspoon vanilla extract

Combine first 5 ingredients in a large saucepan. Bring to a boil over medium heat; cook 4 minutes, stirring frequently. Remove from heat; stir in vanilla. Yield: 2 cups.

Cream Cheese Frosting

1 (8-ounce) package cream
   cheese, softened
½ cup butter or margarine,
   softened

1 (16-ounce) package
   powdered sugar, sifted
1 teaspoon vanilla extract

Combine cream cheese and butter; beat at medium speed of an electric mixer until smooth. Gradually add sugar, beating until light and fluffy. Stir in vanilla. Yield: 3 cups.   Beth Burkhart Parrott

Taste of the Town—Second Serving
The Charity League of Lexington, North Carolina

Coconut Cake with Lemon Filling

1 cup butter
2 cups sugar
4 eggs
3 cups all-purpose flour
1 tablespoon baking powder
⅛ teaspoon salt

1 cup milk
2 teaspoons vanilla extract
Lemon Filling
Frosting (recipe follows)
Flaked coconut

Cream butter; gradually add sugar, beating well at medium speed of an electric mixer. Add eggs, one at a time, beating well after each addition. Combine flour, baking powder, and salt; add to creamed mixture alternately with milk, beginning and ending with flour mixture. Mix after each addition. Stir in vanilla.

Pour batter into 3 greased and floured 8-inch round cakepans. Bake at 350° for 20 to 25 minutes or until a wooden pick inserted in center comes out clean. Let cool in pans 10 minutes; remove from pans, and let cool completely on wire racks. Spread Lemon Filling between layers; spread frosting on top and sides of cake. Sprinkle with flaked coconut. Yield: one 3-layer cake.

Lemon Filling

½ cup butter
½ cup sugar
¼ cup grated lemon rind

⅓ cup plus 1 teaspoon fresh
   lemon juice
2 eggs, beaten

Combine first 4 ingredients in top of a double boiler; bring water to a boil. Reduce heat to low; cook until butter melts, stirring occasionally. Add eggs; cook until thickened. Let cool completely. Yield: 1¼ cups.

Frosting

2 cups sugar
⅛ teaspoon cream of tartar
⅛ teaspoon salt

1 cup water
3 egg whites
2 teaspoons vanilla extract

Combine first 4 ingredients in a saucepan. Cook over medium heat, stirring constantly, until clear. Cook, without stirring, to hard ball stage (250° to 268°). Beat egg whites (at room temperature) until soft peaks form. Continue to beat, slowly adding syrup mixture. Add vanilla; beat until stiff peaks form. Yield: 3¼ cups.

Thymes Remembered
The Junior League of Tallahassee, Florida

Custard-Filled Poppyseed Cake

¾ cup milk
½ cup poppyseeds
¾ cup butter, softened
1½ cups sugar
3 cups all-purpose flour
1 tablespoon baking powder
¼ teaspoon salt
1 teaspoon vanilla extract
4 egg whites
Filling (recipe follows)
Frosting (recipe follows)

Combine milk and poppyseeds in a small bowl; chill 2 hours.

Cream butter; gradually add sugar, beating well at medium speed of an electric mixer.

Combine flour, baking powder, and salt; add to creamed mixture alternately with milk mixture, beginning and ending with flour mixture. Mix after each addition. Stir in vanilla.

Beat egg whites (at room temperature) at high speed until stiff peaks form; gently fold whites into creamed mixture. Pour batter into 3 greased and floured 8-inch round cakepans. Bake at 350° for 20 to 25 minutes or until a wooden pick inserted in center comes out clean. Let cool in pans 10 minutes; remove from pans, and let cool completely on wire racks.

Spread filling between cake layers; spread frosting on top and sides of cake. Yield: one 3-layer cake.

Filling

½ cup sugar
3 tablespoons cornstarch
2 tablespoons all-purpose flour
¼ teaspoon salt
1½ cups milk
4 egg yolks, beaten
½ cup chopped walnuts
1 teaspoon clear vanilla extract

Combine sugar, cornstarch, flour, and salt in a medium saucepan, stirring well.

Combine milk and egg yolks; gradually add to sugar mixture, stirring well. Bring to a boil over medium heat, stirring constantly. Remove from heat, and stir in walnuts and vanilla. Let cool completely. Yield: 2¼ cups.

Frosting

1 (8-ounce) package cream cheese, softened
½ cup butter, softened
1 (16-ounce) package powdered sugar, sifted
1 teaspoon vanilla extract

Beat cream cheese and butter at medium speed of an electric mixer until blended. Gradually add sugar, beating until light and fluffy. Stir in vanilla. Yield: 3 cups.

Bound to Please
The Junior League of Boise, Idaho

Swedish Torte

½ cup unsalted butter, softened
1½ cups sugar, divided
4 eggs, separated
¾ cup all-purpose flour
1 teaspoon baking powder
¼ cup milk
½ teaspoon vanilla extract
½ teaspoon almond extract
⅛ teaspoon salt
¼ cup chopped pecans or chopped blanched almonds
1 cup whipping cream, whipped
2 cups strawberries, sliced

Cream butter; gradually add ½ cup sugar, beating well at medium speed of an electric mixer. Add egg yolks, one at a time, beating well after each addition.

Combine flour and baking powder in a small bowl. Add flour mixture to creamed mixture alternately with milk, beginning and ending with flour mixture. Mix well after each addition. Stir in vanilla. Spoon batter into 2 greased and floured 10-inch springform pans. Set aside.

Beat egg whites (at room temperature), almond extract, and salt at high speed of electric mixer 1 minute. Gradually add remaining 1 cup sugar, 1 tablespoon at a time, beating until stiff peaks form and sugar dissolves (2 to 4 minutes). Spread half of meringue over cake batter in each pan; sprinkle with chopped pecans. Bake at 325° for 45 to 50 minutes or until meringue appears to be dry. Let cool in pans 10 minutes; carefully remove sides of pans, and let cool completely on wire racks.

Combine whipped cream and strawberries in a bowl. Place one cake layer, meringue side up, on a serving plate; spoon strawberry mixture over cake layer. Top with second cake layer, meringue side up. Yield: 10 to 12 servings.

Delicious Decisions
The Junior League of San Diego, California

Chocolate-Cinnamon Torte

1½ cups butter, softened
2 cups sugar
2 eggs
2¾ cups all-purpose flour
2 tablespoons ground
  cinnamon

4 cups whipping cream
⅓ cup sifted powdered sugar
2 tablespoons cocoa
12 maraschino cherries
12 walnut halves
Semisweet chocolate curls

Cream butter; gradually add 2 cups sugar, beating well. Add eggs, one at a time, beating well after each addition.

Combine flour and cinnamon; add to creamed mixture, beating well. Divide dough into 10 equal portions. Press into 10 greased, floured, and wax paper-lined 8-inch round cakepans. (Layers may be baked in batches.) Bake at 375° for 8 to 12 minutes or until golden brown. Remove from pans; remove wax paper, and let layers cool completely on wire racks.

Beat whipping cream until foamy; gradually add powdered sugar, beating until soft peaks form. Reserve ⅓ cup sweetened whipped cream. Spread remaining sweetened whipped cream between torte layers. Stir cocoa into reserved sweetened whipped cream; spread on top of torte. Alternately place cherries and walnut halves around outer edge of torte. Sprinkle chocolate curls in center of torte. Chill thoroughly. Yield: one 8-inch torte.

Company's Coming
The Junior League of Kansas City, Missouri

Applesauce Cake Roll

3 eggs
¾ cup sugar
1 cup all-purpose flour
½ teaspoon baking powder
½ teaspoon baking soda
¼ teaspoon salt

½ teaspoon ground cinnamon
¼ teaspoon ground cloves
½ cup applesauce
¼ cup raisins
1 tablespoon sugar
Filling (recipe follows)

Grease bottom and sides of a 15- x 10- x 1-inch jellyroll pan with vegetable oil; line with wax paper. Grease and flour wax paper; set pan aside. Beat eggs at high speed of an electric mixer until foamy. Gradually add ¾ cup sugar, beating until thick and lemon colored (5 to 6 minutes).

Combine flour and next 5 ingredients; gradually fold into egg mixture. Fold in applesauce and raisins. Spread batter in prepared pan. Bake at 375° for 12 to 15 minutes or until a wooden pick inserted in center comes out clean.

Sprinkle 1 tablespoon sugar in a 15- x 10-inch rectangle on a towel. When cake is done, immediately loosen from sides of pan, and turn out onto sugared towel. Carefully peel off wax paper. Starting at narrow end, roll up cake and towel together; let cool completely on a wire rack, seam side down. Unroll cake. Spread with filling, and carefully reroll cake, without towel. Place cake on a serving plate, seam side down. Chill. Yield: 8 to 10 servings.

Filling

**1 (8-ounce) package cream
  cheese, softened**

**¼ cup sugar
2 teaspoons milk**

Beat cream cheese until light and fluffy. Gradually add sugar, beating well. Add milk; beat until smooth. Yield: 1 cup.

Quiltie Ladies Scrapbook
Variable Star Quilters
Souderton, Pennsylvania

Peanut Butter Cupcakes

**1¾ cups all-purpose flour
1 tablespoon baking powder
½ teaspoon salt
¾ cup sugar
1 cup milk**

**½ cup creamy peanut butter
¼ cup butter or margarine
2 eggs
¾ teaspoon vanilla extract
⅔ cup milk chocolate morsels**

Combine first 9 ingredients in a large mixing bowl; beat at low speed of an electric mixer just until blended. Beat at high speed 2 minutes. Spoon batter into greased muffin pans, filling two-thirds full. Sprinkle chocolate morsels over each cupcake. Bake at 350° for 18 to 20 minutes or until a wooden pick inserted in center comes out clean. Remove from pans, and let cool completely on wire racks. Yield: 16 cupcakes.

Crème de LA Coast
Small World Guild—Childrens Hospital of Orange County,
California

Raspberry Swirl Cheesecake with Whole Berry Sauce

15 amaretti cookies, crushed (about ¾ cup)
¾ cup vanilla wafer crumbs
2 tablespoons butter, melted
1 (10-ounce) package frozen raspberries, thawed
1½ cups sugar, divided
5 (8-ounce) packages cream cheese, softened
3 tablespoons all-purpose flour

Dash of salt
1½ teaspoons lemon juice
½ teaspoon almond extract
5 eggs
2 egg yolks
¼ cup whipping cream
2 tablespoons framboise or other raspberry-flavored brandy
Whole Berry Sauce

Combine crumbs and butter; stir well. Firmly press crumb mixture in bottom of a 10-inch springform pan. Chill. Place raspberries in container of an electric blender or food processor; process until smooth. Press raspberry puree through a sieve; discard seeds. Combine raspberry puree and ½ cup sugar, stirring well; set aside.

Beat cream cheese until light and fluffy. Add remaining 1 cup sugar, flour, salt, lemon juice, and almond extract; beat 5 minutes. Add eggs and egg yolks, one at a time, beating well after each addition. Add cream; mix well. Stir in brandy. Pour batter into prepared pan. Pour raspberry mixture over batter; swirl with knife.

Bake at 425° for 10 minutes; reduce temperature to 350°, and bake for 1 hour and 5 minutes. Turn oven off. Let cheesecake cool in oven 1 hour. Remove from oven; let cool to room temperature on a wire rack. Cover and chill 8 hours. Remove sides of pan. Serve with Whole Berry Sauce. Yield: 12 to 14 servings.

Whole Berry Sauce

1 (10-ounce) package frozen raspberries in syrup, thawed

½ cup red currant jelly
2 teaspoons cornstarch
1 tablespoon water

Drain raspberries, reserving syrup. Combine syrup and jelly in a saucepan; cook over medium heat until jelly dissolves, stirring occasionally. Combine cornstarch and water. Add to syrup mixture, and cook until thickened. Stir in raspberries. Yield: 1⅓ cups.

The Mystic Seaport All Seasons Cookbook
Mystic Seaport Museum Stores
Mystic, Connecticut

Cookies & Candies

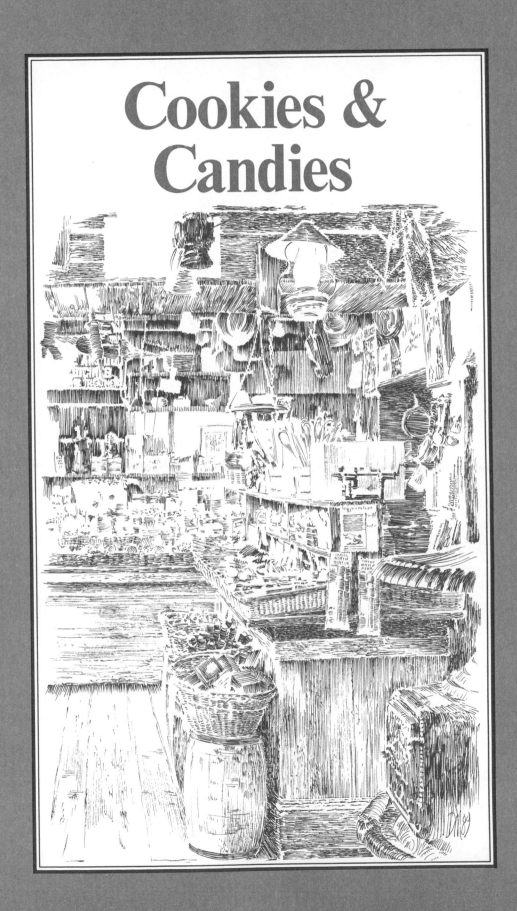

Weston, Vermont, is home to an old-time general store, complete with potbellied stove, gadgets, and penny candy. A handwritten sign next to the candy counter reads "Count your candy and tell the clerk how much you owe."

Alabama Cookies

1 cup shortening
1 cup sugar
1 cup firmly packed brown
sugar
2 eggs
1 teaspoon vanilla extract

1½ cups all-purpose flour
1 teaspoon salt
2 cups regular oats, uncooked
2 cups chopped pecans
1 cup crisp rice cereal
1 cup flaked coconut

Cream shortening; gradually add sugars, beating well at medium speed of an electric mixer. Add eggs and vanilla, beating well.

Combine flour and salt; add to creamed mixture, mixing well. Stir in oats and remaining ingredients. Drop dough by heaping teaspoonfuls onto greased cookie sheets. Bake at 325° for 10 to 12 minutes. Let cool slightly on cookie sheets; remove to wire racks to cool completely. Yield: 6 dozen.   Shirley Smithson Langston

A Samford Celebration Cookbook
Samford University Auxiliary
Birmingham, Alabama

Granola Cookies

2 cups regular oats, uncooked
1 cup firmly packed brown
sugar
1 cup butter, melted
2 eggs, beaten
¼ cup frozen orange juice
concentrate, thawed
1 teaspoon baking soda
1½ cups all-purpose flour

1 (12-ounce) package
semisweet chocolate
morsels
1 cup raisins
1 cup unsalted dry roasted
peanuts
1 teaspoon ground cinnamon
1 teaspoon vanilla extract
¼ teaspoon salt

Combine first 4 ingredients in a bowl; stir well. Combine orange juice concentrate and soda; add to oat mixture, stirring well. Add flour and remaining ingredients, stirring well to combine. Cover and chill at least 1 hour. Drop dough by tablespoonfuls onto greased cookie sheets. Bake at 375° for 10 minutes or until lightly browned. Let cool on wire racks. Yield: 6 dozen.   Carlin Weaver

Elizabeth H. Brown Humane Society Cookbook
Elizabeth H. Brown Humane Society, Inc.
Orleans, Vermont

Lemon-Zucchini Cookies

¾ cup butter, softened
¾ cup sugar
1 egg
1 teaspoon grated lemon rind
2 cups all-purpose flour
1 teaspoon baking powder
½ teaspoon salt
1 cup peeled, shredded
  zucchini
1 cup chopped walnuts
1 cup sifted powdered sugar
1½ tablespoons lemon juice

Cream butter; gradually add ¾ cup sugar, beating well at medium speed of an electric mixer. Add egg and lemon rind, beating well.

Combine flour, baking powder, and salt; stir well. Add to creamed mixture, mixing well. Stir in zucchini and walnuts.

Drop dough by rounded teaspoonfuls onto greased cookie sheets. Bake at 350° for 10 minutes. Remove to wire racks. Combine powdered sugar and lemon juice; stir well. Drizzle over warm cookies; let cool completely. Yield: 4 dozen.   Kim Olson

One Hundred Years of Sharing
Calvary Covenant Church Women
Evansville, Minnesota

Orange Marmalade Cookies

½ cup shortening
1 cup orange marmalade
1 egg
1 teaspoon vanilla extract
2 cups all-purpose flour
½ teaspoon baking soda
½ teaspoon salt
¼ cup chopped pecans,
  raisins, or chopped candied
  mixed fruit

Cream shortening; add orange marmalade, beating well at medium speed of an electric mixer until light and fluffy. Add egg and vanilla; beat well.

Combine flour, soda, and salt; stir well. Add to creamed mixture, mixing well. Stir in pecans.

Drop dough by rounded teaspoonfuls 2 inches apart onto ungreased cookie sheets. Bake at 350° for 12 to 15 minutes or until cookies are lightly browned. Let cool completely on wire racks. Yield: 4 dozen.   Priscilla La Pointe, Carrie Bates

Recipes Begged, Borrowed, Stolen
Highland Grange #48
Huntington, Massachusetts

Peanut Butter Honeys

½ cup shortening
½ cup creamy peanut butter
½ cup sugar
1 egg
½ cup honey

1½ cups all-purpose flour
¼ teaspoon baking powder
¼ teaspoon baking soda
¼ teaspoon salt

Cream shortening and peanut butter; gradually add sugar, beating well at medium speed of an electric mixer. Add egg and honey; stir well. Combine flour, baking powder, soda, and salt; stir well. Gradually add to peanut butter mixture, mixing well.

Drop dough by rounded teaspoonfuls onto greased cookie sheets. Bake at 350° for 10 to 12 minutes or until cookies are lightly browned. Let cool slightly on cookie sheets; remove cookies to wire racks to cool completely. Yield: 4½ dozen.   Emily Smith

Knollwood Cooks II
Christian Women's Guild, Knollwood United Methodist Church
Granada Hills, California

Gingersnaps

¾ cup shortening
1 cup sugar
¼ cup light molasses
1 egg, beaten
2 cups all-purpose flour
2 teaspoons baking soda

¼ teaspoon salt
1 teaspoon ground ginger
1 teaspoon ground cinnamon
1 teaspoon ground cloves
Additional sugar

Cream shortening; gradually add 1 cup sugar, beating well at medium speed of an electric mixer. Add molasses and beaten egg, beating well.

Combine flour and next 5 ingredients; stir well. Add to creamed mixture, mixing well. Cover and chill 1 hour.

Shape dough into 1-inch balls; roll in sugar. Place 2 inches apart on lightly greased cookie sheets. Bake at 375° for 12 to 15 minutes. Let cool 2 minutes on cookie sheets; remove to wire racks to cool completely. Yield: 4 dozen.

Rave Revues
Lakewood Center Associates, Lakewood Center for the Arts
Lake Oswego, Oregon

Molasses Sugar Cookies

¾ cup shortening
1 cup sugar
¼ cup molasses
2 cups all-purpose flour
2 teaspoons baking soda
½ teaspoon salt
1 teaspoon ground cinnamon
½ teaspoon ground ginger
½ teaspoon ground cloves
Additional sugar

Cream shortening; gradually add 1 cup sugar, beating well at medium speed of an electric mixer. Add molasses, beating well.

Combine flour and next 5 ingredients, stirring well; add to creamed mixture, and mix well.

Shape dough into 1-inch balls; roll in sugar. Place 2 inches apart on greased cookie sheets. Bake at 375° for 6 to 8 minutes. Let cool on wire racks. Yield: 3 dozen.   Marlene Fenger

Calvary Collections
Calvary Lutheran Church
Kalispell, Montana

Chocolate Kiss Peanut Butter Cookies

1 cup butter or margarine, softened
⅔ cup creamy peanut butter
1 cup sugar
1 cup firmly packed brown sugar
2 eggs
2 teaspoons vanilla extract
3 cups all-purpose flour
2 teaspoons baking soda
1 teaspoon salt
Additional sugar
2 (9-ounce) packages milk chocolate kisses, unwrapped

Cream butter and peanut butter; gradually add 1 cup sugar and brown sugar, beating at medium speed of an electric mixer until light and fluffy. Add eggs and vanilla, beating well. Combine flour, baking soda, and salt; add to creamed mixture, mixing well.

Shape dough into 1-inch balls; roll in sugar. Place 2 inches apart on ungreased cookie sheets. Bake at 375° for 8 minutes. Press a chocolate kiss into top of each cookie; bake an additional 2 minutes. Let cool on wire racks. Yield: 10½ dozen.   Nicole Kelly

Port's Galley
The Port Council of Port of Portland, Oregon

Pecan Pie Cookies

1 cup butter or margarine,
  softened
½ cup sugar
2 eggs, separated
½ cup dark corn
  syrup

2½ cups all-purpose
  flour
Pecan Filling

Cream butter in a large mixing bowl at medium speed of an electric mixer. Gradually add sugar, beating well at medium speed of electric mixer. Add egg yolks, one at a time, beating after each addition. Add corn syrup, beating well. Gradually stir in flour. Cover dough, and chill 2 to 3 hours.

Shape dough into 1-inch balls. Place 2 inches apart on greased cookie sheets. Beat egg whites (at room temperature) with a wire whisk until foamy. Brush balls lightly with beaten egg whites. Bake at 350° for 6 to 7 minutes. Remove from oven.

Shape ½ teaspoon Pecan Filling into a ball; repeat procedure with remaining filling. Press one Pecan Filling ball into center of each cookie. Return cookies to oven, and bake an additional 6 to 8 minutes or until cookies are lightly browned. (Centers of cookies will be soft.)

Let cookies cool on cookie sheets 5 minutes. Remove cookies to wire racks, and let cool completely. Yield: about 4 dozen.

Pecan Filling

½ cup sifted powdered
  sugar
¼ cup butter or
  margarine

3 tablespoons dark corn
  syrup
½ cup chopped pecans

Combine sugar, butter, and corn syrup in a medium saucepan. Cook over medium heat, stirring constantly, until thickened and bubbly. Remove from heat. Stir in chopped pecans. Chill thoroughly. Yield: ¾ cup.   Lee Milliken

Academic Apron
The Middlesex School
Concord, Massachusetts

Peanut Butter Cookies with a Chocolate Bite

½ cup shortening
¾ cup creamy peanut butter, divided
½ cup sugar
¼ cup light corn syrup
1 tablespoon milk

1½ cups all-purpose flour
½ teaspoon baking soda
¼ teaspoon salt
¼ cup semisweet chocolate morsels

Combine shortening and ½ cup peanut butter in a large mixing bowl; beat at medium speed of an electric mixer until creamy. Gradually add sugar, beating at medium speed of electric mixer. Add corn syrup and milk, beating well.

Combine flour, soda, and salt, and stir well. Add flour mixture to creamed mixture, mixing well. Shape dough into a 10-inch roll; wrap in wax paper, and chill at least 2 hours.

Unwrap roll, and cut dough into ¼-inch slices; place half of slices 2 inches apart on ungreased cookie sheets. Spoon ½ teaspoon of remaining ¼ cup peanut butter into center of each cookie. Press 4 chocolate morsels into each peanut butter center. Top with remaining cookie slices; seal edges with a fork.

Bake cookies at 350° for 10 to 12 minutes. Let cool completely on wire racks. Yield: about 2 dozen.

Gourmet LA
The Junior League of Los Angeles, California

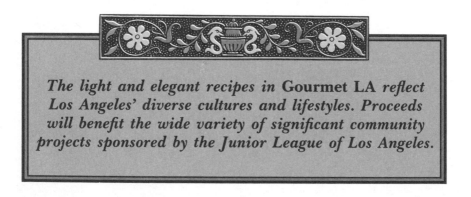

The light and elegant recipes in Gourmet LA *reflect Los Angeles' diverse cultures and lifestyles. Proceeds will benefit the wide variety of significant community projects sponsored by the Junior League of Los Angeles.*

Simple Sesames

2 cups butter, softened
1½ cups sugar
3 cups all-purpose flour
1 cup sesame seeds

2 cups shredded coconut
½ cup finely chopped
 blanched almonds, toasted

Cream butter; gradually add sugar, beating well at medium speed of an electric mixer. Add flour, beating well. Stir in sesame seeds, coconut, and almonds.

Shape dough into three 5-inch rolls; wrap in wax paper, and chill at least 3 hours. Unwrap rolls, and cut into ¼-inch slices; place 1 inch apart on ungreased cookie sheets. Bake at 300° for 25 to 30 minutes or until lightly browned. Let cookies cool completely on wire racks. Yield: 4 dozen.

Jackson Hole à la Carte
The Jackson Hole Alliance for Responsible Planning
Jackson, Wyoming

Ice Box Cinnamon Cookies

1 cup butter, softened
1 cup sugar
1 cup firmly packed brown
 sugar
2 eggs
3½ cups all-purpose flour

1 teaspoon baking soda
¼ teaspoon salt
1 tablespoon ground
 cinnamon
1 cup finely chopped pecans
 or walnuts

Cream butter; gradually add sugars, beating at medium speed of an electric mixer until light and fluffy. Add eggs, one at a time, beating well after each addition. Combine flour, soda, salt, and cinnamon; stir well. Add to creamed mixture, beating well. Stir in pecans. Shape dough into two 10-inch rolls; wrap in wax paper, and chill at least 8 hours.

Unwrap rolls, and cut into ¼-inch slices; place 2 inches apart on greased cookie sheets. Bake at 350° for 10 to 12 minutes. Let cool on wire racks. Yield: 6½ dozen.   Betsy Mathews

Keeping the Feast
The Episcopal Church Women of St. Thomas Church
Abingdon, Virginia

Mom's Sugar Cookies

5 cups all-purpose flour
2 teaspoons baking powder
Dash of salt
1 cup butter

3 eggs, beaten
3 cups sugar
1 tablespoon vanilla extract
1 teaspoon ground mace

Combine flour, baking powder, and salt in a large bowl; cut in butter with a pastry blender until mixture resembles coarse meal.

Combine eggs, sugar, vanilla, and mace in a large bowl; beat at medium speed of an electric mixer until smooth. Add to flour mixture, beating until smooth. Shape dough into a ball; wrap in wax paper, and chill at least 2 hours.

Divide dough in half; store 1 portion in refrigerator. Roll dough to 1/16-inch thickness on a lightly floured surface. Cut with a 2-inch cookie cutter, and place on lightly greased cookie sheets.

Bake at 375° for 8 to 10 minutes or until edges are lightly browned. Let cool on wire racks. Repeat procedure with remaining dough. Yield: 10½ dozen.   Deborah Nasteff

A Collection of Recipes
The Worcester Country School Development Office
Berlin, Maryland

Here's My Heart Cookies

1 cup unsalted butter,
  softened
½ cup firmly packed brown
  sugar
2½ cups all-purpose flour

1 teaspoon vanilla extract
7 (1-ounce) squares semisweet
  chocolate
¾ cup finely chopped pecans
  or walnuts

Cream butter; gradually add sugar, beating at medium speed of an electric mixer. Add flour and vanilla; mix well. Shape dough into a ball; wrap in wax paper, and chill 2 hours.

Roll dough to ¼-inch thickness on a lightly floured surface. Cut with a 2½-inch heart-shaped cookie cutter; place 2 inches apart on ungreased cookie sheets. Bake at 300° for 25 to 30 minutes or until edges are lightly browned. Let cool on wire racks.

Place chocolate in top of a double boiler; bring water to a boil. Reduce heat to low; cook until chocolate melts, stirring occasionally. Remove double boiler from heat, leaving chocolate over hot water.

Dip half of each cookie in melted chocolate to coat both sides; sprinkle with chopped pecans. Place cookies on wire racks; let stand until chocolate is firm. Yield: 2½ dozen.

The Mystic Seaport All Seasons Cookbook
Mystic Seaport Museum Stores
Mystic, Connecticut

Out-of-This-World Pumpkin Bars

2 cups sugar	1 teaspoon baking soda
2 cups cooked, mashed pumpkin	½ teaspoon ground cinnamon
4 eggs, beaten	1 cup chopped pecans or walnuts
¾ cup butter, melted	Frosting (recipe follows)
2 cups all-purpose flour	
2 teaspoons baking powder	

Combine sugar, pumpkin, beaten eggs, and melted butter in a large bowl; stir well.

Combine flour, baking powder, soda, and cinnamon in a medium bowl; stir well. Add flour mixture to pumpkin mixture, stirring well. Stir in chopped pecans.

Pour batter into a greased 15- x 10- x 1-inch jellyroll pan. Bake at 325° for 25 to 35 minutes or until a wooden pick inserted in center comes out clean. Let cool in pan on a wire rack. Spread with frosting; cut into bars. Yield: 4 dozen.

Frosting

3 cups sifted powdered sugar	1 tablespoon half-and-half
1 (3-ounce) package cream cheese, softened	1 teaspoon vanilla extract
¼ cup plus 2 tablespoons butter, softened	

Combine all ingredients in a bowl; beat until smooth. Yield: about 2 cups.   Betty Lou Hammargren

Sinfully Good
The Catholic Library Association
Haverford, Pennsylvania

Apricot Spice Bars

⅓ cup butter, softened
1½ cups firmly packed brown
  sugar
½ cup honey
3 eggs
1¾ cups all-purpose flour
1 teaspoon baking powder

1 teaspoon salt
1 teaspoon ground cinnamon
½ teaspoon ground cloves
1 (6-ounce) package dried
  apricots, finely chopped
1 cup chopped walnuts
Glaze (recipe follows)

Cream butter; gradually add sugar, beating until light and fluffy. Add honey, beating well. Add eggs, one at a time, beating after each addition. Combine flour and next 4 ingredients; stir well. Add flour mixture to honey mixture, stirring well. Fold in apricots and walnuts. (Batter will be stiff.) Spread batter in a greased and floured 15- x 10- x 1-inch jellyroll pan. Bake at 350° for 20 to 25 minutes. Let cool in pan on a wire rack 15 minutes; brush with glaze. Let cool completely, and cut into bars. Yield: 4 dozen.

Glaze

¾ cup sifted powdered sugar   1 tablespoon lemon juice

Combine sugar and lemon juice in a small bowl; stir until smooth. Yield: ⅓ cup.   Carla Kretschman

Country Cuisine
The Women's Club of Arvada, Wyoming

Cheesecake Bars

¼ cup plus 1 tablespoon
  butter, softened
⅓ cup firmly packed light
  brown sugar
1 cup all-purpose flour
¼ cup chopped pecans
1 (8-ounce) package cream
  cheese, softened

½ cup sugar
1 egg
2 tablespoons milk
1 tablespoon fresh lemon
  juice
½ teaspoon vanilla extract

Cream butter; gradually add brown sugar, beating well at medium speed of an electric mixer. Stir in flour and pecans. Set aside 1 cup flour mixture. Press remaining flour mixture in bottom of an

8-inch square baking pan. Bake at 350° for 12 to 15 minutes. Remove from oven, and set aside.

Beat cream cheese in a medium bowl at high speed until smooth. Gradually add ½ cup sugar, beating until mixture is light and fluffy. Add egg and remaining ingredients, mixing well. Spread cream cheese mixture evenly over crust. Sprinkle reserved flour mixture evenly over batter. Bake at 350° for 25 minutes. Let cool to room temperature in pan on a wire rack; chill thoroughly. Cut into bars. Yield: about 1½ dozen.

Savannah Style
The Junior League of Savannah, Georgia

Lemon Squares

1½ cups all-purpose flour
1½ cups firmly packed brown
  sugar, divided
½ cup butter or margarine
2 eggs, beaten
2 tablespoons all-purpose
  flour
½ teaspoon baking powder

¼ teaspoon salt
½ teaspoon vanilla extract
1¼ cups flaked coconut
½ cup chopped pecans
1 cup sifted powdered sugar
2 tablespoons lemon juice
1 tablespoon butter or
  margarine, melted

Combine 1½ cups flour and ½ cup brown sugar in a medium bowl; cut in ½ cup butter with a pastry blender until mixture resembles coarse meal. Press flour mixture in bottom of a 13- x 9- x 2-inch baking pan. Bake at 275° for 10 minutes. Remove from oven, and set aside.

Combine eggs, remaining 1 cup brown sugar, 2 tablespoons flour, baking powder, salt, and vanilla; stir well. Stir in coconut and chopped pecans. Spoon mixture evenly over crust; bake at 350° for 20 to 25 minutes.

Combine powdered sugar, lemon juice, and melted butter in a small mixing bowl, stirring until smooth. Drizzle glaze over warm lemon squares. Let cool in pan on a wire rack; cut into squares. Yield: 3 dozen.   Ruth Apperson

Calling All Cooks Two
The Telephone Pioneers of America
Birmingham, Alabama

Brickle Blonde Brownies

½ cup butter or margarine, softened
1 cup sugar
½ cup firmly packed brown sugar
2 eggs
1 teaspoon vanilla extract

1½ cups all-purpose flour
1 teaspoon baking powder
½ teaspoon salt
1 (6-ounce) package almond brickle chips

Cream butter; gradually add sugars, beating at medium speed of an electric mixer until light and fluffy. Add eggs and vanilla, and beat well.

Combine flour, baking powder, and salt in a small bowl; stir well. Add flour mixture to creamed mixture, mixing well. Stir in almond brickle chips.

Spread batter in a well-greased 13- x 9- x 2-inch baking pan. Bake at 350° for 30 to 35 minutes or until lightly browned. Let cool in pan on a wire rack; cut into bars. Yield: 4 dozen.   Dave Mathiot

Mothers of Twins Cookbook
Twice as Nice, Mothers of Twins Club
Gillette, Wyoming

The Junior League of Gaston County, North Carolina, creators of Southern Elegance, *offers a recipe collection that reflects North Carolina's relaxed, gracious style of entertaining and their celebration of family and friends. Proceeds from the sale of their cookbook will help fund a variety of league-sponsored community projects.*

Apricot Balls

10 ounces dried apricots,
   finely chopped
2 cups sugar
3 tablespoons grated orange
   rind
3 tablespoons orange juice
1 cup finely chopped pecans
Powdered sugar

Combine apricots, 2 cups sugar, orange rind, and juice in top of a double boiler; bring water to a boil. Reduce heat to low; cook 10 to 12 minutes, stirring occasionally. Remove from heat; let cool.

Add chopped pecans to cooled apricot mixture. Shape mixture into 1-inch balls, and roll in powdered sugar. Store in an airtight container. Yield: 4 dozen.   Betty Matthews

Southern Elegance
The Junior League of Gaston County, North Carolina

Christmas White Fudge

2¼ cups sugar
½ cup sour cream
¼ cup milk
2 tablespoons butter
1 tablespoon light corn syrup
¼ teaspoon salt
2 teaspoons clear vanilla
   extract
½ cup candied cherries,
   quartered
1 cup chopped walnuts

Combine sugar, sour cream, milk, butter, corn syrup, and salt in a 2-quart saucepan. Cook over low heat, stirring constantly, until sugar dissolves. Cover and cook over medium heat 2 to 3 minutes to wash down sugar crystals from sides of pan. Uncover and cook to soft ball stage (238°), stirring occasionally. Remove from heat. Let mixture cool 30 minutes or until lukewarm (110°). Add vanilla; beat with a wooden spoon 2 to 3 minutes or until mixture thickens and begins to lose its gloss. Quickly stir in candied cherries and chopped walnuts. Pour mixture into a buttered 9-inch square pan. Let cool completely before cutting into squares. Store in an airtight container. Yield: 1½ pounds.   Elaine Jarvis

M.A.E.H. Cook Book
The Michigan Association of Extension Homemakers
Hastings, Michigan

Caramel Popcorn

5 quarts freshly popped
popcorn
1 cup butter or margarine
2 cups firmly packed brown
sugar

½ cup light corn syrup
1 teaspoon salt
1 teaspoon vanilla extract
½ teaspoon baking soda

Place popcorn in a lightly greased roasting pan; set aside.

Melt butter in a large saucepan; stir in sugar, corn syrup, and salt. Cook over medium heat, stirring frequently, until candy thermometer registers 248°. Remove from heat; stir in vanilla and soda. Pour caramel mixture over popcorn; stir well. Bake at 225° for 1 hour, stirring every 15 minutes. Let cool completely; store in an airtight container. Yield: 5 quarts.   Stephanie Fishback

CordonBluegrass
The Junior League of Louisville, Kentucky

Orange Candied Nuts

3 cups pecan or walnut
halves
2 tablespoons butter or
margarine
½ cup sugar, divided

½ cup light corn syrup
¼ cup grated orange rind
3 tablespoons orange juice
1 teaspoon grated lemon rind

Place pecans in a 13- x 9- x 2-inch baking pan. Bake at 250° for 5 minutes. Remove from oven, and set aside.

Melt butter in a medium saucepan. Add ¼ cup sugar, corn syrup, orange rind, juice, and lemon rind, stirring well. Bring mixture to a boil over medium heat, stirring constantly. Boil, without stirring, for 5 minutes. Pour syrup over pecans, stirring gently to coat well.

Bake at 250° for 1 hour, stirring frequently. Sprinkle with remaining ¼ cup sugar. Spread onto greased baking sheets. Separate pecans with a fork. Let cool completely. Store in an airtight container. Yield: 3 cups.

Parishables
St. Paul's Episcopal Church
Cleveland Heights, Ohio

Desserts

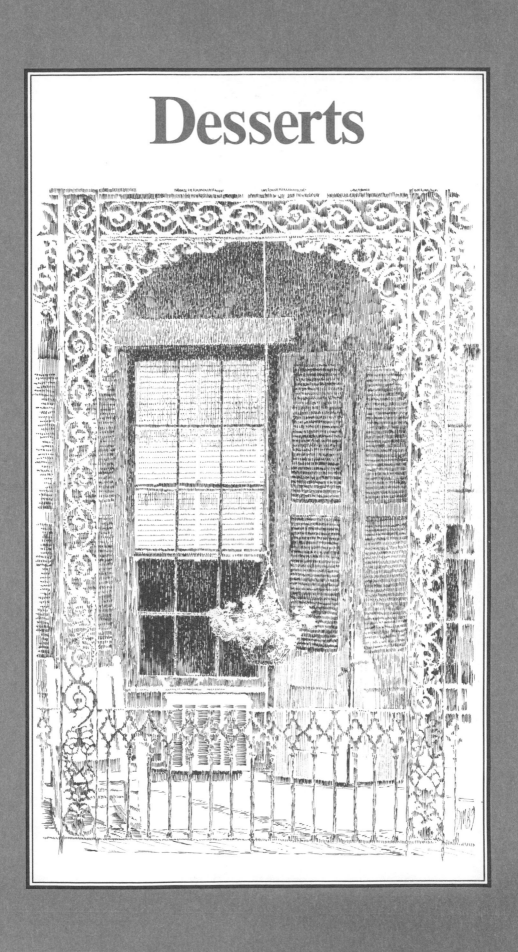

An ornate wrought iron balcony in the distinctive city of New Orleans is typical of Creole architecture. The iron grillwork was designed by local craftsmen who blended native architectural ingenuity with the French colonial traditions of eastern Canada and West Indian Spanish colonial styles.

Continental Peaches

3 large ripe peaches, peeled
  and halved
1 tablespoon light rum or
  rum extract
¼ cup plus 2 tablespoons
  sour cream

3 tablespoons brown sugar
2 tablespoons sliced
  almonds

Arrange peach halves, cut side up, in a 9-inch pieplate; sprinkle evenly with rum. Spoon 1 tablespoon sour cream into center of each peach half; sprinkle brown sugar and sliced almonds evenly over peach halves.

Bake at 350° for 25 to 30 minutes or until sugar caramelizes. Serve warm. Yield: 6 servings.   Beverly Anderson Dorsey

Cook 'em Horns: The Quickbook
The Ex-Students Association of the University of Texas
Austin, Texas

Baked Pears in Caramel Sauce

6 medium-size firm pears,
  peeled and cored
¼ cup sugar

¼ cup unsalted butter
1 cup whipping cream

Cut pears in half lengthwise. Arrange pear halves, cut side down, in a lightly greased 11- x 7- x 2-inch baking dish. Sprinkle with sugar, and dot with butter.

Bake at 425° for 35 minutes or until pears are tender. Pour whipping cream evenly over pears. Bake an additional 10 to 15 minutes, basting pears frequently with whipping cream. Serve warm. Yield: 6 servings.   Marie Weitzman

Pesach Potpourri
The Sinai Akiba Academy
Los Angeles, California

Ginger Pears

2 cups water
1 cup sugar
1 (3-inch) stick cinnamon
2 (3- x ¼-inch) strips lemon
  rind

1 (2- x ¼-inch) slice ginger
1 teaspoon whole cloves
8 medium-size ripe pears,
  peeled and cored
Whipped cream

Combine water, sugar, cinnamon stick, lemon rind strips, ginger, and cloves in a large Dutch oven. Bring to a boil; reduce heat, and simmer 5 minutes. Add pears to liquid in Dutch oven. Cover and simmer 15 to 20 minutes or until pears are tender. Transfer pears and syrup to a medium bowl. Cover and chill thoroughly. Drain pears, discarding syrup.

To serve, place pears in individual dessert dishes; pipe whipped cream into pear cavities. Yield: 8 servings.   Marie Krebs

Favorite Recipes
The Sponsor's Club, Robert Louis Stevenson School
Pebble Beach, California

Brandied Cherries Jubilee

2 cups Burgundy or other
  dry red wine
1 cup superfine sugar
3 cups pitted fresh sweet
  cherries or 2 (16-ounce)
  cans pitted dark sweet
  cherries, drained

3 tablespoons lemon juice
1 tablespoon cornstarch
¼ cup kirsch
¼ cup brandy
Vanilla ice cream

Bring wine to a boil in a large saucepan over medium heat. Add sugar; cook 5 minutes or until sugar dissolves, stirring occasionally. Add cherries; simmer 8 to 10 minutes or until cherries are tender. (If using canned cherries, cook until thoroughly heated.)

Transfer cherries to a bowl, using a slotted spoon; reserve liquid in pan. Bring liquid to a boil over high heat; cook 10 minutes or until liquid is reduced by one third. Combine lemon juice and cornstarch, stirring well. Add cornstarch mixture to reduced liquid, stirring well; boil 1 minute or until slightly thickened, stirring constantly. Stir in kirsch and cherries. Remove from heat, and set aside. Place brandy in a small, long handled saucepan; heat until warm (do not boil). Remove from heat. Ignite with a long match; pour over cherry mixture. Stir until flames die down. Serve immediately over ice cream. Yield: 8 servings.

Libretto
The Opera Society of Fort Lauderdale, Florida

Caramel Apples with Rum and Ice Cream

¾ cup unsalted butter
1⅓ cups sugar
1 teaspoon lemon juice
4 large cooking apples,
    peeled and thinly sliced

1½ tablespoons dark rum
Coffee ice cream

Melt butter in a large skillet over medium heat. Add sugar and lemon juice; cook, stirring constantly, until sugar melts and syrup is golden brown. Stir in apple slices, and cook 3 to 5 minutes. Remove from heat; stir in rum. Serve apples warm over coffee ice cream. Yield: 6 servings.   Jimmy Rohr

Hemi-demi-semi Flavors
The Chamber Music Society of the North Shore
Glencoe, Illinois

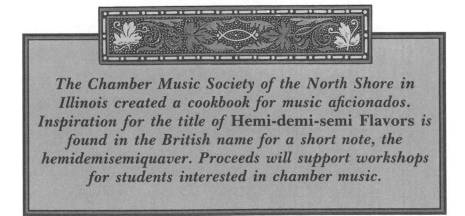

The Chamber Music Society of the North Shore in Illinois created a cookbook for music aficionados. Inspiration for the title of **Hemi-demi-semi Flavors** *is found in the British name for a short note, the hemidemisemiquaver. Proceeds will support workshops for students interested in chamber music.*

Deluxe Peach Ice Cream

6 cups mashed fresh ripe
  peaches
2½ cups sugar, divided
3 eggs
2 tablespoons all-purpose
  flour

½ teaspoon salt
4 cups milk
1 cup whipping cream
1 tablespoon vanilla extract

Combine peaches and 1 cup sugar in a large bowl; stir well, and set aside.

Beat eggs at medium speed of an electric mixer until foamy. Combine remaining 1½ cups sugar, flour, and salt; stir well. Gradually add to beaten eggs, beating until mixture thickens. Add milk, beating well.

Pour egg mixture into a Dutch oven. Cook over low heat, stirring constantly, until mixture thickens and coats a metal spoon (about 15 minutes). Let cool to room temperature.

Stir in whipping cream and vanilla. Add peach mixture, stirring well. Pour into freezer can of a 5-quart hand-turned or electric freezer. Freeze according to manufacturer's instructions. Let ripen 1 hour before serving. Yield: about 1 gallon.   David Susina

From the Hills
The Lutheran Church of Vestavia Hills, Alabama

Pistachio Brittle Ice Cream

1⅓ cups shelled pistachios,
  toasted
4 cups milk
4 cups whipping cream

14 egg yolks, beaten
1⅓ cups sugar
2 teaspoons vanilla extract
Pistachio Brittle

Position knife blade in food processor bowl; add pistachios, and process until pistachios are ground.

Combine ground pistachios, milk, and whipping cream in a large Dutch oven; bring just to a boil over medium heat. Remove from heat, and let stand 30 minutes. Strain mixture; discard pistachios.

Combine egg yolks and sugar in a large saucepan; beat with a wire whisk until thick and lemon colored. Gradually add milk mixture, beating constantly with a wire whisk. Cook over medium heat until mixture thickens and coats a metal spoon. Remove from heat, and let cool completely. Stir in vanilla and Pistachio Brittle. Pour into freezer can of a 1-gallon hand-turned or electric freezer. Freeze according to manufacturer's instructions. Let ripen at least 1 hour before serving. Yield: 2 quarts.

Pistachio Brittle

⅔ cup shelled pistachios, coarsely chopped and toasted

1 tablespoon unsalted butter, melted

¾ cup sugar

3 tablespoons water

Sauté pistachios in butter in a skillet until lightly browned. Remove from heat, and set aside.

Combine sugar and water in skillet. Bring to a boil over medium heat; cook, stirring constantly, until sugar melts and syrup is light golden brown. Stir in pistachios. Pour mixture in a thin layer onto a greased baking sheet. Let cool. Break into pieces. Yield: 1½ cups.

Gourmet LA
The Junior League of Los Angeles, California

Praline Ice Cream

4 eggs, separated

4 cups half-and-half

2 (14-ounce) cans sweetened condensed milk

2½ cups milk

⅔ cup maple-flavored syrup

1 teaspoon maple flavoring

½ teaspoon salt

5 pralines, coarsely chopped

2 (1.4-ounce) English toffee-flavored candy bars, coarsely chopped

Combine egg yolks and next 6 ingredients in a large bowl; stir well. Add pralines and candy; stir well, and set aside.

Beat egg whites (at room temperature) at high speed of an electric mixer until stiff peaks form. Fold into egg yolk mixture. Pour into freezer can of a 1-gallon hand-turned or electric freezer. Freeze according to manufacturer's instructions. Let ripen 1 hour, if desired, before serving. Yield: 1 gallon.

South of the Fork
The Junior League of Dallas, Texas

Arctic Snow

6 large coconut macaroons,
 crushed
½ cup chopped pecans

½ gallon vanilla ice cream,
 softened
¾ cup cream sherry

Spread crushed macaroons on a baking sheet. Bake at 350° for 5 minutes, stirring occasionally. Set aside, and let cool.

Spread pecans in a single layer on baking sheet. Bake at 350° for 10 minutes, stirring occasionally. Set aside, and let cool.

Combine softened ice cream and sherry in a large mixing bowl; beat at medium speed of an electric mixer until smooth. Layer half of ice cream mixture, macaroon crumbs, and pecans in individual dessert dishes. Repeat layers, using remaining ice cream, macaroon crumbs, and pecans. Cover and freeze 8 hours or until firm. Yield: 16 servings.

Gourmet by the Bay
The Dolphin Circle of the King's Daughters and Sons
Virginia Beach, Virginia

Raspberry Ice Cream Crunch

1½ cups crushed crisp rice
 cereal
1 cup flaked coconut
¼ cup firmly packed brown
 sugar

¼ cup butter or margarine,
 melted
½ gallon vanilla ice cream,
 softened
Raspberry Sauce

Combine crushed cereal, coconut, brown sugar, and melted butter in a medium bowl; stir well. Press half of cereal mixture in bottom of a 9-inch square baking pan. Spread softened ice cream over cereal layer. Sprinkle remaining cereal mixture over ice cream. Cover and freeze 3 hours or until firm. Cut into squares. Serve with Raspberry Sauce. Yield: 9 servings.

Raspberry Sauce

3 (10-ounce) packages frozen
 raspberries, thawed
3 tablespoons cornstarch
3 tablespoons water

¾ cup sugar
1½ tablespoons lemon
 juice
Dash of salt

Drain raspberries, reserving 1½ cups raspberry juice. Set raspberries and juice aside.

Combine cornstarch and water in a small bowl, stirring well. Combine raspberry juice, cornstarch mixture, sugar, lemon juice, and salt in a heavy saucepan. Cook over medium heat until mixture thickens, stirring occasionally. Remove from heat; add raspberries, stirring well. Let cool. Serve over Raspberry Ice Cream Crunch, reserving any remaining Raspberry Sauce for other uses. Yield: about 4 cups.   Barbara Watson

Recipes Begged, Borrowed, Stolen
Highland Grange #48
Huntington, Massachusetts

Frozen Strawberry Dessert

1 cup all-purpose flour
¼ cup firmly packed brown
   sugar
½ cup chopped walnuts
½ cup butter, melted
2 egg whites
1 cup sugar

2 cups sliced fresh
   strawberries
2 tablespoons lemon
   juice
1 cup whipping cream,
   whipped

Combine first 4 ingredients in a small bowl; stir well. Press mixture in bottom of a 13- x 9- x 2-inch baking dish. Bake at 350° for 20 minutes. Let cool 10 minutes; crush into crumbs. Sprinkle two-thirds crumb mixture in bottom of 13- x 9- x 2-inch baking dish; set aside.

Combine egg whites (at room temperature), 1 cup sugar, strawberries, and lemon juice in a large mixing bowl; beat at high speed of an electric mixer 10 minutes.

Fold whipped cream into strawberry mixture. Spoon mixture over crumbs; top with remaining crumb mixture. Cover and freeze 8 hours or until firm. Cut into squares, and serve immediately. Yield: 12 servings.   Pat Ketchpel

RSVP—Recipes Shared Very Proudly
First Church of Christ
Simsbury, Connecticut

Chocolate-Coffee Sundae Squares

1⅓ cups crushed vanilla
  wafers
¼ cup finely chopped
  walnuts
¼ cup butter, melted
3 egg whites
2 tablespoons instant coffee
  granules

Dash of salt
½ cup sugar
1 cup whipping cream,
  whipped
Fudge Sauce
Walnut halves

Combine crushed vanilla wafers, chopped walnuts, and melted butter in a medium bowl; stir well. Press mixture in bottom of a 9-inch square baking pan. Bake at 375° for 10 minutes. Set aside, and let crust cool.

Combine egg whites (at room temperature), coffee granules, and salt in a medium mixing bowl; beat at high speed of an electric mixer just until foamy. Gradually add sugar, 1 tablespoon at a time, beating until stiff peaks form and sugar dissolves (2 to 4 minutes). Fold in whipped cream.

Spread egg white mixture over cooled crust. Cover and freeze 8 hours or until firm.

Let dessert stand at room temperature at least 5 minutes before serving. Cut into squares. Top each square with warm Fudge Sauce and a walnut half. Yield: 16 servings.

Fudge Sauce

½ cup semisweet chocolate
  morsels
⅓ cup light corn
  syrup

⅓ cup evaporated
  milk

Combine chocolate and corn syrup in top of a double boiler; bring water to a boil. Reduce heat to low; cook until chocolate melts, stirring occasionally. Remove from heat, and stir in evaporated milk. Yield: 1 cup.

Margaret H. Brown

CordonBluegrass
The Junior League of Louisville, Kentucky

Frozen Lemon Torte

1 cup all-purpose flour
2 tablespoons powdered
  sugar
3 tablespoons finely chopped
  blanched almonds
½ cup butter, melted
5 eggs, separated
1 cup sugar, divided
1½ teaspoons grated lemon
  rind

½ cup fresh lemon
  juice
2 cups whipping cream,
  whipped
Fresh raspberries
  (optional)
Lemon slices (optional)

Combine flour, powdered sugar, chopped almonds, and melted butter in a medium bowl, stirring just until dry ingredients are moistened. Shape mixture into a ball. Press dough firmly in bottom and ½ inch up the sides of a 9-inch springform pan; prick bottom of pastry with a fork. Bake at 425° for 8 to 10 minutes. Let crust cool completely on a wire rack.

Combine egg yolks, ½ cup sugar, lemon rind, and lemon juice in top of a double boiler; bring water to a boil. Reduce heat to low; cook until thickened, stirring constantly. Remove from heat, and let cool 30 minutes. Cover and chill 2 hours.

Beat egg whites (at room temperature) at high speed of an electric mixer just until foamy. Gradually add remaining ½ cup sugar, 1 tablespoon at a time, beating until stiff peaks form and sugar dissolves (2 to 4 minutes).

Gently fold beaten egg whites and whipped cream into chilled lemon mixture. Pour into prepared crust; cover and freeze 8 hours or until firm.

Let dessert stand at room temperature at least 15 minutes before serving. Carefully remove sides of springform pan; if desired, garnish with fresh raspberries and lemon slices. Yield: 8 to 10 servings.

Stanford University Medical Center Auxiliary Cookbook
Stanford University Medical Center Auxiliary
Palo Alto, California

Apricot Fantasia

1 (17-ounce) can apricot
halves in light syrup,
undrained
1 envelope unflavored gelatin
¾ cup sugar
1 tablespoon apricot brandy
(optional)

1 cup whipping cream,
whipped
Chocolate sauce (recipe
follows)
Chocolate curls (optional)

Drain apricot halves, reserving syrup. Set apricot halves aside. Sprinkle gelatin over apricot syrup in a small saucepan; let stand 1 minute. Cook over low heat, stirring until gelatin dissolves. Let cool to room temperature.

Place apricot halves in a large bowl; beat 2 minutes at medium speed of an electric mixer. Add dissolved gelatin, sugar, and, if desired, apricot brandy, mixing well. Cover and chill apricot mixture until it reaches the consistency of unbeaten egg white. Fold in whipped cream.

Layer apricot mixture and chocolate sauce in each of 6 parfait glasses, beginning and ending with apricot mixture. Garnish with chocolate curls, if desired. Yield: 6 servings.

Chocolate Sauce

4 (1-ounce) squares semisweet
chocolate
¼ cup water

2 tablespoons sugar
2 tablespoons butter or
margarine

Combine all ingredients in top of a double boiler; bring water to a boil. Reduce heat to low; cook until chocolate and butter melt, stirring constantly. Let sauce cool to room temperature before using. Yield: ½ cup.   Eva Kopcha

A Book of Favorite Recipes
Sisterhood of SS. Cyril and Methodius Orthodox Church
Terryville, Connecticut

Big Apple Mousse

2 pounds cooking apples,
  peeled and sliced
1½ cups firmly packed light
  brown sugar
1 (3-inch) stick cinnamon
1 cup water
2 tablespoons fresh lemon
  juice

4 envelopes unflavored
  gelatin
¾ cup cold water
5 cups whipping cream
½ cup sugar
1 tablespoon Calvados or
  other apple-flavored brandy
  (optional)

Combine first 5 ingredients in a large Dutch oven. Bring to a boil; cover, reduce heat, and simmer 30 minutes or until apples are tender. Remove from heat; let cool 30 minutes. Remove and discard cinnamon stick.

Combine gelatin and cold water in a saucepan; let stand 1 minute. Cook over low heat, stirring constantly, until gelatin dissolves. Add to apple mixture, stirring well. Cover and chill 1½ hours. Beat apple mixture until soft peaks form.

Beat whipping cream at high speed of electric mixer until foamy; gradually add sugar and, if desired, Calvados, beating until soft peaks form. Gently fold whipped cream into apple mixture. Spoon mousse into a large serving bowl; cover and chill thoroughly. Yield: 16 servings.   Mario M. Cuomo

Capital Connoisseur
The Lawrence Center Independence House
Schenectady, New York

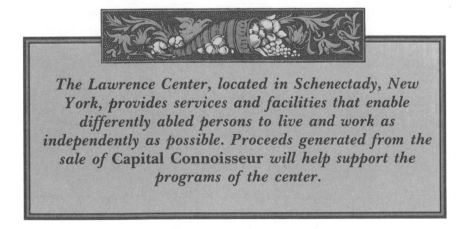

The Lawrence Center, located in Schenectady, New York, provides services and facilities that enable differently abled persons to live and work as independently as possible. Proceeds generated from the sale of **Capital Connoisseur** *will help support the programs of the center.*

Lemon Mousse with Blueberries

5 eggs, separated
1 cup sugar, divided
½ cup fresh lemon juice
1 cup whipping cream,
  whipped

2½ teaspoons grated lemon
  rind
4 cups fresh blueberries
Fresh mint sprigs

Place egg yolks in top of a double boiler; bring water to a boil. Reduce heat to low; cook, beating at medium speed of an electric mixer, until thick and lemon colored. Gradually add ¾ cup sugar, beating well. Add lemon juice, and cook, stirring constantly, until mixture thickens and coats a metal spoon. Remove from heat, and let cool to room temperature.

Beat egg whites (at room temperature) at high speed of electric mixer until stiff peaks form. Fold beaten egg whites into lemon mixture. Fold in whipped cream and lemon rind. Cover mousse, and chill 8 hours.

Place blueberries in bottom of a 2-quart soufflé dish. Sprinkle with remaining ¼ cup sugar. Spoon mousse over blueberries. Garnish with mint sprigs. Yield: 6 servings.   Barbara McCarthy

Southern Elegance
The Junior League of Gaston County, North Carolina

Pumpkin Soufflé

1 envelope unflavored gelatin
¼ cup rum
4 eggs
⅔ cup sugar
1 cup cooked, mashed
  pumpkin
½ teaspoon ground cinnamon

½ teaspoon ground ginger
¼ teaspoon ground mace
¼ teaspoon ground cloves
1 cup whipping cream
Sweetened whipped cream
  (optional)
Candied fruit (optional)

Sprinkle gelatin over rum in a small saucepan; let stand 1 minute. Cook over low heat, stirring constantly, until gelatin dissolves. Set gelatin mixture aside.

Beat eggs at medium speed of an electric mixer. Gradually add sugar; beat well. Add pumpkin, cinnamon, ginger, mace, and cloves, stirring well.

Add reserved gelatin mixture and 1 cup whipping cream to pumpkin mixture; beat at medium speed until well blended. Pour mixture into an ungreased 1-quart soufflé dish. Cover and chill 8 hours. If desired, garnish with sweetened whipped cream and candied fruit. Yield: 6 servings.   Mary E. Bolstand

Taste of the Town—Second Serving
The Charity League of Lexington, North Carolina

Apple Pudding Soufflé

1 cup peeled, chopped
  cooking apple
¼ cup butter, melted
8 slices bread, cut into
  ½-inch cubes (about
  3 cups)
2 cups milk

½ cup sugar
½ cup raisins or currants
1 teaspoon grated lemon rind
1 teaspoon vanilla extract
¼ teaspoon salt
3 eggs, separated

Sauté chopped apple in butter in a large skillet until tender. Add bread cubes, and cook until lightly browned. Remove from heat, and set aside.

Place milk in a medium saucepan, and heat thoroughly (do not boil). Remove from heat; add apple mixture, sugar, raisins, lemon rind, vanilla, and salt, stirring well.

Beat egg yolks in a small bowl at high speed of an electric mixer until thick and lemon colored; add beaten yolks to apple mixture, stirring well.

Beat egg whites (at room temperature) in a medium bowl at high speed of electric mixer until stiff peaks form. Fold beaten egg whites into apple mixture.

Spoon into an ungreased 2½-quart soufflé dish. Place dish in a larger shallow pan; add water to larger pan to a depth of 1 inch. Bake at 350° for 45 minutes. Serve warm or at room temperature. Yield: 6 to 8 servings.   Jini Taylor

Pegasus Presents
Pegasus of Germantown, Tennessee

Applesauce Pudding

1 (16-ounce) can applesauce
1 cup sugar
1 cup graham cracker crumbs
1 cup milk

2 eggs, beaten
1 tablespoon lemon juice
½ cup butter, melted

Combine applesauce, sugar, graham cracker crumbs, milk, eggs, and lemon juice in a medium bowl; stir well. Stir in melted butter. Pour mixture into a greased 1½-quart baking dish. Bake at 350° for 50 to 60 minutes. Yield: 6 servings.

Stir Crazy!
The Junior Welfare League of Florence, South Carolina

The Demon's Float

1¼ cups sugar, divided
1 cup sifted cake flour
2 teaspoons baking powder
¼ teaspoon salt
1 tablespoon plus ¾ teaspoon
   cocoa
½ cup milk
2 tablespoons margarine,
   melted

1 teaspoon vanilla extract
½ cup chopped pecans or
   walnuts
½ cup firmly packed brown
   sugar
¼ cup plus 1½ teaspoons
   cocoa
1 cup boiling water
Whipped cream

Sift together ¾ cup sugar, cake flour, baking powder, salt, and 1 tablespoon plus ¾ teaspoon cocoa in a large bowl. Add milk, melted margarine, and vanilla to dry ingredients, beating at medium speed of an electric mixer until mixture is smooth. Stir in chopped pecans. Pour batter into a well-greased 9-inch square baking pan.

Combine remaining ½ cup sugar, brown sugar, ¼ cup plus 1½ teaspoons cocoa, and boiling water in a medium bowl, stirring well. Pour sugar mixture evenly over cake batter. Bake at 350° for 40 minutes. Serve cake warm with a dollop of whipped cream. Yield: 6 to 8 servings.

The Farmer's Daughters
The National Multiple Sclerosis Society
St. Charles, Arkansas

Trifle

1 (10-ounce) commercial
pound cake, sponge cake,
or jellyroll cake
1 to 1½ cups raspberry jam
½ cup cream sherry or fruit
juice
8 coconut macaroons,
crushed

Soft Custard
2 cups whipping cream
1 teaspoon vanilla extract
1 tablespoon sugar
¼ cup slivered blanched
almonds, toasted

Slice cake into 2½- x 1-inch slices. Spread jam on one side of each slice of cake. Line bottom and sides of a 12-cup trifle bowl with cake slices, jam-covered sides toward center of bowl. Sprinkle cake slices with cream sherry, and top with crushed coconut macaroons. Cover and chill 8 hours.

Pour chilled Soft Custard over macaroons; cover and chill 2 hours. Combine whipping cream and vanilla; beat at high speed of an electric mixer until foamy. Gradually add sugar, beating until soft peaks form. Spread whipped cream over trifle, and sprinkle with slivered almonds. Yield: 8 to 10 servings.

Soft Custard

⅓ cup sugar
2 tablespoons cornstarch
⅛ teaspoon salt

2 cups milk
3 eggs, beaten
1 teaspoon vanilla extract

Combine sugar, cornstarch, and salt in a medium saucepan; stir well. Gradually add milk; cook over medium heat, stirring constantly, until mixture thickens and comes to a boil. Boil 1 minute, stirring constantly. Remove from heat.

Gradually stir about one-fourth of hot milk mixture into beaten eggs; add to remaining hot milk mixture, stirring constantly. Cook over medium heat, stirring constantly, until mixture thickens (do not boil). Remove from heat, and stir in vanilla. Cover custard with plastic wrap, gently pressing directly on custard. Chill thoroughly. Yield: 2½ cups.

The Minnesota Ethnic Food Book
The Minnesota Historical Society Press
St. Paul, Minnesota

Lemon Cups

1 cup sugar
¼ cup all-purpose flour
⅛ teaspoon salt
2 tablespoons butter or
  margarine, melted
2 teaspoons grated lemon
  rind

¼ cup plus 1 tablespoon
  lemon juice
3 eggs, separated
1½ cups milk

Combine first 3 ingredients in a large bowl; stir well. Add butter, lemon rind, and lemon juice; stir well. Set aside.

Beat egg yolks at high speed of an electric mixer until thick and lemon colored. Add beaten egg yolks and milk to lemon mixture, stirring well.

Beat egg whites (at room temperature) at high speed until stiff peaks form; fold egg whites into lemon mixture. Pour mixture into eight 6-ounce greased custard cups. Place custard cups in a shallow baking pan; pour hot water into baking pan to a depth of 1 inch. Bake at 325° for 45 minutes or until custard is set. Let cool. Yield: 8 servings.

Kitty Conrad

Keeping the Feast
The Episcopal Church Women of St. Thomas Church
Abingdon, Virginia

The Florida Federation of Women's Clubs donate proceeds from the sale of The Florida Cooking Adventure *to the Hacienda Girls' Ranch. The club's theme, "The Keys to Caring and Sharing," is reflected in their book with the use of keys as border art and the sharing of treasured recipes from caring people.*

Valentine Pineapple Hearts

¼ cup sugar
1 envelope unflavored gelatin
½ teaspoon salt
2 eggs, beaten
1 cup milk
1 cup whipping cream, divided
1 (20-ounce) can pineapple slices in heavy syrup, undrained

2 (3-ounce) packages cream cheese, softened
2 teaspoons vanilla extract
½ teaspoon almond extract
1 teaspoon cornstarch
1 (10-ounce) package frozen raspberries, thawed

Combine first 3 ingredients in top of a double boiler; stir well, and set aside.

Combine eggs, milk, and ½ cup whipping cream in a medium bowl; beat at medium speed of an electric mixer until blended. Add egg mixture to gelatin mixture, stirring well; let stand 1 minute. Bring water to a boil; reduce heat to low, and cook, stirring constantly, 15 minutes or until mixture coats a metal spoon. Remove from heat, and set aside.

Drain pineapple, reserving ¾ cup syrup. Chill 8 pineapple slices, reserving remaining slices for other uses.

Combine remaining ½ cup whipping cream, ½ cup reserved pineapple syrup, softened cream cheese, and vanilla and almond extracts in a large bowl; beat at medium speed of electric mixer until mixture is smooth. Add gelatin mixture; beat at low speed until ingredients are combined.

Spoon mixture into eight ½-cup lightly oiled heart-shaped molds. Chill at least 8 hours.

Combine remaining ¼ cup reserved pineapple syrup and cornstarch in a small saucepan; stir well. Add raspberries, stirring to combine. Bring to a boil over medium heat, stirring constantly until mixture thickens. Press raspberry mixture through a sieve to remove seeds; discard seeds. Chill sauce thoroughly.

To serve, place chilled pineapple slices on individual dessert plates. Unmold gelatin hearts onto pineapple slices. Serve with raspberry sauce. Yield: 8 servings.   Bernice Jansen

The Florida Cooking Adventure
The Florida Federation of Women's Clubs
Lakeland, Florida

Cranberry-Hazelnut Baskets

⅓ cup hazelnuts
8 sheets commercial frozen
  phyllo pastry, thawed
1 cup unsalted butter, melted
¼ cup plus 2 tablespoons
  fine, dry breadcrumbs
10 ounces cream cheese,
  softened

½ cup plus 1½ teaspoons
  sifted powdered sugar
1 tablespoon plus ¾ teaspoon
  grated lemon rind
1 tablespoon plus ½ teaspoon
  fresh lemon juice
Cranberry Topping

Place hazelnuts in a single layer on a baking sheet; bake at 350° for 10 to 20 minutes. Rub briskly with a towel to remove skins; discard skins. Coarsely chop hazelnuts, and set aside.

Place 1 sheet of phyllo on a damp towel (keep remaining phyllo covered). Brush phyllo with melted butter, and sprinkle with 1 tablespoon breadcrumbs. Layer 3 more sheets phyllo on first sheet, brushing each with melted butter and sprinkling second and third layer with breadcrumbs. (Do not sprinkle crumbs on top layer.) Repeat procedure with remaining phyllo, butter, and breadcrumbs. Cut each stack of phyllo into 3-inch squares.

Brush miniature (1¾-inch) muffin pans with melted butter. Place 1 square of layered phyllo in each muffin cup, pressing gently in center to form a shell. Bake at 350° for 8 to 10 minutes or until golden. Gently remove from pan, and let cool on wire racks.

Combine cream cheese and next 3 ingredients; beat at medium speed of an electric mixer until smooth. Spoon about 1½ teaspoons cheese mixture into each phyllo basket; top with Cranberry Topping. Sprinkle with chopped hazelnuts. Yield: about 3½ dozen.

Cranberry Topping

1 (12-ounce) package fresh
  cranberries
1½ cups sugar

½ cup plus 1½ teaspoons
  water

Combine all ingredients in a medium saucepan; bring to a boil over medium heat, stirring constantly. Cook 3 minutes or until cranberry skins pop. Remove from heat; let cool. Cover and chill at least 3 hours. Yield: 2⅔ cups.

Finely Tuned Foods
The Symphony League of Leawood, Kansas

Eggs & Cheese

More than 1.8 billion pounds of high quality cheese is produced in the state of Wisconsin each year. Wisconsin cheesemakers lead the United States in the production of many cheese varieties, including Cheddar, Colby, Brick, Muenster, and Italian cheeses. Colby, Brick, and Cold Pack cheese are Wisconsin originals.

Crab-Stuffed Eggs

12 hard-cooked eggs
1 (6-ounce) can crabmeat, drained and flaked
½ cup mayonnaise
1 teaspoon prepared mustard
¼ teaspoon salt
⅛ teaspoon pepper
1 (2-ounce) jar sliced pimiento, drained
Fresh parsley sprigs

Slice eggs in half lengthwise, and carefully remove yolks. Mash yolks with a fork; add crabmeat and next 4 ingredients, stirring well. Spoon yolk mixture into egg whites. Garnish with pimiento slices and fresh parsley sprigs. Yield: 12 servings.   Janet Tysse

From the Hills
The Lutheran Church of Vestavia Hills, Alabama

Cottage Cheese Toast (Blitzen)

12 slices sandwich bread
½ cup milk
1 cup cottage cheese
1 egg
1 tablespoon sugar
1½ teaspoons grated orange rind
⅛ teaspoon salt
3 tablespoons butter, melted
2 tablespoons sugar
1 teaspoon ground cinnamon
Orange slices

Dip one side of 6 bread slices in milk. Place bread on an ungreased baking sheet, milk side up.

Combine cottage cheese, egg, 1 tablespoon sugar, orange rind, and salt, stirring well. Spread 2 tablespoons cottage cheese mixture over each bread slice on baking sheet. Dip one side of remaining 6 bread slices in milk. Place on top of cottage cheese mixture, milk side down. Gently press edges together to seal. Brush top bread slices with melted butter.

Combine 2 tablespoons sugar and cinnamon; stir well, and sprinkle over buttered bread. Bake at 400° for 10 minutes or until lightly browned. Garnish with orange slices. Serve immediately. Yield: 6 servings.   The Sisters of St. Francis, Hankinson

Heritage Cookbook
The Catholic Diocese of Fargo, North Dakota

Overnight Caramel French Toast

1 cup firmly packed brown
  sugar
½ cup butter
2 tablespoons light corn
  syrup

12 slices sandwich bread
6 eggs, beaten
1½ cups milk
1 teaspoon vanilla extract
¼ teaspoon salt

Combine sugar, butter, and corn syrup in a small saucepan; cook over medium heat until thickened, stirring constantly. Pour syrup mixture into a 13- x 9- x 2-inch baking dish. Place 6 slices of bread on top of syrup mixture. Top with remaining 6 slices of bread.

Combine eggs, milk, vanilla, and salt, stirring until blended. Pour egg mixture evenly over bread slices. Cover and chill 8 hours. Bake, uncovered, at 350° for 40 to 45 minutes or until lightly browned. Serve immediately. Yield: 6 servings.   Dolores Swanson

Thou Preparest a Table Before Me
East Avenue United Methodist Church Women
York, Nebraska

Delaware Farmers' Breakfast

6 slices bacon, cut into 2-inch
  pieces
3 large baking potatoes,
  peeled, cubed, and cooked
1 small green pepper, chopped

2 tablespoons chopped onion
½ cup (2 ounces) shredded
  Cheddar cheese
6 eggs, beaten
Salt and pepper to taste

Cook bacon in a large skillet until crisp; drain, reserving 3 tablespoons drippings in skillet. Set bacon aside.

Sauté potatoes, pepper, and onion in drippings until potatoes are browned. Sprinkle cheese over potatoes; stir until cheese melts. Pour beaten eggs over potatoes; cook over low heat until eggs are set. Add salt and pepper to taste. Top with reserved bacon. Serve immediately. Yield: 6 to 8 servings.   Charlotte Givens

The Delaware Heritage Cookbook
The Delaware Heritage Commission
Wilmington, Delaware

Fancy Egg Scramble

1 cup diced Canadian bacon
  or cooked ham
¼ cup chopped green onions
¼ cup plus 1 tablespoon
  butter or margarine, melted
12 eggs, beaten
½ pound fresh mushrooms,
  sliced
2 tablespoons butter or
  margarine
2 tablespoons all-purpose
  flour

½ teaspoon salt
⅛ teaspoon pepper
2 cups milk
1 cup (4 ounces) shredded
  sharp Cheddar cheese
2 cups soft breadcrumbs
1 tablespoon plus 1 teaspoon
  butter or margarine, melted
⅛ teaspoon paprika

Sauté bacon and green onions in 3 tablespoons melted butter in a large skillet over medium heat until onion is tender. Add eggs; cook, without stirring, until mixture begins to set on bottom. Draw a spatula across bottom of pan to form large curds. Continue cooking until eggs are thickened but still moist (do not stir constantly). Remove from heat, and set aside.

Sauté sliced mushrooms in 2 tablespoons melted butter in a small skillet until mushrooms are tender. Remove from heat, and set mushrooms aside.

Melt 2 tablespoons butter in a large saucepan over low heat; add flour, salt, and pepper, stirring until smooth. Cook 1 minute, stirring constantly. Gradually add milk; cook over medium heat, stirring constantly, until thickened and bubbly. Add cheese, stirring until cheese melts. Fold egg mixture and sautéed mushrooms into cheese sauce.

Spoon mixture into a 13- x 9- x 2-inch baking dish. Combine breadcrumbs, 1 tablespoon plus 1 teaspoon melted butter, and paprika in a small bowl, stirring well. Sprinkle breadcrumb mixture evenly over egg mixture. Cover casserole, and chill at least 8 hours. Bake, uncovered, at 350° for 30 minutes. Serve immediately. Yield: 8 to 10 servings.

Rave Revues
Lakewood Center Associates, Lakewood Center for the Arts
Lake Oswego, Oregon

Simsbury Scramble

2½ cups milk
1 (8-ounce) package cream
　cheese, softened
12 eggs, beaten
2 tablespoons chopped fresh
　chives or green onions

1½ teaspoons salt
¼ teaspoon pepper
½ cup butter, melted
1 cup (4 ounces) shredded
　Cheddar cheese
Chopped fresh parsley

Heat milk thoroughly in a medium saucepan (do not boil). Add cream cheese, stirring until smooth. Add eggs and next 3 ingredients, beating with a wire whisk until blended.

Place melted butter in a 13- x 9- x 2-inch baking dish. Pour egg mixture over butter. Bake at 350° for 1 hour. Sprinkle with shredded Cheddar cheese and chopped fresh parsley. Serve immediately. Yield: 8 to 10 servings.　　　　　　　　　　Joanne Johnson

RSVP—Recipes Shared Very Proudly
First Church of Christ
Simsbury, Connecticut

Broccoli Frittata

3 tablespoons vegetable oil
2 cups chopped broccoli
1 cup thinly sliced fresh
　mushrooms
1 cup thinly sliced onion
½ cup chopped green pepper
8 eggs, lightly beaten

¾ cup milk
¾ cup freshly grated
　Parmesan cheese
½ teaspoon salt
½ teaspoon dried whole basil
⅛ teaspoon pepper

Heat oil in a 10-inch ovenproof skillet. Sauté broccoli, mushrooms, onion, and green pepper 5 minutes or until broccoli is crisp-tender. Let cool slightly.

Combine eggs and remaining ingredients; stir well. Add egg mixture to vegetable mixture in skillet, stirring well. Bake at 325° for 20 to 25 minutes until eggs are set and a knife inserted in center comes out clean. Cut frittata into wedges, and serve immediately. Yield: 8 servings.

From Scratch Cookbook
The Assistance League® of Glendale, California

Vegetable Frittata

1 medium onion, chopped
3 tablespoons olive oil
2 small zucchini, sliced
1 large sweet red pepper, cut into ¼-inch strips
3 medium baking potatoes, peeled, sliced, and cooked
8 pitted ripe olives, sliced
8 eggs, beaten

½ cup grated Parmesan cheese
⅓ cup milk
2 tablespoons chopped fresh parsley
1 teaspoon salt
¼ teaspoon ground white pepper

Sauté chopped onion in olive oil in a 10-inch ovenproof skillet over medium heat 5 minutes. Add sliced zucchini and sweet red pepper strips, and sauté an additional 5 minutes. Stir in potatoes and sliced olives. Remove skillet from heat, and set vegetable mixture aside.

Combine beaten eggs and remaining ingredients in a medium bowl, stirring well. Pour egg mixture over vegetables in skillet. Bake at 350° for 35 to 40 minutes or until eggs are set and top is golden brown. Cut frittata into wedges, and serve immediately. Yield: 8 servings.

Dining In
The Young Woman's League of Westport, Connecticut

The Westport Young Woman's League offers a peek into the culinary lives of its members with Dining In, *a celebration of its thirtieth anniversary. In its thirty years, the league has raised more than $500,000 to help preserve the quality of life in Westport by funding community educational programs.*

24-Hour Wine and Cheese Omelets

1 (1-pound) loaf French bread
¼ cup plus 2 tablespoons
  unsalted butter, melted
3 cups (12 ounces) shredded
  Swiss cheese
2 cups (8 ounces) shredded
  Monterey Jack cheese
9 thin slices salami, coarsely
  chopped
16 eggs
¾ cup milk
½ cup Chablis or other dry
  white wine

4 green onions, minced
1 tablespoon hot prepared
  mustard
¼ teaspoon freshly ground
  pepper
⅛ teaspoon ground red
  pepper
1½ cups sour cream
1 cup freshly grated
  Parmesan cheese

Break bread into small pieces; spread evenly over the bottom of two 13- x 9- x 2-inch baking dishes. Drizzle butter over bread. Sprinkle Swiss and Monterey Jack cheeses and salami over bread. Combine eggs and next 6 ingredients; beating with a wire whisk until foamy. Pour egg mixture evenly over bread mixture in each dish. Cover and chill 8 hours.

Bake omelets, covered, at 325° for 1 hour. Remove from oven; spread sour cream evenly over omelet in each dish. Sprinkle Parmesan cheese evenly over each sour cream layer. Continue to bake, uncovered, 12 to 15 minutes or until tops of omelets are lightly browned. Yield: 16 to 20 servings.   Karen Johnson

Crème de la Congregation
Our Saviors Lutheran Church
Lafayette, California

Green Chiles and Cheese

3 (4-ounce) cans whole green
  chiles, undrained
4 cups (16 ounces) shredded
  Cheddar cheese
4 eggs

2 cups milk
1 cup all-purpose flour
1 to 2 teaspoons salt
1 teaspoon pepper

Drain chiles, reserving liquid. Rinse chiles in cold water; remove and discard seeds. Place half of chiles in a buttered 2-quart baking dish. Sprinkle 2 cups cheese over chiles. Repeat layers, using remaining chiles and cheese.

Combine reserved liquid from chiles, eggs, and remaining ingredients, beating well at medium speed of an electric mixer. Pour egg mixture over layered chiles and cheese. Cover and bake at 325° for 30 minutes. Remove cover, and continue to bake 30 to 35 minutes or until lightly browned. Yield: 8 servings.

Company's Coming
The Junior League of Kansas City, Missouri

New Mexican Pepper Casserole

2 tablespoons butter, melted
2 tablespoons vegetable oil
1½ cups finely chopped
 onion
3 cloves garlic, crushed
½ teaspoon salt
1 teaspoon ground cumin
½ teaspoon dry mustard
½ teaspoon chili powder
2 medium-size green peppers,
 cut into ¼-inch strips
2 medium-size sweet red
 peppers, cut into ¼-inch
 strips
2 medium-size sweet yellow
 peppers, cut into ¼-inch
 strips
8 ounces Cheddar cheese,
 thinly sliced
1½ cups sour cream
4 eggs, lightly beaten
Paprika

Combine melted butter and vegetable oil in a large skillet; place over medium heat until hot. Add onion, garlic, salt, cumin, dry mustard, and chili powder; sauté until onion is tender. Add peppers; sauté 10 minutes, stirring occasionally.

Layer half the pepper mixture in a greased 11- x 7- x 2-inch baking dish. Top with half the cheese slices; repeat layers, using remaining pepper mixture and cheese slices.

Combine sour cream and eggs in a medium bowl; beat with a wire whisk until blended. Pour egg mixture evenly over pepper mixture. Sprinkle evenly with paprika. Cover and bake at 375° for 30 minutes. Remove cover, and bake casserole an additional 15 minutes. Yield: 6 to 8 servings.

License to Cook New Mexico Style
New Mexico Federation of Business and Professional Women
Albuquerque, New Mexico

Boursin Cheese Quiche

Pastry for one 9-inch pie
1 cup (4 ounces) shredded
 Swiss cheese, divided
¼ cup chopped green onions
¼ cup chopped ripe olives

8 cherry tomatoes, halved
3 eggs, beaten
½ cup whipping cream
1 (5-ounce) package Boursin
 cheese, softened

Line a 9-inch quiche dish with pastry. Trim excess pastry around edges. Prick bottom and sides of pastry with a fork. Bake at 400° for 3 minutes; remove from oven, and gently prick with a fork. Bake an additional 5 minutes. Set aside, and let cool.

Sprinkle ¾ cup shredded Swiss cheese over bottom of pastry shell. Top with chopped green onions, chopped olives, and cherry tomato halves. Set aside.

Combine eggs, whipping cream, and Boursin cheese in container of an electric blender or food processor; process until mixture is smooth. Pour egg mixture over vegetables in pastry shell. Sprinkle with remaining ¼ cup Swiss cheese. Bake at 375° for 40 to 50 minutes or until quiche is set. Let stand 5 minutes before serving. Yield: one 9-inch quiche.

Second Round, Tea-Time at the Masters®
The Junior League of Augusta, Georgia

Salmon Quiche

1 cup whole wheat flour
⅔ cup (2.6 ounces) shredded
 Cheddar cheese
½ cup slivered blanched
 almonds, chopped
¼ cup vegetable oil
½ teaspoon salt
¼ teaspoon paprika
1 (15½-ounce) can red
 salmon, drained and flaked

1 (8-ounce) carton sour cream
3 eggs, beaten
½ cup (2 ounces) shredded
 Cheddar cheese
¼ cup mayonnaise
1 tablespoon grated onion
¼ teaspoon dried whole
 dillweed
⅛ teaspoon hot sauce

Combine flour, ⅔ cup cheese, and almonds in a medium bowl; stir well. Add oil, salt, and paprika; stir well. Reserve ½ cup flour mixture. Press remaining flour mixture on bottom and up sides of a 10-inch quiche dish. Bake at 400° for 10 minutes.

Combine salmon and remaining ingredients in a medium bowl; stir well. Pour salmon mixture into prepared quiche dish. Sprinkle with reserved flour mixture. Bake at 325° for 45 minutes or until quiche is set. Let stand 10 minutes before serving. Yield: one 10-inch quiche.

Gladys Howes

The Ashfield Cookbook
The Ladies' Circle of the First Congregational Church
Ashfield, Massachusetts

Spinach and Sausage Pie

2 (10-ounce) packages frozen chopped spinach, thawed
1 pound mild Italian sausage
5 eggs
1 egg, separated
4 cups (16 ounces) shredded mozzarella cheese
1 cup ricotta cheese
1 small clove garlic, crushed
½ teaspoon salt
⅛ teaspoon pepper
Pastry for double-crust 10-inch pie
1 tablespoon water

Drain spinach well, pressing between paper towels until barely moist. Set aside.

Remove and discard casing from sausage. Cook sausage in a large skillet over medium heat until browned, stirring to crumble. Drain well; set aside.

Combine spinach, 5 eggs, 1 egg white, mozzarella cheese, ricotta cheese, garlic, salt, and pepper in a large bowl; stir well. Add sausage; stir well.

Place half of pastry in a 10-inch pieplate; trim off excess pastry along edges. Spoon spinach mixture into pastry shell. Top with remaining half of pastry; fold edges under and flute. Cut slits in top crust to allow steam to escape.

Combine remaining egg yolk and 1 tablespoon water in a small bowl; beat lightly with a wire whisk. Brush top of pastry with egg yolk mixture. Bake at 375° for 1 hour and 15 minutes or until crust is lightly browned. Let pie stand 10 minutes before serving. Yield: 10 servings.

Viola Malachuk

Our Town Cookbook
The Historical Society of Peterborough, New Hampshire

Pizza Rustica

1 (10-ounce) package frozen chopped spinach
1 (16-ounce) carton ricotta cheese
1 cup (4 ounces) shredded mozzarella cheese
¼ pound salami, chopped
½ cup butter or margarine, softened
¼ cup (1 ounce) shredded provolone cheese
¼ cup grated Parmesan cheese
2 eggs, lightly beaten
½ teaspoon salt
¼ teaspoon ground nutmeg
⅛ teaspoon pepper
2 cups all-purpose flour
1 teaspoon salt
½ cup shortening
2 eggs, lightly beaten
1 egg
1 tablespoon water

Cook spinach according to package directions. Drain well. Combine spinach, ricotta cheese, and next 9 ingredients in a large bowl; stir well, and set aside.

Combine flour and 1 teaspoon salt in a large mixing bowl; cut in shortening with a pastry blender until mixture resembles coarse meal. Add 2 lightly beaten eggs, stirring just until dry ingredients are moistened.

Divide dough into 4 equal portions. Roll one portion to ⅛-inch thickness on a lightly floured surface; place in a 9-inch pieplate. Spoon half of cheese mixture into crust. Roll another portion of dough to ⅛-inch thickness. Place over filling; fold edges under and flute. Cut slits in top crust to allow steam to escape. Repeat procedure with remaining 2 portions of dough and cheese mixture.

Combine 1 egg and 1 tablespoon water; beat with a wire whisk. Brush egg mixture over pizzas. Bake at 375° for 45 minutes or until golden brown. Yield: two 9-inch pizzas.   Evelyn Spadaccino

Favorite Italian Recipes
St. Theresa Guild of Holy Rosary Church
Bridgeport, Connecticut

Fish & Shellfish

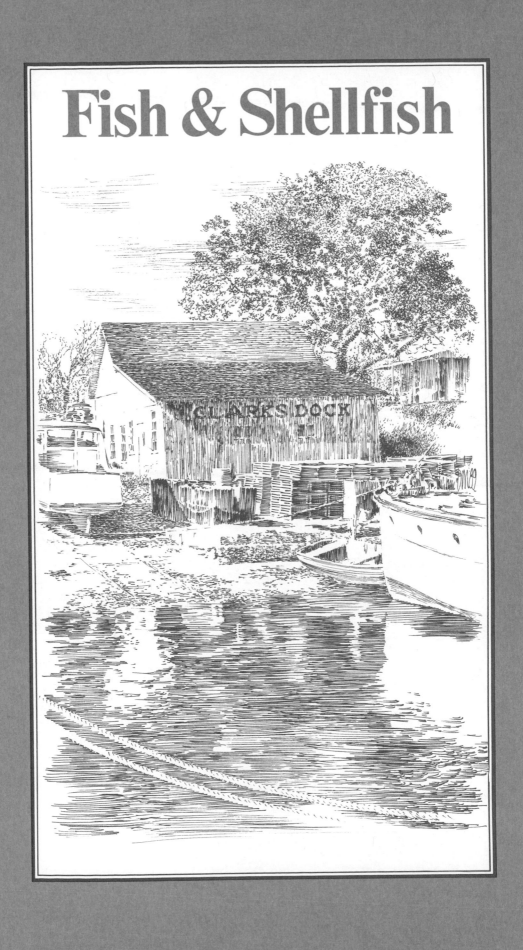

CLARK'S DOCK

Fishing boats are docked at a harbor in Niantic, Connecticut, so named for the North American Indian tribe of the eastern woodland region. Connecticut successfully maintains a unique blend of modern city life with a commitment to the environment of its harbors, beaches, hills, and village greens.

Spinach-Stuffed Fish Rolls

1 (10-ounce) package frozen
   chopped spinach, thawed
¼ cup grated Parmesan cheese
2 tablespoons grated onion
¼ teaspoon hot sauce
4 (6-ounce) flounder or other
   fish fillets

2 tablespoons butter or
   margarine
1 clove garlic, minced
Paprika
Hot cooked brown rice

Drain spinach; press between paper towels to remove excess moisture. Combine spinach and next 3 ingredients; stir well.

Spoon one-fourth of spinach mixture onto each fillet, and roll up to enclose filling; secure with wooden picks. Place rolls, seam side down, in an 11- x 7- x 2-inch baking dish.

Melt butter in a saucepan over low heat; remove from heat, and stir in garlic. Brush over fish rolls; sprinkle with paprika. Bake at 350° for 30 minutes or until fish flakes easily when tested with a fork. Serve over rice. Yield: 4 servings.   Lois Besmer

Woman to Woman Cookbook
The Zonta Club of the Black Hills
Rapid City, South Dakota

A Honey of a Fish

¼ cup honey
¼ cup Dijon mustard
2 tablespoons lemon juice
1 teaspoon curry powder

½ teaspoon salt
4 (¾-inch-thick) grouper or
   other fish fillets (about 1½
   pounds)

Combine first 5 ingredients; stir well. Place fillets in a 13- x 9- x 2-inch baking dish; brush with half of honey mixture. Turn fillets; brush with remaining honey mixture. Cover and marinate in refrigerator 15 minutes. Remove fillets from marinade, reserving marinade. Place fillets on a lightly greased rack in a roasting pan. Broil 4 inches from heat 10 to 12 minutes or until fish flakes easily when tested with a fork, basting occasionally with reserved marinade. Yield: 4 servings.   Florence Bober Sigel

A Rainbow of Kosher Cuisine
The Baltimore Chapter of Hadassah
Baltimore, Maryland

Halibut Casserole Supreme

2 quarts water
½ teaspoon salt
1 pound halibut fillets
1 cup cooked wide egg
   noodles
2 hard-cooked eggs, diced
1 cup chopped celery
½ cup chopped green
   pepper
1 tablespoon butter, melted
3 tablespoons butter
3 tablespoons all-purpose
   flour

1½ cups milk
¾ cup (6 ounces)
   shredded Cheddar
   cheese
½ cup mayonnaise
1 teaspoon salt
⅛ teaspoon paprika
1 cup soft breadcrumbs
1 tablespoon butter,
   melted

Bring water and ½ teaspoon salt to a boil in a large Dutch oven; add halibut fillets. Cover, reduce heat, and simmer 10 to 15 minutes or until fish flakes easily when tested with a fork. Drain well, and flake fish.

Combine fish, cooked noodles, and eggs in a large bowl; toss gently, and set aside.

Sauté celery and green pepper in 1 tablespoon melted butter in a skillet over medium heat until tender. Add sautéed vegetables to fish mixture; toss gently.

Melt 3 tablespoons butter in a heavy saucepan over low heat; add flour, stirring until smooth. Cook 1 minute, stirring constantly. Gradually add milk; cook over medium heat, stirring constantly until mixture is thickened and bubbly. Add shredded Cheddar cheese, mayonnaise, 1 teaspoon salt, and paprika, stirring well. Add cheese sauce to fish mixture, stirring well. Pour mixture into an 11- x 7- x 2-inch baking dish.

Combine breadcrumbs and 1 tablespoon melted butter in a small bowl; stir well. Sprinkle breadcrumb mixture evenly over fish mixture in baking dish. Bake at 350° for 30 minutes or until casserole is thoroughly heated. Yield: 6 servings.   Karen Bivins

Pioneers of Alaska Cookbook
The Pioneers of Alaska Auxiliary #4
Anchorage, Alaska

Fish in Foil

1 cup finely chopped onion
½ cup clam juice
½ cup tomato juice or
  vegetable juice cocktail
⅓ cup chopped green
  pepper
¼ cup chopped fresh
  mushrooms
¼ cup vegetable oil
1 to 2 tablespoons all-purpose
  flour
2 cloves garlic, crushed
1 teaspoon Worcestershire
  sauce
2 dashes of hot sauce
¼ cup Chablis or other dry
  white wine (optional)
3 tablespoons capers
1½ teaspoons salt
1½ teaspoons pepper
6 (4- to 6-ounce) orange
  roughy or other fish fillets

Combine first 10 ingredients in a medium saucepan, and stir well. Bring to a boil; reduce heat, and simmer, uncovered, 5 minutes. Remove from heat, and stir in wine, if desired. Add capers, salt, and pepper, stirring well.

Place each fish fillet on a large piece of heavy-duty aluminum foil; top fillets evenly with sauce. Fold edges of foil over fish, and wrap securely. Bake at 350° for 45 minutes or until fish flakes easily when tested with a fork. Remove fish from foil before serving. Yield: 6 servings.   John Lang

Two and Company
St. Thomas' Church, Garrison Forest
Owings Mills, Maryland

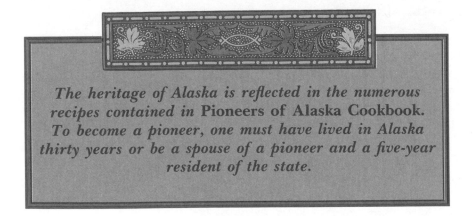

The heritage of Alaska is reflected in the numerous recipes contained in Pioneers of Alaska Cookbook. *To become a pioneer, one must have lived in Alaska thirty years or be a spouse of a pioneer and a five-year resident of the state.*

Poached Salmon with Dill-Cucumber Sauce

4 quarts water
1 (25.4-ounce) bottle Chablis
   or other dry white wine
2 medium carrots, scraped
   and chopped
1 medium onion, chopped
10 black peppercorns

½ lemon
1 teaspoon salt
¼ teaspoon pepper
1 (5- to 6-pound) dressed
   whole salmon
Dill-Cucumber Sauce

Fill a 10-quart fish poacher with 4 quarts water. Add wine, chopped carrot, chopped onion, peppercorns, ½ lemon, salt, and pepper. Bring mixture to a boil; cover, reduce heat, and simmer 30 minutes.

Wrap whole salmon in cheesecloth. Carefully place salmon on rack in fish poacher. Place fish poacher over 2 surface units; cover and cook over medium-low heat 40 to 50 minutes or until salmon is soft to the touch.

Transfer salmon to a large platter; remove cheesecloth. Let fish cool slightly; cover and chill thoroughly. Remove skin and spine from salmon before serving. Serve with Dill-Cucumber Sauce. Yield: 10 to 12 servings.

Dill-Cucumber Sauce

1 cup mayonnaise
½ cup chopped fresh parsley
¼ cup chopped fresh chives
¼ cup chopped fresh
   dillweed
2 to 3 tablespoons dry
   vermouth

1 tablespoon fresh lemon
   juice
1 medium cucumber, seeded
   and chopped

Position knife blade in food processor bowl. Add all ingredients except cucumber to processor bowl; process until mixture is smooth. Cover and chill at least 1 hour. Stir in chopped cucumber. Yield: about 2½ cups.

Libretto
The Opera Society of Fort Lauderdale, Florida

Barbecued Salmon

2 large onions
2 cups water
2 cups tomato juice
1 cup catsup
½ cup firmly packed brown
sugar
½ cup vinegar

2 tablespoons Worcestershire
sauce
1 teaspoon garlic salt
1 teaspoon chili powder
2 bay leaves
4 whole cloves
4 (8-ounce) salmon steaks

Cut onions into ½-inch slices, and separate into rings. Combine onion rings and water in a saucepan; bring to a boil over medium heat. Reduce heat, and simmer, uncovered, 20 minutes. Add tomato juice and next 8 ingredients, stirring well; simmer 1 hour. Remove and discard bay leaves and cloves. Set sauce aside.

Brown salmon steaks on both sides in a large nonstick skillet; place salmon in a 13- x 9- x 2-inch baking dish. Pour sauce over salmon, and bake at 350° for 30 minutes or until fish flakes easily when tested with a fork. Yield: 4 servings.   The Family of Claire Longpré

Symphony of Tastes
The Youth Symphony of Anchorage, Alaska

Turtle Creek Sole

2 pounds sole fillets
½ cup finely chopped onion
¼ cup butter, melted
¾ cup sour cream
2 teaspoons grated lemon
rind

1 tablespoon fresh lemon
juice
½ teaspoon dried whole
dillweed
Salt and pepper to taste

Place fillets in a 13- x 9- x 2-inch baking dish; set aside.

Sauté onion in butter in a small skillet until tender. Remove from heat, and stir in sour cream and remaining ingredients. Pour sauce over fillets. Bake, uncovered, at 350° for 12 to 15 minutes or until fish flakes easily when tested with a fork. Serve immediately. Yield: 6 to 8 servings.

South of the Fork
The Junior League of Dallas, Texas

Lemonade Sole

1 pound sole or other fish
    fillets
1 tablespoon butter, melted
3 tablespoons frozen
    lemonade concentrate,
    thawed
½ cup sour cream or
    mayonnaise
3 tablespoons grated
    Parmesan cheese
2 tablespoons chopped fresh
    parsley

2 tablespoons finely chopped
    green onions
½ teaspoon dried whole
    tarragon
¼ teaspoon salt
⅛ teaspoon ground white
    pepper
Additional ground white
    pepper
Paprika

Place fillets in a lightly greased 11- x 7- x 2-inch baking dish.
Brush with butter; drizzle with lemonade concentrate. Combine
sour cream and next 6 ingredients, and stir well; spread over fillets.
Broil 6 inches from heat 8 to 10 minutes or until fish flakes easily
when tested with a fork. Remove fillets to a serving platter. Sprinkle
with pepper and paprika. Yield: 4 servings.

The Mystic Seaport All Seasons Cookbook
Mystic Seaport Museum Stores
Mystic, Connecticut

Grilled Fish with Garlic Buerre Rouge

6 (6-ounce) red snapper or
    other fish fillets (about
    ¾-inch thick)
½ cup olive oil
¼ cup plus 1 tablespoon
    fresh lemon juice, divided
½ cup chopped fresh
    cilantro, divided
4 cloves garlic, sliced
Salt and freshly ground
    pepper to taste

¼ cup unsalted butter,
    divided
¼ cup chopped purple onion
2 jalapeño peppers, seeded
    and minced
4 cloves garlic, minced
2 medium tomatoes, peeled
    and chopped
Lemon wedges
Fresh cilantro sprigs

Place fillets in a 13- x 9- x 2-inch baking dish. Combine olive oil, ¼
cup lemon juice, ¼ cup chopped cilantro, 4 sliced garlic cloves, salt,

and freshly ground pepper in a jar; cover tightly, and shake vigorously. Pour marinade mixture over fillets; cover and marinate in refrigerator 8 hours, turning once.

Melt 2 tablespoons butter in a large skillet. Sauté onion, jalapeño peppers, and 4 minced garlic cloves until tender. Add tomatoes and remaining 1 tablespoon lemon juice. Cook over medium heat 10 minutes, stirring occasionally. Add remaining 2 tablespoons butter, stirring until butter melts; reduce heat, and keep warm.

Remove fillets from marinade, discarding marinade. Grill fillets over low coals 8 to 10 minutes on each side or until fish flakes easily when tested with a fork.

Stir remaining ¼ cup chopped cilantro into tomato mixture. Pour sauce over fillets. Garnish with lemon wedges and fresh cilantro sprigs. Serve immediately. Yield: 6 servings.   Beverly Stone

Delicious Decisions
The Junior League of San Diego, California

Grilled Red Snapper
with Ginger and Sesame Oil

1 (3- to 4-pound) dressed whole red snapper	2 tablespoons fresh lemon juice
½ cup rice wine vinegar	2 tablespoons sesame oil
3 shallots, minced	2 teaspoons minced fresh ginger
1 clove garlic, minced	
3 tablespoons soy sauce	¼ cup sesame seeds, toasted

Place snapper in a large shallow dish. Combine vinegar and next 6 ingredients, stirring well. Pour marinade mixture over snapper. Cover and marinate in refrigerator at least 2 hours. Remove snapper from marinade, reserving marinade.

Grill fish over hot coals 5 to 7 minutes on each side or until fish flakes easily when tested with a fork, basting frequently with reserved marinade. Sprinkle fish with toasted sesame seeds. Yield: 6 to 8 servings.

Off the Hook
The Junior League of Stamford-Norwalk
Darien, Connecticut

Swordfish Provençal

1 cup diced celery
⅔ cup chopped leek
⅓ cup olive oil
2 to 3 tablespoons minced
  garlic
2 (14.5-ounce) cans whole
  tomatoes, undrained,
  seeded, and chopped
1 bay leaf
1 tablespoon chopped fresh
  parsley
1 teaspoon dried whole basil
1 teaspoon dried whole
  oregano
½ teaspoon freshly ground
  pepper
⅛ teaspoon dried whole
  marjoram
⅛ teaspoon dried whole
  thyme
4 (6-ounce) swordfish steaks,
  skinned
¼ cup Sauterne or other
  sweet white wine
Hot cooked rice

Sauté celery and leek in hot olive oil in a large skillet over medium heat 5 minutes. Add garlic, and sauté 2 minutes or until tender. Add tomatoes and next 7 ingredients; stir well. Bring to a boil; reduce heat, and simmer 10 minutes. Remove and discard bay leaf.

Arrange steaks in an 11- x 7- x 2-inch baking dish; sprinkle with wine. Pour sauce over steaks. Bake at 350° for 20 to 25 minutes or until fish flakes easily when tested with a fork. Serve with rice. Yield: 4 servings.   Cheri Fry

Pot Luck
Village Green
Temple, New Hampshire

Broiled Swordfish Steaks with Horseradish Sauce

4 (6- to 8-ounce) swordfish
  steaks (about 1-inch thick),
  skinned
½ teaspoon freshly ground
  pepper
¼ cup mayonnaise
1 teaspoon Dijon mustard
Fresh parsley sprigs
Horseradish Sauce

Place swordfish steaks on a lightly greased rack in a roasting pan; sprinkle with pepper. Combine mayonnaise and mustard; stir well.

Spread half of mayonnaise mixture over steaks. Broil 6 inches from heat 6 to 7 minutes. Turn steaks; spread with remaining mayonnaise mixture. Broil 4 to 5 minutes or until fish flakes easily when tested with a fork. Garnish with parsley; serve with Horseradish Sauce. Yield: 4 servings.

Horseradish Sauce

½ **cup whipping**
   cream
½ **teaspoon salt**

2 **tablespoons prepared**
   horseradish, drained
Dash of hot sauce

Beat whipping cream at high speed of an electric mixer until foamy; add salt, beating until stiff peaks form. Fold in horseradish and hot sauce. Yield: 1 cup.   Jeanne Clark

A Slice of Nantucket
St. Mary's Guild, St. Mary-Our Lady of the Isle Church
Nantucket, Massachusetts

Baked Trout with Garden Herbs

2 **dressed trout (about 1¾**
   pounds)
Salt and pepper to taste
3 **tablespoons chopped fresh**
   parsley
2 **tablespoons minced green**
   onions
2 **teaspoons minced fresh**
   sage

2 **teaspoons chopped fresh**
   chives
1 **teaspoon minced fresh**
   rosemary
1 **teaspoon minced fresh**
   thyme
1 **clove garlic, minced**
¼ **cup unsalted butter**
Lemon wedges

Sprinkle trout with salt and pepper to taste. Combine parsley and next 6 ingredients in a small bowl; stir well. Stuff half of herb mixture into fish cavities. Place fish in a buttered 13- x 9- x 2-inch baking dish; dot fish with butter. Bake at 350° for 20 to 25 minutes or until fish flakes easily when tested with a fork. Garnish with lemon wedges. Yield: 2 servings.   Madeline Hunter

Favorite Recipes from Friends
The Town Hill School
Lakeville, Connecticut

Grilled Tuna Santa Fe

6 (6- to 8-ounce) tuna
  fillets
½ cup fresh lime juice
½ cup beer
3 tablespoons vegetable
  oil
1 tablespoon plus 1 teaspoon
  ground cumin

1 tablespoon plus 1 teaspoon
  Dijon mustard
4 cloves garlic, minced
½ teaspoon salt
Salsa Fresca
Sliced avocado

Place fillets in a 13- x 9- x 2-inch baking dish.

Combine lime juice, beer, vegetable oil, cumin, Dijon mustard, minced garlic, and salt in a small bowl; stir well. Pour marinade mixture over fillets. Cover and marinate in refrigerator 2 hours, turning once.

Remove fillets from marinade, reserving marinade. Grill fillets over medium coals 5 minutes on each side or until fish flakes easily when tested with a fork, basting frequently with reserved marinade. Top grilled tuna fillets with Salsa Fresca and sliced avocado. Yield: 6 servings.

Salsa Fresca

2 large ripe tomatoes,
  coarsely chopped
1 small onion, chopped
½ medium-size green pepper,
  chopped
3 cloves garlic, minced
4 pickled jalapeño peppers,
  seeded and chopped

2 teaspoons pickled jalapeño
  pepper juice
½ cup chopped fresh cilantro
1½ cups tomato juice
½ teaspoon salt

Position knife blade in food processor bowl; add tomatoes, onion, green pepper, minced garlic, jalapeño peppers, and jalapeño pepper juice to processor bowl, and pulse 3 or 4 times. Add cilantro, tomato juice, and salt; pulse until mixture is well blended and chunky. Yield: 4½ cups.

Gourmet LA
The Junior League of Los Angeles, California

Scalloped Seafood

1 pound flounder, perch, or
  haddock fillets
2 tablespoons vegetable oil
¾ pound unpeeled
  medium-size fresh shrimp
6 cups water
¾ pound fresh sea scallops
1 teaspoon salt
6 black peppercorns
2 bay leaves
¼ cup butter
¼ cup all-purpose flour

1¾ cups milk
¼ cup chopped fresh
  parsley
1 tablespoon lemon juice
1¼ teaspoons Worcestershire
  sauce
1 teaspoon salt
¼ teaspoon pepper
¼ cup fine, dry breadcrumbs
2 tablespoons butter, melted
Hot cooked rice

Sauté fish fillets in vegetable oil on both sides in a large skillet until fillets are lightly browned. Place fillets in a greased 2-quart casserole, and set aside.

Peel and devein shrimp. Place 6 cups water in a large saucepan, and bring to a boil. Add shrimp, sea scallops, 1 teaspoon salt, peppercorns, and bay leaves, and cook 3 to 5 minutes. Drain seafood mixture well. Remove and discard peppercorns and bay leaves. Set cooked shrimp and scallops aside.

Melt ¼ cup butter in a saucepan over low heat; add flour, stirring until smooth. Cook 1 minute, stirring constantly. Gradually add milk; cook over medium heat, stirring constantly, until mixture is thickened and bubbly. Remove from heat.

Add chopped fresh parsley, lemon juice, Worcestershire sauce, 1 teaspoon salt, and pepper to white sauce; stir well. Add cooked shrimp and scallops, stirring gently; pour seafood mixture over fish fillets in casserole.

Combine breadcrumbs and melted butter; sprinkle evenly over seafood mixture. Bake at 400° for 30 minutes. Serve over rice. Yield: 8 servings.

Cal Poly Pomona 50th Anniversary
The Home Economics Alumni Association
Pomona, California

Seafood and Artichoke Casserole

2 (14-ounce) cans artichoke
hearts, drained and
quartered
3 cups water
1 pound unpeeled
medium-size fresh shrimp
1 pound fresh lump
crabmeat, drained and
flaked
½ pound fresh mushrooms,
sliced
2 tablespoons butter, melted
¼ cup plus 1½ teaspoons
butter

¼ cup plus 1½ teaspoons
all-purpose flour
1½ cups half-and-half
¼ cup dry sherry
1 tablespoon Worcestershire
sauce
½ teaspoon salt
⅛ teaspoon ground white
pepper
¼ cup freshly grated
Parmesan cheese
Paprika
Chopped fresh parsley
Hot cooked rice (optional)

Arrange artichoke hearts in a buttered 3-quart baking dish, and
set aside.

Bring 3 cups water to a boil in a medium saucepan; add shrimp,
and cook 3 to 5 minutes. Drain well; rinse with cold water. Peel and
devein shrimp. Arrange shrimp and crabmeat over artichoke hearts
in baking dish.

Sauté sliced mushrooms in 2 tablespoons melted butter in a small
skillet until tender. Arrange sautéed mushrooms evenly over seafood layer.

Melt ¼ cup plus 1½ teaspoons butter in a heavy saucepan over
low heat; add flour, stirring until smooth. Cook 1 minute, stirring
constantly. Gradually add half-and-half; cook over medium heat,
stirring constantly, until mixture is thickened and bubbly. Add
sherry, Worcestershire sauce, salt, and pepper; stir well. Pour sauce
over mushrooms. Sprinkle freshly grated Parmesan cheese and
paprika evenly over sauce.

Bake casserole at 375° for 20 minutes. Sprinkle with chopped
fresh parsley. Serve casserole with hot cooked rice, if desired. Yield:
6 to 8 servings.

Noel Haeberle

An Apple a Day
The Auxiliary to the Boyd County Medical Society
Ashland, Kentucky

Swiss-Crab Casserole

½ cup chopped celery
¼ cup chopped onion
¼ cup chopped green pepper
¼ cup butter, melted
¼ cup all-purpose flour
1 teaspoon salt
2 cups milk
2 cups cooked rice
2 cups fresh lump crabmeat, drained and flaked
2 cups (8 ounces) shredded Swiss cheese

1 (4-ounce) can sliced mushrooms, drained
⅓ cup sliced pitted ripe olives
¼ cup sliced almonds, toasted
2 tablespoons butter, melted
⅓ cup fine, dry breadcrumbs
3 (3- x 1-inch) strips Swiss cheese
Fresh parsley sprigs

Sauté first 3 ingredients in ¼ cup butter over medium heat until tender. Reduce heat to low; add flour and salt, and stir until smooth. Cook 1 minute, stirring constantly. Gradually add milk; cook over medium heat, stirring constantly, until thickened and bubbly.

Combine rice and next 5 ingredients; add sauce, stirring to combine. Spoon mixture into a 2-quart casserole. Combine 2 tablespoons butter and breadcrumbs; sprinkle over casserole. Bake at 350° for 25 minutes. Remove from oven, and arrange cheese on top of casserole. Bake an additional 5 minutes or until cheese melts. Garnish with parsley. Yield: 6 servings.   Pat Szabo

More Memoirs of a Galley Slave
The Kodiak Fishermen's Wives Association
Kodiak, Alaska

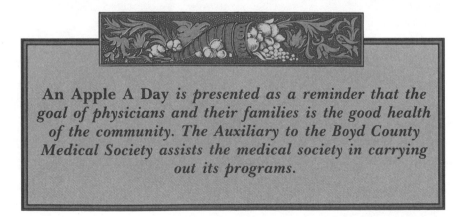

An Apple A Day *is presented as a reminder that the goal of physicians and their families is the good health of the community. The Auxiliary to the Boyd County Medical Society assists the medical society in carrying out its programs.*

Vodka Steamed Scallops

1 pound fresh bay scallops
1 tablespoon vodka
½ teaspoon cornstarch
¼ cup chopped green onions
1 tablespoon minced fresh
  ginger

1 tablespoon chopped fresh
  cilantro
2 cloves garlic, crushed
1 tablespoon peanut oil
1 tablespoon soy sauce
Hot cooked rice

Combine scallops, vodka, and cornstarch in a large bowl, tossing gently. Place scallops on a steaming rack. Combine green onions, ginger, and cilantro; sprinkle over scallops. Place steaming rack over boiling water; cover and steam 5 minutes. Remove scallops to a serving bowl.

Sauté garlic in oil in a small skillet until lightly browned; stir in soy sauce. Pour mixture over scallops. Serve immediately over rice. Yield: 4 servings.

Finely Tuned Foods
The Symphony League of Leawood, Kansas

Scampi Capriccio di Diana

3 cups water
1 pound unpeeled
  medium-size fresh shrimp
2½ tablespoons butter or
  margarine
3 tablespoons all-purpose
  flour
2 tablespoons chopped green
  onions
1½ cups milk
½ cup whipping cream

½ teaspoon salt
½ teaspoon lemon juice
⅛ teaspoon ground white
  pepper
⅛ teaspoon ground nutmeg
1 cup (4 ounces) shredded
  Swiss cheese, divided
2 tablespoons grated
  Parmesan cheese
Paprika
Chopped fresh parsley

Bring 3 cups water to a boil; add shrimp, and cook 3 to 5 minutes. Drain well; rinse with cold water. Peel and devein shrimp. Place shrimp in a greased 1-quart casserole. Set aside.

Melt butter in a saucepan over low heat; add flour and onions, stirring until blended. Cook 1 minute, stirring constantly. Gradually add milk; cook over medium heat, stirring constantly, until thickened and bubbly. Gradually add cream, stirring well. Add salt and next 3 ingredients, stirring well. Remove from heat; add ½ cup Swiss cheese, stirring until cheese melts. Pour sauce over shrimp; sprinkle with remaining ½ cup Swiss cheese and Parmesan cheese. Sprinkle with paprika. Bake at 350° for 20 to 25 minutes or until hot and bubbly. Garnish with chopped fresh parsley. Yield: 4 servings.

Lasting Impressions
The Saint Joseph's Hospital of Atlanta Auxiliary
Atlanta, Georgia

Shrimp and Feta Cheese

1 large onion, chopped	⅛ teaspoon pepper
2 cloves garlic, minced	1 pound unpeeled
2 tablespoons butter, melted	medium-size fresh shrimp
6 large tomatoes, peeled and chopped	¼ cup butter, melted
	2 tablespoons cognac
1 tablespoon chopped fresh basil	1 tablespoon ouzo or other anise-flavored liqueur
½ teaspoon sugar	⅔ cup crumbled feta cheese
½ teaspoon cumin seeds	Chopped fresh parsley
¼ teaspoon salt	

Sauté onion and garlic in 2 tablespoons melted butter in a large skillet until tender. Add tomatoes and next 5 ingredients, stirring well; cook, uncovered, over low heat 20 to 30 minutes, stirring occasionally. Remove from heat; set aside.

Peel, devein, and butterfly shrimp, leaving tails intact. Sauté shrimp in ¼ cup melted butter in a medium skillet 3 minutes. Remove from heat.

Place cognac in a small long-handled saucepan; heat just until warm (do not boil). Remove from heat. Ignite with a long match, and pour over shrimp. Repeat procedure with ouzo.

Combine shrimp and tomato mixtures; place in a 13- x 9- x 2-inch baking dish. Sprinkle top with feta cheese. Bake at 375° for 20 minutes or until bubbly. Garnish with chopped fresh parsley. Yield: 4 to 6 servings.

A Taste of Almost Heaven
The Monongalia Arts Center
Morgantown, West Virginia

Oriental Kabobs

1 cup soy sauce
1 cup honey
1 cup cream sherry
2 teaspoons grated orange
    rind
1 teaspoon garlic powder
1¼ pounds unpeeled large
    fresh shrimp
2½ pounds boneless pork
    loin, trimmed and cut into
    1-inch cubes

1 pound fresh mushrooms
1 (8-ounce) can pineapple
    chunks, drained
1 medium-size green pepper,
    cut into 1-inch pieces
1 medium-size sweet red
    pepper, cut into 1-inch
    pieces

Combine soy sauce, honey, sherry, orange rind, and garlic powder in a large bowl; stir well, and set aside.

Peel and devein shrimp. Add shrimp, pork, and mushrooms to
marinade mixture, stirring well. Cover and marinate in refrigerator
8 hours.

Remove shrimp, pork, and mushrooms from marinade, reserving
marinade. Alternate shrimp, pork, mushrooms, pineapple chunks,
and pepper pieces on metal skewers. Grill over medium-hot coals 8
minutes or until done, turning and basting frequently with reserved
marinade. Yield: 6 to 8 servings.

The Golden Apple Collection
White Plains Auxiliary of the White Plains Hospital Center
White Plains, New York

Meats

An old-time water well serves as a reminder of prosperous days-gone-by in Texas when fresh meat was so abundant that it was given away. Even in larger towns, butchers had a hard time selling sirloin steak at 20 cents per pound.

Black-Tie Standing Rib Roast

2 teaspoons salt
1 teaspoon freshly ground
  pepper
1 teaspoon dried whole
  thyme
1 (10-pound) standing rib
  roast
⅔ cup water
¼ cup plus 1½ tablespoons
  butter, divided
2 tablespoons lemon juice

¼ teaspoon salt
½ pound small fresh
  mushrooms, sliced
½ cup minced shallots
1 cup canned diluted beef
  broth
½ cup Madeira
1 tablespoon tomato paste
Salt and freshly ground
  pepper to taste

Combine 2 teaspoons salt, 1 teaspoon pepper, and thyme; stir well. Sprinkle mixture evenly over roast; set aside.

Combine water, 1½ tablespoons butter, lemon juice, and ¼ teaspoon salt in a medium saucepan. Bring to a boil over medium-high heat. Add mushrooms; cover, reduce heat, and cook 5 minutes. Drain mushrooms, reserving liquid. Set mushrooms aside. Add water to liquid to measure 1 cup; set aside.

Place roast, fat side up, on a rack in a shallow roasting pan. Insert meat thermometer, making sure it does not touch fat or bone. Bake at 500° for 10 minutes. Reduce oven temperature to 350°; bake 3 hours or until meat thermometer registers 140° (rare), 160° (medium), or 170° (well done).

Remove roast to a serving platter. Drain off drippings, reserving 1 cup drippings. Return 1 cup drippings to pan. Add remaining ¼ cup butter to drippings; cook over medium-high heat until butter melts. Add shallots, and sauté until tender. Stir in reserved mushroom liquid, beef broth, wine, and tomato paste. Reduce heat to low, and cook 15 to 20 minutes or until liquid is reduced to 2 cups. Add reserved mushrooms, and cook until thoroughly heated. Add salt and pepper to taste. Serve sauce with roast. Yield: 12 to 14 servings.

Simply Sensational
TWIGS, The Auxiliary of the Children's Medical Center
Dayton, Ohio

Barbecued Pot Roast

1 (3-pound) beef blade roast
2 teaspoons salt
¼ teaspoon pepper
3 tablespoons shortening, melted
1 (8-ounce) can tomato sauce
½ cup water
3 medium onions, thinly sliced
2 cloves garlic, minced
¼ cup vinegar

¼ cup lemon juice
¼ cup catsup
1 tablespoon Worcestershire sauce
2 tablespoons brown sugar
½ teaspoon dry mustard
¼ teaspoon paprika
2 tablespoons all-purpose flour
2 tablespoons water

Sprinkle roast with salt and pepper. Brown roast in shortening in a Dutch oven over medium-high heat. Reduce heat to low; cover and cook 1½ hours. Drain; discard drippings. Add tomato sauce, ½ cup water, onion, and garlic to Dutch oven. Combine vinegar and next 6 ingredients, stirring well; pour over roast. Cover and cook 1 hour or until meat is tender. Remove roast to a serving platter, reserving liquid in Dutch oven. Combine flour and 2 tablespoons water, stirring until smooth; stir into liquid in Dutch oven. Cook over medium heat, stirring constantly, until thickened and bubbly. Spoon 1 cup sauce over roast; serve remaining sauce with roast. Yield: 6 to 8 servings.   Elaine Schleusener

Woman to Woman Cookbook
The Zonta Club of the Black Hills
Rapid City, South Dakota

Grandmother's Buttermilk Pot Roast

1 tablespoon all-purpose flour
1 tablespoon dry mustard
1½ teaspoons salt
¼ teaspoon pepper
1 (3- to 4-pound) beef blade roast
1 tablespoon vegetable oil
1 beef-flavored bouillon cube
⅓ cup hot water

1½ cups buttermilk, divided
6 medium carrots, scraped and cut into 2-inch pieces
1 pound fresh brussels sprouts or 1 (10-ounce) package frozen brussels sprouts, thawed
¼ cup plus 2 tablespoons all-purpose flour

Combine 1 tablespoon flour, mustard, salt, and pepper; dredge roast in flour mixture. Brown roast in hot oil in a large Dutch oven. Dissolve bouillon cube in hot water; pour over roast. Cover and simmer 1½ hours. Add ½ cup buttermilk, carrots, and brussels sprouts; cover and simmer 1 hour or until roast and vegetables are tender. Remove roast and vegetables to a platter; keep warm. Reserve drippings in Dutch oven.

Combine remaining 1 cup buttermilk and ¼ cup plus 2 tablespoons flour in a small bowl; stir well. Stir flour mixture into liquid in Dutch oven. Cook over medium heat, stirring constantly, until mixture is thickened and bubbly. Serve gravy with roast. Yield: 6 to 8 servings.   John L. Huston

A Book of Favorite Recipes
Sisterhood of SS. Cyril and Methodius Orthodox Church
Terryville, Connecticut

Tenderloin of Beef

1 cup Burgundy or other dry
  red wine
1 cup soy sauce
½ cup vegetable oil
1 teaspoon dried whole
  thyme
1 bay leaf

1 (4- to 5-pound) beef
  tenderloin, trimmed
5 cloves garlic
1 teaspoon salt
1 teaspoon pepper
5 slices bacon

Combine first 5 ingredients; stir well, and set aside.

Rub tenderloin with garlic. Make 5 slits in tenderloin, and insert 1 garlic clove into each slit; sprinkle tenderloin with salt and pepper. Place in a large shallow dish; pour marinade over tenderloin. Cover and marinate in refrigerator 8 hours, turning occasionally.

Drain meat; discard marinade. Place tenderloin on a rack in a roasting pan. Place bacon slices on top of beef; insert meat thermometer into thickest portion of tenderloin, making sure it does not touch fat. Bake at 425° for 25 to 30 minutes or until thermometer registers 140° (rare), 150° (medium rare), or 160° (medium). Let stand 10 minutes before slicing. Yield: 10 to 12 servings.

Finely Tuned Foods
The Symphony League of Leawood, Kansas

Beef Tenderloin
with Mustard-Tarragon Sauce

1 (2-pound) beef tenderloin, trimmed
2 tablespoons vegetable oil
½ teaspoon salt
½ teaspoon pepper
3 tablespoons unsalted butter, softened
2 tablespoons Dijon mustard
1 cup Chablis or other dry white wine
¼ cup minced shallots
1½ tablespoons minced fresh tarragon or 2 teaspoons dried whole tarragon
1 tablespoon whipping cream
8 cornichons (gherkins), cut into julienne strips (optional)
Salt and pepper to taste

Rub tenderloin with oil; sprinkle with ½ teaspoon each of salt and pepper. Place on a rack in a roasting pan. Insert meat thermometer into thickest portion of tenderloin, making sure it does not touch fat. Bake at 425° for 30 minutes or until thermometer registers 140° (rare), 150° (medium rare), or 160° (medium). Transfer to a platter. Cover; let stand 10 minutes before slicing. Combine butter and mustard; stir well. Cover and chill. Combine wine, shallots, and tarragon; cook over medium-high heat until reduced to 3 tablespoons. Stir in cream and, if desired, cornichons. Cook over low heat until heated (do not boil). Add butter mixture, stirring until smooth. Add salt and pepper. Serve sauce with tenderloin. Yield: 6 servings.

Celebrated Seasons
The Junior League of Minneapolis, Minnesota

The beautiful change of seasons in Minneapolis signals a change of tastes and special reasons to celebrate. A tour through the seasons becomes the focal point of the **Celebrated Seasons** *cookbook from the Junior League of Minneapolis.*

Flank Steak Broil

1 (1½-pound) flank steak
⅔ cup catsup
½ cup water
⅓ cup lemon juice
2 teaspoons Worcestershire
    sauce
1 teaspoon celery seeds

1 bay leaf
½ teaspoon coarsely ground
    pepper
¼ teaspoon dried whole basil,
    crushed
Dash of hot pepper sauce

Score steak diagonally across grain at ¾-inch intervals. Place meat in a shallow dish; set aside. Combine catsup and remaining ingredients, stirring well. Pour marinade mixture over steak; cover and marinate in refrigerator 8 hours, turning occasionally.

Remove meat from marinade, reserving marinade. Remove and discard bay leaf from marinade.

Grill steak over hot coals 5 minutes on each side or to desired degree of doneness. To serve, slice steak diagonally across grain into thin slices. Boil marinade 5 minutes, and serve marinade with steak. Yield: 4 to 6 servings.

Con Mucho Gusto
The Desert Club of Mesa, Arizona

Marinated Flank Steak

1 (2-pound) flank steak
1 small onion, finely chopped
¾ cup vegetable oil
¼ cup soy sauce

3 tablespoons honey
2 tablespoons cider vinegar
1½ teaspoons garlic salt
1½ teaspoons ground ginger

Score steak diagonally across grain at ¾-inch intervals. Place meat in a shallow dish. Combine oil and remaining ingredients in a small bowl; stir well. Pour marinade mixture over steak; cover and marinate in refrigerator 8 hours, turning occasionally.

Remove meat from marinade; discard marinade. Grill steak over medium coals 8 minutes on each side or to desired degree of doneness. To serve, slice steak diagonally across grain into thin slices. Yield: 6 to 8 servings.

Savannah Style
The Junior League of Savannah, Georgia

Chinese Pepper Steak

1 (1-pound) flank steak
2 tablespoons vegetable oil
1 teaspoon salt
½ teaspoon pepper
2 green peppers, cut into
  1-inch pieces
1 sweet yellow pepper, cut
  into 1-inch pieces
1 sweet red pepper, cut into
  1-inch pieces
1 cup diagonally sliced celery
2 medium carrots, scraped
  and cut into julienne strips

½ cup chopped onion
1 clove garlic, minced
1½ cups canned diluted beef
  broth
3 tablespoons cornstarch
¾ cup water
¼ cup Madeira
1 tablespoon soy sauce
1 (8-ounce) can sliced water
  chestnuts, drained
1 cup firmly packed torn
  spinach
Hot cooked rice

Trim excess fat from steak; partially freeze steak. Slice steak across grain into 2- x ⅛-inch strips. Pour oil around top of pre-heated wok, coating sides; heat at medium high (325°) for 2 minutes. Add steak, salt, and pepper; increase temperature to high (375°), and stir-fry 4 to 5 minutes. Add green pepper pieces and next 6 ingredients; stir-fry 2 minutes. Add beef broth; cover and cook 3 to 5 minutes.

Combine cornstarch and water, stirring until smooth. Add wine and soy sauce to cornstarch mixture, stirring well. Add to steak mixture, and cook, stirring constantly, until thickened and bubbly. Add water chestnuts and spinach, stirring well; cook 1 minute. Serve over rice. Yield: 6 servings.

Lasting Impressions
The Saint Joseph's Hospital of Atlanta Auxiliary
Atlanta, Georgia

Stars and Stripes

½ pound boneless sirloin steak
2 tablespoons vegetable oil
2 tablespoons minced fresh
  ginger
1 small sweet red pepper, cut
  into julienne strips

4 green onions, diagonally
  sliced
3 tablespoons soy sauce
3 starfruit, thinly
  sliced
Hot cooked rice

Partially freeze steak; slice diagonally across grain into 3- x ¼-inch strips. Set aside.

Pour oil around top of preheated wok, coating sides; heat at medium high (325°) for 2 minutes. Add ginger, and stir-fry 1 minute. Add steak, and stir-fry 1 minute. Stir in pepper and onions; stir-fry 1 minute. Add soy sauce and starfruit; stir-fry until starfruit are thoroughly heated. Serve over rice. Yield: 4 servings.

Make It Miami
The Guild of the Museum of Science, Inc.
Miami, Florida

Beef Parmigiana

1½ pounds boneless round
　steak
⅓ cup grated Parmesan
　cheese
⅓ cup fine, dry breadcrumbs
1 egg, beaten
⅓ cup vegetable oil
1 medium onion, chopped
1 clove garlic, minced
1 tablespoon butter or
　margarine, melted

1 (8-ounce) can tomato paste
1 teaspoon salt
½ teaspoon sugar
½ teaspoon dried whole
　marjoram
¼ teaspoon pepper
2 cups hot water
8 ounces mozzarella cheese,
　sliced

Trim excess fat from steak; pound steak to ¼-inch thickness, using a meat mallet. Cut steak into serving-size pieces. Combine Parmesan cheese and breadcrumbs. Dip steak in beaten egg, and dredge in Parmesan cheese mixture. Heat oil in a large skillet to 375°. Fry steak in hot oil until browned, turning once. Drain on paper towels.

Sauté onion and garlic in butter in a large skillet until tender. Add tomato paste and next 4 ingredients, stirring well. Gradually add hot water, stirring constantly. Bring to a boil, and cook 5 minutes.

Place steak in a 13- x 9- x 2-inch baking dish; top with two-thirds tomato sauce. Top with cheese slices. Pour remaining tomato sauce over cheese. Cover and bake at 350° for 1 hour. Yield: 6 servings.

From Scratch Cookbook
The Assistance League® of Glendale, California

Boeuf au Fromage

1 pound boneless sirloin or
round steak
½ cup all-purpose flour
½ teaspoon salt
½ teaspoon pepper
2 tablespoons peanut oil
2 tablespoons butter, melted

1 cup canned diluted beef
broth
1 tablespoon sour cream
2 tablespoons commercial
Roquefort salad dressing
2 tablespoons grated
Parmesan cheese

Partially freeze steak; slice diagonally across grain into 2- x ¼-inch strips. Set aside. Combine flour, salt, and pepper in a small bowl. Reserve 1 tablespoon flour mixture. Dredge steak strips in remaining flour mixture.

Brown steak in hot oil and butter in a skillet. Drain on paper towels, reserving drippings in skillet. Add beef broth to drippings; cook over low heat until thoroughly heated. Remove from heat; let cool slightly. Stir in sour cream. Add 1 tablespoon reserved flour mixture, stirring well. Cook over medium heat, stirring constantly, until thickened (do not boil). Return beef to skillet, stirring to combine. Spoon beef mixture into a greased 11- x 7- x 2-inch baking dish. Drizzle with dressing, and sprinkle with Parmesan cheese. Broil 6 inches from heat 3 minutes or until lightly browned. Yield: 4 servings.   Susan Walgreen Kessler and Jim Kessler

Cook 'em Horns: The Quickbook
The Ex-Students Association of the University of Texas
Austin, Texas

Glazed Corned Beef

1 (3-pound) corned beef
brisket
Whole cloves
1 (8¼-ounce) can pineapple
slices, undrained

1 cup firmly packed brown
sugar
1 tablespoon dry mustard

Place brisket in a large Dutch oven; add water to cover. Bring to a boil. Remove from heat; drain. Add fresh water to cover. Bring to a boil; cover, reduce heat, and simmer 3 hours or until brisket is tender. Drain well.

Place brisket, fat side up, on a rack in a roasting pan. Score fat in a diamond design, and stud with whole cloves.

Drain pineapple, reserving juice. Set pineapple slices aside. Combine brown sugar, mustard, and 3 tablespoons reserved pineapple juice, stirring well. Brush glaze over brisket. Bake at 375° for 25 minutes, basting frequently with any remaining glaze and juice. Remove brisket to a serving platter; garnish with pineapple slices. Yield: 4 to 6 servings.   Riva Chase

What's Cooking?
The Sisterhood of Temple Shalom
Succasunna, New Jersey

Mother's Meat Loaf

1½ pounds lean ground   ⅛ teaspoon pepper
  beef   2 eggs, lightly beaten
⅔ cup soft breadcrumbs   1 cup milk
⅓ cup chopped onion   Piquant Sauce
1 teaspoon salt

Combine ground beef, breadcrumbs, chopped onion, salt, pepper, beaten eggs, and milk in a large bowl; stir well. Shape meat mixture into a 12- x 7-inch loaf; place in a 13- x 9- x 2-inch baking pan. Bake at 350° for 1 hour and 15 minutes.

Remove meat loaf from oven, and pour Piquant Sauce over top of loaf. Return meat loaf to oven, and bake an additional 15 minutes. Transfer meat loaf to a serving platter. Yield: 6 servings.

Piquant Sauce

¾ cup firmly packed brown   1½ teaspoons dry mustard
  sugar   ¾ teaspoon Worcestershire
¾ cup catsup   sauce

Combine all ingredients in a small bowl, stirring well. Yield: about 1¼ cups.   Earl Ann Lenert Bumpus

A Samford Celebration Cookbook
Samford University Auxiliary
Birmingham, Alabama

Sauerbrated Meat Loaf

1½ pounds ground beef
½ pound ground pork
1 medium onion, finely chopped
½ cup soft breadcrumbs
½ cup gingersnap crumbs
2 eggs, beaten
3 tablespoons cider vinegar
2 teaspoons salt

1½ teaspoons prepared
  mustard
¼ cup firmly packed brown
  sugar
3 tablespoons cider vinegar
3 tablespoons catsup
1 tablespoon prepared
  mustard

Combine ground beef, ground pork, chopped onion, bread-crumbs, gingersnap crumbs, beaten eggs, 3 tablespoons vinegar, salt, and 1½ teaspoons mustard in a large bowl; stir well. Shape meat mixture into a loaf; place in a 9- x 5- x 3-inch loafpan.

Combine brown sugar, 3 tablespoons vinegar, catsup, and 1 tablespoon mustard in a small bowl, and stir well. Pour glaze over meat loaf, and bake at 350° for 1 hour and 15 minutes. Yield: 8 servings.

Janet Sturrock

Chestnut Hill Cookbook
The Chestnut Hill Senior Services Center
Philadelphia, Pennsylvania

Pocket Gyros with Yogurt Sauce

1¼ pounds lean ground beef
1¼ pounds lean ground lamb
1 medium onion, finely chopped
2 large cloves garlic, finely
  chopped
¼ cup chopped fresh oregano
1 tablespoon fresh thyme
  sprigs, crushed

¾ teaspoon salt
1½ teaspoons freshly ground
  pepper
8 (6-inch) pita bread rounds,
  cut in half crosswise
3 medium tomatoes, chopped
1 large onion, thinly sliced
Yogurt Sauce

Combine ground beef, ground lamb, chopped onion, garlic, oreg-ano, thyme, salt, and pepper in a large bowl; stir well. Shape meat mixture into a loaf, and place in a 9- x 5- x 3-inch loafpan. Bake at 350° for 1½ hours. Remove from pan, and let cool.

Slice meat loaf into ¼-inch-thick slices. Fill pita bread round halves with meat slices. Top with chopped tomato, sliced onion, and Yogurt Sauce. Yield: 8 servings.

Yogurt Sauce

1 cup plain yogurt
¼ cup finely chopped
   cucumber
¼ cup finely chopped onion

1 clove garlic, minced
2 teaspoons olive oil
¼ teaspoon salt
¼ teaspoon pepper

Combine all ingredients in a medium bowl; stir well. Cover and chill thoroughly. Yield: 1¼ cups.

Gatherings
The Junior League of Milwaukee, Wisconsin

Chinese Meatballs

2½ pounds ground beef or
   ground turkey
2 eggs, beaten
3 tablespoons finely chopped
   onion
1¼ teaspoons salt
¾ teaspoon ground ginger
2 large green peppers, cut
   into 1-inch pieces
2 large sweet red peppers,
   cut into 1-inch pieces

2 (20-ounce) cans pineapple
   chunks in juice, undrained
1 cup canned diluted chicken
   broth, divided
½ cup sugar
½ cup white vinegar
3 tablespoons cornstarch
2 teaspoons soy sauce
Hot cooked rice

Combine beef, eggs, onion, salt, and ginger in a large bowl; stir well. Shape meat mixture into 1½-inch balls. Brown meatballs in a skillet over medium heat; drain well.

Add pepper pieces, pineapple chunks with juice, and ⅓ cup chicken broth to meatballs in skillet. Simmer 10 minutes, stirring occasionally.

Combine remaining ⅔ cup chicken broth, sugar, vinegar, cornstarch, and soy sauce, stirring until smooth. Add to meatballs, and cook until mixture is thickened and bubbly. Serve over rice. Yield: 6 to 8 servings.   Lois England

The Florida Cooking Adventure
The Florida Federation of Women's Clubs
Lakeland, Florida

Moving Day Casserole

1 (12-ounce) package medium
  egg noodles
1 pound ground beef
2 (8-ounce) cans tomato sauce
¾ cup flat beer
1 teaspoon salt
½ teaspoon dried whole
  oregano

2 drops of hot sauce
1 (8-ounce) package cream
  cheese, softened
1 cup cottage cheese
½ cup sour cream
¼ cup chopped green pepper
  (optional)

Cook noodles according to package directions; drain well, and set noodles aside.

Cook ground beef in a large skillet over medium heat until browned, stirring to crumble meat. Add tomato sauce and next 4 ingredients; stir well. Remove from heat, and set aside.

Combine cheeses, sour cream, and, if desired, green pepper; stir well. Place half the noodles in an ungreased shallow 3-quart casserole. Top with cheese mixture; place remaining noodles over cheese mixture. Spoon beef mixture over noodles. Bake at 350° for 30 minutes. Yield: 6 servings.   Louise J. Nichols

Pioneers of Alaska Cookbook
The Pioneers of Alaska Auxiliary #4
Anchorage, Alaska

Polenta Beef Casserole

1 pound ground beef
½ pound fresh mushrooms,
  sliced
1 cup chopped green pepper
1 medium onion, finely
  chopped
1 clove garlic, minced
1 cup soft breadcrumbs
1 egg, beaten
1 teaspoon salt

½ teaspoon dried whole
  oregano, crushed
½ teaspoon pepper
½ teaspoon hot sauce
2½ cups water
1 teaspoon salt
¾ cup yellow cornmeal
1 cup (4 ounces) shredded
  Cheddar cheese

Combine first 5 ingredients in a large skillet. Cook over medium heat until meat is browned and vegetables are tender, stirring occasionally to crumble meat. Drain.

Combine breadcrumbs, egg, 1 teaspoon salt, oregano, pepper, and hot sauce in a large bowl; stir well. Add beef mixture to breadcrumb mixture, stirring well. Spoon into an ungreased 11- x 7- x 2-inch baking dish. Set aside.

Bring water and 1 teaspoon salt to a boil in a large saucepan. Gradually add cornmeal, stirring constantly; boil 1 minute or until mixture is thickened. Spoon cornmeal mixture over meat mixture. Cover and bake at 350° for 30 minutes. Remove from oven, and top with shredded cheese. Bake an additional 3 to 5 minutes or until cheese melts. Yield: 6 servings.   Beverly Read

Dobar Tek
The Yugoslav Women's Club
Seattle, Washington

Calf's Liver Veneziano

1½ pounds calf's liver, 1-inch thick
¼ cup all-purpose flour
1½ teaspoons salt
¼ teaspoon pepper
¼ cup butter or margarine, melted
¼ cup olive or vegetable oil, divided
2 pounds onions, thinly sliced
½ teaspoon dried whole sage
¼ cup Chablis or other dry white wine
1 tablespoon lemon juice
2 tablespoons chopped fresh parsley

Slice liver into ¼-inch strips. Combine flour, salt, and pepper; dredge liver in flour mixture. Brown liver in butter and 2 tablespoons oil in a large skillet. Remove liver from skillet, and set aside.

Sauté onion in remaining 2 tablespoons oil 10 minutes or until golden. Add sage; stir well. Cover, reduce heat to low, and cook 5 minutes. Add liver; cook 5 minutes, stirring occasionally. Remove to a serving platter, and keep warm. Reserve drippings in skillet.

Add wine and lemon juice to pan drippings in skillet; bring to a boil, stirring constantly. Pour over liver and onions. Sprinkle with chopped fresh parsley. Yield: 6 to 8 servings.

Favorite Italian Recipes
The St. Theresa Guild of Holy Rosary Church
Bridgeport, Connecticut

Pan-Fried Veal Chops

6 (1-inch-thick) veal loin
  chops (about 3 pounds)
Salt and pepper
¼ cup olive oil, divided
2 or 3 sprigs fresh rosemary
3 Granny Smith apples,
  peeled and coarsely
  chopped

3 large shallots, coarsely
  chopped
2 tablespoons butter, melted
½ pound fresh cranberries
¼ cup port or other sweet
  red wine
1 to 2 tablespoons brown
  sugar

Sprinkle chops with salt and pepper. Heat 2 tablespoons oil and rosemary in a skillet over medium-high heat. Add chops; cook to desired degree of doneness, turning once. Set aside; keep warm.

Sauté apple and shallots in remaining 2 tablespoons oil and butter in a large skillet until apple is crisp-tender. Add cranberries, wine, and brown sugar; stir well. Cook over medium heat 4 minutes or until cranberry skins pop, stirring occasionally. Serve sauce with chops. Yield: 6 servings.

Only in California
The Children's Home Society of California
Los Angeles, California

Veal with Apples

1 medium onion, chopped
¼ cup plus 2 tablespoons
  butter, melted and divided
2 cups peeled, coarsely
  chopped cooking apples
3 slices white bread, cubed
1 clove garlic, minced
1 teaspoon salt

½ teaspoon poultry seasoning
12 (¼-inch-thick) veal cutlets
½ cup all-purpose flour
¾ cup apple juice or cider
2 tablespoons Calvados or
  other apple-flavored brandy
Crab apples
Fresh parsley sprigs

Sauté onion in ¼ cup melted butter in a large skillet until tender. Add apple and next 4 ingredients; stir well. Cook over low heat 1 to 2 minutes. Remove from heat, and set aside.

Place cutlets between sheets of wax paper; flatten to ⅛-inch thickness, using a meat mallet or rolling pin. Spoon apple mixture evenly over each cutlet; fold edges over, roll up, and secure with wooden picks.

Dredge veal in flour; brown in remaining 2 tablespoons butter in skillet. Add apple juice and brandy to skillet; cook over low heat 25 to 30 minutes.

Transfer veal to a serving platter. Garnish with crab apples and fresh parsley sprigs. Yield: 6 servings.   Roberta Jones

Another Taste of Palm Springs
Tiempo de Los Niños, an Auxiliary of Desert Hospital
Palm Springs, California

Veal Scallops with Mushrooms

1 pound fresh mushrooms, sliced
¼ cup minced shallots, divided
½ cup butter, melted and divided
2 cups whipping cream, divided
⅓ cup all-purpose flour
Salt and pepper to taste
4 (¼-inch-thick) veal cutlets
½ cup Chablis or other dry white wine
8 (1-ounce) slices Swiss cheese

Sauté mushrooms and 2 teaspoons shallots in ¼ cup melted butter in a large skillet until tender. Gradually stir in ⅔ cup whipping cream; cook over medium-high heat until mixture is reduced by half. Set aside, and keep warm.

Combine flour and salt and pepper to taste in a small bowl; dredge veal in flour mixture. Brown veal in remaining ¼ cup melted butter in skillet; drain well. Transfer veal to a 2-quart casserole; set aside, and keep warm.

Combine remaining 3 tablespoons plus 1 teaspoon shallots and white wine in a saucepan; cook over medium heat, stirring constantly, until mixture is reduced by one-third. Add remaining 1⅓ cups whipping cream; cook, stirring constantly, until mixture is reduced by half. Remove from heat, and set aside.

Top each cutlet with mushroom mixture and 2 slices of Swiss cheese. Pour wine sauce over cheese. Broil 6 inches from heat 2 to 3 minutes or until cutlets are golden brown and cheese melts. Yield: 4 servings.   Louise Kozisek

Pioneers of Alaska Cookbook
The Pioneers of Alaska Auxiliary #4
Anchorage, Alaska

Braised Lamb Shanks

6 lamb shanks (about 7
   pounds)
1 lemon, cut in half
½ cup all-purpose flour
2 teaspoons salt
½ teaspoon pepper
¼ cup vegetable oil
1 medium onion, chopped

2 cloves garlic, minced
1 cup Burgundy or other dry
   red wine
1 (10-ounce) can consommé
1 cup scraped, sliced carrots
1 cup sliced celery
1 bay leaf

Rub lamb shanks with lemon; discard lemon. Let lamb shanks stand 10 minutes.

Combine flour, salt, and pepper in a small bowl. Dredge shanks in flour mixture; cook in vegetable oil in a large skillet until browned. Transfer shanks to a 5-quart casserole, reserving drippings in skillet.

Sauté onion and garlic in pan drippings until tender. Stir in remaining flour mixture; cook 1 minute, stirring constantly. Gradually add wine and consommé; cook over medium heat, stirring constantly, until mixture thickens slightly. Pour over shanks. Add carrot, celery, and bay leaf. Bake, uncovered, at 350° for 2½ hours.

Remove and discard bay leaf. Arrange lamb shanks on a large serving platter, and spoon carrots and celery around shanks. Yield: 6 servings.   Kay Samuels

Feed My People
Carter-Westminster United Presbyterian Church
Skokie, Illinois

Marinated Lamb Chops

8 (1-inch-thick) lamb loin
   chops
3 tablespoons olive oil
2 tablespoons wine vinegar
1 tablespoon lemon juice
2 teaspoons prepared mustard

1 clove garlic, minced
1 teaspoon dried whole
   rosemary
¼ teaspoon salt
¼ teaspoon ground ginger
1 small onion, thinly sliced

Place lamb chops in an 11- x 7- x 2-inch baking dish; set aside. Combine olive oil and next 7 ingredients, stirring well. Pour marinade mixture over chops; top with sliced onion. Cover and marinate in refrigerator 4 to 5 hours, turning occasionally.

Remove chops from marinade, discarding marinade and onion. Grill chops over hot coals 5 to 8 minutes on each side or to desired degree of doneness. Yield: 8 servings.

Gourmet by the Bay
The Dolphin Circle of the King's Daughters and Sons
Virginia Beach, Virginia

Grilled Lamb Chops

6 (1-inch-thick) lamb loin
chops
2 cups dry sherry

½ cup chopped fresh mint
4 cloves garlic, crushed

Trim excess fat from lamb chops. Place chops in a large shallow baking dish.

Combine sherry, mint, and garlic; stir well. Pour marinade mixture over lamb chops. Cover and marinate in refrigerator 8 hours, turning occasionally.

Remove chops from marinade; discard marinade. Grill chops over medium coals 8 to 10 minutes on each side or to desired degree of doneness. Yield: 6 servings.

Delicious Decisions
The Junior League of San Diego, California

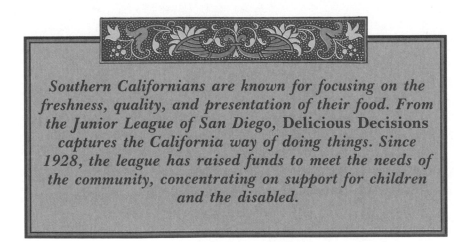

Southern Californians are known for focusing on the freshness, quality, and presentation of their food. From the Junior League of San Diego, Delicious Decisions captures the California way of doing things. Since 1928, the league has raised funds to meet the needs of the community, concentrating on support for children and the disabled.

Spit-Roasted Holiday Pork

1 (5-pound) boneless double
   pork loin roast
4 (4½-ounce) jars strained
   apricot baby food, divided
1 cup ginger ale
⅓ cup honey
¼ cup fresh lemon juice
¼ cup soy sauce
1 small onion, minced

1 small clove garlic, minced
⅛ teaspoon ground ginger
⅛ teaspoon pepper
1 (29-ounce) can whole
   unpeeled apricots, drained
1 tablespoon grated lemon
   rind
¼ cup flaked coconut
Fresh parsley sprigs

Place roast in a shallow dish. Combine 2 jars baby food and next 8 ingredients; stir well. Pour marinade mixture over roast; cover and marinate in refrigerator 8 hours, turning occasionally.

Drain roast; reserve marinade. Insert meat thermometer into thickest part of roast, making sure it does not touch fat. Grill roast over low coals 3 hours or until thermometer registers 160°. Turn and baste roast with marinade during last 30 minutes of grilling time. Remove roast to a platter; brush with 1 jar baby food.

Combine apricots and lemon rind; cook over low heat just until heated. Remove from heat; sprinkle with coconut. Combine remaining jar baby food and any remaining marinade. Bring to a boil; reduce heat, and simmer 5 minutes. Garnish roast with apricots and parsley; serve with apricot sauce. Yield: 10 to 12 servings.

Biscayne Bights and Breezes
The Villagers, Inc.
Coral Gables, Florida

Loin of Pork with Lemon and Herbs

½ cup chopped fresh parsley
¼ cup minced onion
¼ cup grated lemon rind
1 tablespoon chopped fresh
   basil
3 medium cloves garlic,
   crushed

½ cup plus 3 tablespoons
   olive oil, divided
1 (5- to 6-pound) rolled
   boneless pork loin roast
¾ cup dry sherry
Lemon slices
Fresh parsley sprigs

Combine first 5 ingredients; stir well. Add ½ cup oil; stir well. Score roast, and place in a baking dish; rub with herb mixture. Wrap in aluminum foil; chill 8 hours. Remove roast from foil. Place roast, fat side up, on a rack in a roasting pan. Brush with remaining 3 tablespoons oil. Insert meat thermometer into thickest part of roast, making sure it does not touch fat. Bake at 350° for 2½ hours or until thermometer registers 160°. Remove roast to a platter; keep warm.

Skim fat from drippings in pan; discard fat. Add sherry to pan drippings; cook over low heat 2 minutes or until thoroughly heated. Garnish roast with lemon slices and fresh parsley sprigs; serve sauce with roast. Yield: 10 to 12 servings.   Eloise Meigs

An Apple a Day
The Auxiliary to the Boyd County Medical Society
Ashland, Kentucky

Pork Roast with Mushroom Sauce

1 (2-pound) rolled boneless
  pork loin roast
¼ teaspoon salt
⅛ teaspoon pepper
½ pound fresh mushrooms,
  sliced
2 tablespoons lemon juice
¼ cup butter, melted

¼ cup butter
¼ cup all-purpose flour
1¾ cups milk
¼ pound ground cooked ham
1 cup (4 ounces) shredded
  Swiss cheese
Hot cooked rice

Sprinkle roast with salt and pepper; place roast on a rack in a roasting pan. Insert meat thermometer into thickest part of roast, making sure is does not touch fat. Bake at 350° for 1½ to 2 hours or until thermometer registers 160°. Remove roast from pan, reserving pan drippings. Slice roast; transfer slices to an 11- x 7- x 2-inch baking dish. Cover; keep warm.

Combine mushrooms and lemon juice; toss gently. Sauté mushroom mixture in ¼ cup melted butter in a skillet until tender; set aside. Melt ¼ cup butter in a saucepan over low heat; add flour, stirring until smooth. Cook 1 minute, stirring constantly. Gradually add milk; cook over medium heat, stirring constantly, until mixture is thickened and bubbly. Add pan drippings, mushroom mixture, ham, and cheese; stir well. Pour sauce over roast. Bake at 350° for 30 minutes. Serve with rice. Yield: 6 to 8 servings.

Sooner Sampler
The Junior League of Norman, Oklahoma

Pork Tenderloin

1 (12-ounce) jar apricot
  preserves
2 tablespoons dry sherry or
  Madeira
1 tablespoon dry mustard
2 tablespoons honey

½ teaspoon garlic powder
2 (1-pound) pork tenderloins
¼ cup butter, softened
2 teaspoons dried whole
  thyme
Salt and pepper to taste

Combine first 5 ingredients; stir well, and set aside. Place tenderloins on a rack in a roasting pan; spread with butter, and sprinkle with thyme, salt, and pepper. Insert meat thermometer into thickest part of tenderloin. Bake at 350° for 30 to 40 minutes. Remove tenderloins from oven; baste with apricot sauce. Bake an additional 15 minutes or until thermometer registers 160°, basting tenderloins every 5 minutes. Yield: 6 to 8 servings.   Pamela Croy Newton

Georgia on My Menu
The Junior League of Cobb-Marietta, Georgia

Pork, Corn, and Tomato en Brochette with Hot Red Pepper Marinade

⅓ cup olive oil
2 tablespoons red wine
  vinegar
2 green onions, chopped
1 shallot, minced
4 cloves garlic, minced
½ teaspoon salt
2 teaspoons dried whole
  oregano, crushed

1½ tablespoons crushed red
  pepper
Freshly ground pepper to
  taste
1½ pounds pork tenderloin,
  cut into 1-inch cubes
6 ears fresh corn
16 cherry tomatoes

Combine first 9 ingredients; stir well. Add pork; stir well. Cover and marinate in refrigerator 4 hours. Slice each ear of corn into 4 pieces. Remove meat from marinade, reserving marinade. Alternate meat, corn, and tomatoes on eight 12-inch metal skewers. Grill kabobs 6 inches from medium coals 30 minutes or until done, turning and basting frequently with marinade. Yield: 6 servings.

Gourmet LA
The Junior League of Los Angeles, California

Szechwan Pork Chops

2 green onions, minced
2 tablespoons soy sauce
2 large cloves garlic, minced
1 tablespoon sesame oil
2½ teaspoons lemon juice
2 teaspoons chili paste

1 teaspoon sugar
1 teaspoon minced fresh
   ginger
½ teaspoon chili oil
4 (1-inch-thick) pork chops

Combine green onions, soy sauce, garlic, sesame oil, lemon juice, chili paste, sugar, ginger, and chili oil in a small bowl, stirring well. Place pork chops in a large shallow dish. Pour marinade mixture over pork chops; cover and marinate in refrigerator 8 hours, turning occasionally.

Grill chops over medium coals 15 minutes on each side or to desired degree of doneness. Yield: 4 servings.

Rave Revues
Lakewood Center Associates, Lakewood Center for the Arts
Lake Oswego, Oregon

Broiled Mustard-Coated Pork Chops

½ cup Dijon mustard
2 to 3 tablespoons vegetable
   oil
2 to 3 tablespoons soy sauce
2 teaspoons dried whole
   rosemary, crushed

2 cloves garlic, crushed
1½ teaspoons minced fresh
   ginger
4 (1¼-inch-thick) pork chops

Combine Dijon mustard, vegetable oil, soy sauce, rosemary, garlic, and ginger in a small bowl; stir well.

Brush pork chops with mustard mixture, and place on a rack of a broiler pan. Broil 4 to 5 inches from heat 15 minutes on each side or to desired degree of doneness, basting often with remaining mustard mixture. Yield: 4 servings.   Seth Rice

Hemi-demi-semi Flavors
The Chamber Music Society of the North Shore
Glencoe, Illinois

Hazelnut-Coated Pork Cutlets with Port Wine Sauce

1¼ cups hazelnuts, toasted
1 cup fine, dry breadcrumbs
½ teaspoon salt
¼ teaspoon freshly ground pepper
1 (1-pound) pork tenderloin
1 egg, beaten
1 tablespoon water
3 tablespoons vegetable oil
1 tablespoon all-purpose flour

½ cup canned diluted chicken broth
½ cup water
⅓ cup port or other sweet red wine
1 tablespoon coarse-grained mustard
Additional toasted hazelnuts
Watercress or fresh parsley sprigs

Position knife blade in food processor bowl; add 1¼ cups hazelnuts; process until ground. Combine ground hazelnuts, breadcrumbs, salt, and pepper; stir well. Set aside. Slice pork diagonally across grain into ¼-inch slices. Place pork between 2 sheets of wax paper; flatten to ⅛-inch thickness, using a meat mallet.

Combine egg and 1 tablespoon water. Dip pork in egg mixture; dredge in hazelnut mixture. Brown pork in hot oil in a skillet over medium heat. Remove to a platter; keep warm. Add flour to pan drippings, stirring until smooth. Add broth and next 3 ingredients; stir well. Cook over medium heat, stirring occasionally, until sauce is slightly thickened. Spoon sauce around pork slices. Garnish with hazelnuts and watercress. Yield: 4 servings.

One Magnificent Cookbook
The Junior League of Chicago, Illinois

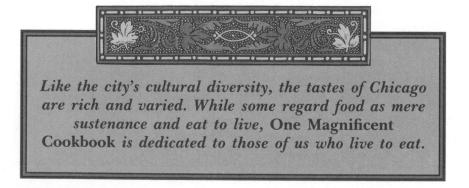

Like the city's cultural diversity, the tastes of Chicago are rich and varied. While some regard food as mere sustenance and eat to live, One Magnificent Cookbook *is dedicated to those of us who live to eat.*

Stir-Fried Pork with Asparagus

1½ pounds fresh asparagus spears
1½ pounds lean boneless pork, cut into strips
1 teaspoon cornstarch
2 teaspoons oyster sauce or low-sodium soy sauce
1 teaspoon dry sherry or rice wine
1 teaspoon minced fresh ginger (optional)
1 clove garlic, minced (optional)
3 tablespoons peanut oil, divided
¼ cup water
½ teaspoon sugar
1 tablespoon water
1 teaspoon cornstarch
½ teaspoon salt
½ teaspoon sesame oil

Snap off tough ends of asparagus. Remove scales from stalks with a knife or vegetable peeler, if desired. Cut asparagus diagonally into 1-inch pieces. Set aside.

Combine pork, 1 teaspoon cornstarch, oyster sauce, sherry, and, if desired, minced ginger and minced garlic in a large bowl. Toss pork mixture gently to coat.

Pour 2 tablespoons peanut oil around top of preheated wok, coating sides; heat at medium high (325°) for 2 minutes. Add pork mixture, and stir-fry 3 minutes. Remove pork mixture from wok, and set aside.

Pour remaining tablespoon peanut oil around top of wok, coating sides. Add reserved asparagus, and stir-fry 10 seconds. Add ¼ cup water and sugar; stir well. Cover and cook 2 minutes or until asparagus is tender.

Combine 1 tablespoon water and 1 teaspoon cornstarch in a small bowl, stirring with a wire whisk until cornstarch mixture is smooth. Add cornstarch mixture to asparagus mixture in wok, stirring well. Add salt, sesame oil, and pork mixture to asparagus mixture in wok, and stir-fry 1 minute or until thoroughly heated. Yield: 6 to 8 servings.   Julaine Chiricosta

Always in Good Taste
St. Anthony of Padua Church
Cincinnati, Ohio

Spareribs Delicious

3 to 4 pounds spareribs
1 medium onion, quartered
1 stalk celery, quartered
4 or 5 black peppercorns
Salt to taste
½ cup chili sauce
¼ cup firmly packed brown
  sugar

¼ cup vinegar
2 cloves garlic, crushed
1½ teaspoons prepared
  horseradish
1 teaspoon chili powder

Cut ribs into serving-size pieces; place in a large Dutch oven. Add water to cover, onion, celery, peppercorns, and salt. Bring water to a boil; cover, reduce heat, and simmer 40 minutes. Drain well. Place ribs, meaty side down, on a rack in a roasting pan. Combine chili sauce and remaining ingredients; stir well. Brush half of sauce on ribs. Bake, uncovered, at 375° for 25 minutes. Turn ribs; baste with remaining sauce. Bake an additional 50 minutes or until ribs are tender. Yield: 4 servings.   Bernadette Dieng

The True Essentials of a Feast
The Library of Congress/LC Cooking Club
Washington, DC

Country Ham Balls

2 pounds ground cooked
  country ham
1 pound pork sausage
2 cups fine, dry breadcrumbs
2 eggs
1½ cups milk

2 cups firmly packed brown
  sugar
1 cup water
1 cup white vinegar
1 tablespoon prepared
  mustard

Combine ham, sausage, breadcrumbs, eggs, and milk; stir well. Shape into 1½-inch balls. Place ham balls in two 13- x 9- x 2-inch baking dishes. Combine brown sugar and remaining ingredients in a saucepan; stir well. Bring to a boil over medium heat; boil 1 minute. Pour over ham balls. Bake at 350° for 45 minutes, basting and turning ham balls after 25 minutes. Yield: 10 to 12 servings.

CordonBluegrass
The Junior League of Louisville, Kentucky

Pasta, Rice & Grains

The prairie dog, named for its barklike call, is a gregarious, grass-eating creature. Once abundant throughout the plains of the western United States and northern Mexico, the prairie dog has been greatly reduced in number. Protected colonies are now located in Wyoming, Texas, Oklahoma, and South Dakota.

Vegetable Fettuccine

3 small zucchini, peeled and cut into julienne strips
2 carrots, scraped and thinly sliced
1 cup sliced fresh mushrooms
4 green onions, chopped
1 clove garlic, minced
¼ cup butter, melted
1 (15-ounce) can garbanzo beans, drained
½ teaspoon salt
½ teaspoon pepper
½ teaspoon dried whole basil, crushed
1 (8-ounce) package fettuccine
1 (8-ounce) package spinach fettuccine
1 cup grated Parmesan cheese, divided
½ cup whipping cream
2 egg yolks, lightly beaten
½ (8-ounce) package cream cheese, softened

Sauté zucchini strips, sliced carrot, sliced mushrooms, chopped green onions, and minced garlic in melted butter in a large skillet 5 minutes. Add garbanzo beans, salt, pepper, and basil; stir well. Remove from heat, and set aside.

Cook fettuccine according to package directions; drain well.

Combine cooked fettuccine and sautéed vegetable mixture in a large Dutch oven. Cook over medium-low heat 5 minutes. Add ¾ cup Parmesan cheese; toss gently to coat fettuccine and vegetables. Remove from heat, and set aside.

Combine whipping cream and egg yolks in a small mixing bowl; beat at medium speed of an electric mixer until foamy. Add whipping cream mixture and cream cheese to fettuccine mixture in Dutch oven. Cook over medium heat until mixture is thickened, stirring occasionally.

Transfer fettuccine mixture to a large serving platter, and sprinkle evenly with remaining ¼ cup Parmesan cheese. Serve immediately. Yield: 8 servings.   Charlotte Plemmons Warren

Cook 'em Horns: The Quickbook
The Ex-Students Association of the University of Texas
Austin, Texas

Hay and Straw Fettuccine with Red Pepper and Mushroom Sauce

3 cloves garlic, minced
½ cup butter, melted
2 sweet red peppers, cut into julienne strips
1 pound fresh mushrooms, sliced
½ cup canned diluted beef broth
¾ cup whipping cream
½ teaspoon salt
3 quarts water
8 ounces uncooked fresh fettuccine
8 ounces uncooked fresh spinach fettuccine
Freshly grated Parmesan cheese

Sauté garlic in melted butter in a large skillet until tender. Add pepper strips and sliced mushrooms, and sauté until tender. Stir in beef broth; reduce heat, and simmer, uncovered, 20 minutes. Stir in whipping cream; simmer 10 minutes or until mixture is slightly thickened, stirring occasionally. Stir in salt. Remove from heat, and set sauce aside.

Bring water to a boil in a large Dutch oven. Add fettuccine, and return water to a boil. Boil 3 to 4 minutes or until fettuccine is tender; drain well.

Place fettuccine on a large serving platter. Pour sauce over fettuccine, tossing gently to combine. Sprinkle with freshly grated Parmesan cheese. Yield: 6 to 8 servings.

South of the Fork
The Junior League of Dallas, Texas

Fettuccine Alfredo

1 (16-ounce) package fettuccine
¾ cup butter
¼ teaspoon garlic powder
2 cups whipping cream
¾ cup grated Parmesan cheese, divided
¼ cup sour cream

Cook fettuccine in a large Dutch oven according to package directions, omitting salt. Drain well, and return cooked fettuccine to Dutch oven.

Melt butter in a small saucepan; stir in garlic powder. Add to fettuccine in Dutch oven. Gradually add whipping cream, ½ cup

Parmesan cheese, and sour cream; cook over low heat, stirring constantly, until thoroughly heated. Remove from heat. Transfer to a serving dish, and sprinkle with remaining ¼ cup Parmesan cheese. Serve immediately. Yield: 6 to 8 servings.   Susan Kosoris

Gingerbread. . . and all the trimmings
The Junior Service League of Waxahachie, Texas

Fettuccine with Mushrooms and Proscuitto

1 pound fresh mushrooms, thinly sliced
3 tablespoons butter, melted
3 tablespoons olive oil
¼ pound proscuitto, chopped
1 cup whipping cream
¼ teaspoon ground nutmeg
3 quarts water
16 ounces uncooked fresh spinach fettuccine

Freshly ground pepper to taste
1 cup freshly grated Parmesan cheese, divided
½ cup chopped fresh Italian parsley

Sauté mushrooms in butter and oil in a large skillet until tender. Add proscuitto, whipping cream, and nutmeg; cook over medium heat 4 to 5 minutes or until mixture is slightly thickened. Set aside, and keep warm.

Bring water to a boil in a large Dutch oven. Add fettuccine, and return water to a boil. Boil 3 to 4 minutes or until fettuccine is tender. Drain well, and return fettuccine to Dutch oven. Add mushroom mixture, pepper, and ½ cup Parmesan cheese; toss gently to combine.

Transfer fettuccine mixture to a large serving platter. Sprinkle with remaining ½ cup Parmesan cheese and chopped fresh parsley. Yield: 4 to 6 servings.   Margaret A. Stack

Movers & Shakers Cookbook
Lake County Public Library
Merrillville, Indiana

Seafood Pasta del Mar

½ pound unpeeled large
  fresh shrimp
3 cloves garlic, minced
3 tablespoons olive oil,
  divided
3 tablespoons butter, melted
  and divided
½ pound fresh sea scallops
½ pound fresh lump
  crabmeat, drained and
  flaked
2 tablespoons Chablis or
  other dry white wine
1 to 2 tablespoons lemon
  juice
2 tablespoons chopped fresh
  parsley

Salt and pepper to taste
2 carrots, scraped and
  diagonally sliced
1 cup broccoli flowerets
1 zucchini, sliced
2 tablespoons chopped fresh
  basil
1 teaspoon dried whole
  oregano
1 (12-ounce) package
  fettuccine
½ cup whipping cream
¼ cup butter
½ cup grated Parmesan
  cheese

Peel and devein shrimp; set shrimp aside. Sauté minced garlic in 2 tablespoons olive oil and 2 tablespoons melted butter in a large skillet. Add shrimp, scallops, and crabmeat to skillet; sauté 5 minutes. Add wine, lemon juice, chopped fresh parsley, and salt and pepper to taste; sauté 2 minutes. Remove skillet from heat; set aside, and keep seafood mixture warm.

Sauté carrot in remaining 1 tablespoon oil and remaining 1 tablespoon melted butter in a skillet for 5 minutes. Add broccoli; sauté 5 minutes. Add sliced zucchini, and sauté 2 minutes. Stir in basil and oregano. Remove from heat; set aside, and keep warm.

Cook fettuccine in a large Dutch oven according to package directions; drain well. Return fettuccine to Dutch oven.

Combine whipping cream, ¼ cup butter, and Parmesan cheese in a medium saucepan; stir well. Cook over medium heat, stirring until butter melts.

Add seafood mixture, vegetable mixture, and sauce to fettuccine; toss gently to combine. Yield: 4 to 6 servings.

Only in California
The Children's Home Society of California
Los Angeles, California

Spaghetti alla Carbonara

¼ pound bacon, cut into
  1½-inch pieces
½ cup chopped onion
2 tablespoons butter, melted
¼ cup Chablis or other dry
  white wine
3 eggs, beaten
½ cup freshly grated
  Parmesan cheese

2 tablespoons minced fresh
  parsley
½ teaspoon freshly ground
  pepper
1 (16-ounce) package
  spaghetti

Sauté bacon and chopped onion in melted butter in a small skillet until bacon is crisp and onion is tender. Stir in wine, and simmer, uncovered, 10 minutes. Remove skillet from heat; set aside, and keep warm.

Combine eggs, Parmesan cheese, parsley, and pepper in a large bowl; stir well. Set aside.

Cook spaghetti according to package directions; drain well. Immediately add hot spaghetti to egg mixture, and toss gently to coat. Add bacon mixture; toss gently, and serve spaghetti immediately. Yield: 8 servings.

Wilma Zoldoske

The Scott & White Collection
The Scott and White Memorial Hospital Auxiliary
Temple, Texas

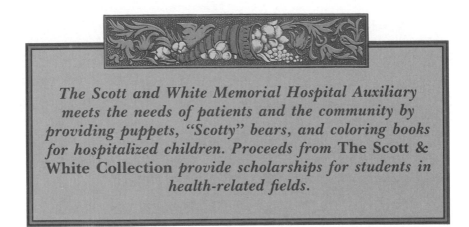

The Scott and White Memorial Hospital Auxiliary meets the needs of patients and the community by providing puppets, "Scotty" bears, and coloring books for hospitalized children. Proceeds from **The Scott & White Collection** *provide scholarships for students in health-related fields.*

Tomato and Mozzarella Sauce with Pasta

6 to 8 ripe tomatoes, peeled, seeded, and coarsely chopped
2 cups (8 ounces) shredded mozzarella cheese
¼ cup minced fresh basil
¼ cup plus 1 tablespoon olive oil
2 cloves garlic, minced
1 tablespoon minced fresh parsley
Salt and pepper to taste
1 (16-ounce) package spaghetti

Combine first 7 ingredients; stir well. Cover and let stand at room temperature 1 hour. Cook spaghetti according to package directions; drain well. Immediately transfer hot spaghetti to a large serving bowl. Pour sauce over hot cooked spaghetti, tossing gently to combine. Yield: 6 to 8 servings.   Cindy Looney

Sampler
The Women's Art Guild, Laguna Gloria Art Museum
Austin, Texas

Spaghetti Pie

6 ounces uncooked spaghetti
⅓ cup grated Parmesan cheese
2 eggs, beaten
2 tablespoons butter or margarine
1 pound ground beef
½ cup chopped onion
¼ cup chopped green pepper
1 (7½-ounce) can whole tomatoes, undrained and chopped
1 (6-ounce) can tomato paste
1 teaspoon sugar
1 teaspoon dried whole oregano
½ teaspoon garlic salt
1 cup cottage cheese
½ cup (2 ounces) shredded mozzarella cheese

Cook spaghetti according to package directions; drain well. Combine spaghetti, Parmesan cheese, eggs, and butter, tossing gently to combine. Pour into a greased 10-inch pieplate. Set aside.
Combine ground beef, onion, and green pepper in a large skillet. Cook over medium heat until meat is browned and vegetables are

tender, stirring to crumble meat. Drain. Add tomatoes and next 4 ingredients; cook 5 minutes, stirring occasionally. Set aside.

Spread cottage cheese over spaghetti mixture in pieplate. Top with beef mixture, and bake at 350° for 20 minutes. Sprinkle with mozzarella cheese, and bake an additional 5 minutes or until cheese melts. Yield: 6 servings.   Mrs. Richard Gelb

As You Like It
St. Bernard's School
New York, New York

Opening Night "Show-Off"

9 cups water
3 pounds unpeeled
  medium-size fresh shrimp
1 (7-ounce) package
  vermicelli or thin spaghetti
½ cup butter or margarine
½ cup all-purpose flour
1 cup canned diluted chicken
  broth
1 cup whipping cream

1 cup (4 ounces) shredded
  Swiss cheese
¼ cup dry sherry
¼ teaspoon ground white
  pepper
1 (6-ounce) can sliced
  mushrooms, drained
¼ cup grated Parmesan cheese
1 (2-ounce) package slivered
  almonds

Bring water to a boil; add shrimp, and cook 3 to 5 minutes. Drain; rinse with cold water. Chill. Peel and devein shrimp. Set aside.

Cook vermicelli according to package directions. Drain well.

Melt butter in a heavy saucepan over low heat; add flour, stirring until smooth. Cook 1 minute, stirring constantly. Gradually add broth and cream; cook over medium heat, stirring constantly, until mixture is thickened and bubbly. Add Swiss cheese, sherry, and white pepper, stirring until cheese melts. Remove from heat; add shrimp, vermicelli, and mushrooms, stirring gently to combine.

Spoon mixture into a 13- x 9- x 2-inch baking dish. Sprinkle with Parmesan cheese and slivered almonds. Broil 6 inches from heat 2 to 3 minutes or until lightly browned. Serve immediately. Yield: 10 to 12 servings.   Mickey Hale

Critics' Choice
The Corinth Theatre Arts Guild
Corinth, Mississippi

Vermicelli with Broccoli Pesto Sauce

4 cups broccoli flowerets
3 tablespoons pine nuts,
   toasted and divided
1 clove garlic, quartered
¼ cup freshly grated
   Parmesan cheese
¼ cup coarsely chopped
   fresh parsley

1 teaspoon dried whole basil
⅓ cup olive oil
Salt and pepper to taste
1 (12-ounce) package
   vermicelli

Cook broccoli in a small amount of boiling water 5 minutes or until tender. Drain; rinse with cold water, and drain well. Reserve ½ cup flowerets for garnish; set broccoli aside.

Place 2 tablespoons pine nuts and garlic in container of an electric blender or food processor; process until minced. Add 3½ cups broccoli flowerets, Parmesan cheese, parsley, and basil; process until broccoli is minced, scraping sides of container, if necessary. With blender running, add oil in a slow, steady stream until mixture is combined. Add salt and pepper to taste. Set aside.

Cook vermicelli according to package directions; drain well. Transfer vermicelli to a large serving platter. Pour sauce over hot cooked vermicelli, tossing gently to combine. Top with reserved ½ cup broccoli flowerets. Sprinkle with remaining 1 tablespoon pine nuts. Yield: 4 to 6 servings.   Lorraine Kilby

A Cook's Book of Recipes from the Pacific Northwest
The Rosehill Community Center
Mukilteo, Washington

Proceeds from the sale of A Cook's Book of Recipes from the Pacific Northwest *will help fund restoration of the old Rosehill elementary school which today houses the Rosehill Community Center.*

Chicken and Goat Cheese Wonton Ravioli

¼ cup dry vermouth
2 tablespoons minced shallots
2 tablespoons tamari
¼ cup whipping cream
¾ cup unsalted butter
½ cup ground cooked chicken
3 ounces goat cheese, crumbled
2 tablespoons minced green onions
1 teaspoon minced fresh ginger
¼ teaspoon ground white pepper
1 egg, lightly beaten
1 teaspoon water
⅛ teaspoon salt
36 wonton wrappers
2½ cups canned diluted chicken broth
Fresh chervil or parsley sprigs

Combine vermouth, shallots, and tamari in a saucepan; cook over medium heat until liquid is reduced to 2 tablespoons. Add whipping cream, and cook until reduced to 2 tablespoons. Reduce heat to low; add butter, 1 tablespoon at a time, stirring constantly with a wire whisk until butter melts. Set aside, and keep warm.

Combine chicken, cheese, green onions, ginger, and white pepper; stir well, and set aside.

Combine beaten egg, water, and salt in a small bowl; stir well, and set aside.

Place 1 wonton wrapper on work surface. Spoon 1 rounded teaspoon chicken mixture in center of wrapper. Brush ¾ inch around edges of wrapper with egg mixture. Carefully place another wrapper over chicken mixture; press edges together to seal. Using a fluted pastry wheel, cut through both wonton wrappers to remove excess dough. Repeat procedure with remaining wrappers and chicken mixture.

Bring chicken broth to a boil in a large skillet over medium heat. Add about one-third of the ravioli; reduce heat, and simmer 4 to 6 minutes. Remove ravioli carefully from broth, using a slotted spoon; drain ravioli in a colander. Repeat procedure with remaining ravioli.

Spoon reserved sauce onto a large serving platter; top with ravioli. Garnish with fresh chervil sprigs. Yield: 4 servings.

One Magnificent Cookbook
The Junior League of Chicago, Illinois

Cold Shrimp with Pasta

1½ quarts water
2 pounds unpeeled small
   fresh shrimp
2 (8-ounce) packages small
   seashell macaroni
1 cup finely chopped celery
6 green onions, minced
1½ cups mayonnaise

¼ cup chili sauce
2 tablespoons capers
1 tablespoon fresh lemon
   juice
1 teaspoon celery seeds
¼ teaspoon salt
¼ teaspoon freshly ground
   white pepper

Bring water to a boil; add shrimp, and cook 3 to 5 minutes. Drain well; rinse with cold water. Chill. Peel and devein shrimp.

Cook macaroni according to package directions; drain well. Combine macaroni, shrimp, chopped celery, and green onions in a large bowl; toss gently.

Combine mayonnaise and remaining ingredients; stir well. Pour over shrimp mixture; toss gently to combine. Cover and chill at least 2 hours. Yield: 8 to 10 servings.

Treasured Recipes from Camargo to Indian Hill
The Indian Hill Historical Society
Cincinnati, Ohio

Sour Cream Noodle Bake

1 (8-ounce) package medium
   egg noodles
1 cup cottage cheese
1 (8-ounce) carton sour cream
½ cup chopped onion
¼ cup chopped green pepper
1½ pounds ground beef
2 (6-ounce) cans tomato paste

1 (4-ounce) can sliced
   mushrooms, undrained
1 teaspoon salt
½ teaspoon garlic salt
⅛ teaspoon pepper
¾ cup (3 ounces) shredded
   Cheddar cheese

Cook noodles according to package directions; drain well. Combine noodles, cottage cheese, sour cream, chopped onion, and chopped green pepper, tossing gently; set aside.

Cook beef in a large skillet until browned, stirring to crumble; drain. Add tomato paste, mushrooms, salt, garlic salt, and pepper, stirring well; simmer 5 minutes.

Spoon half of the noodle mixture in the bottom of a 3-quart baking dish; top with half of the meat mixture. Repeat layers; sprinkle evenly with shredded Cheddar cheese. Bake at 350° for 30 minutes or until cheese melts and mixture is thoroughly heated. Yield: 6 to 8 servings.   Eileen Anderson Nelson

One Hundred Years of Sharing
Calvary Covenant Church Women
Evansville, Minnesota

Noodles with Spinach and Ham

1 (16-ounce) package medium egg noodles
1½ pounds fresh spinach
1 tablespoon lemon juice
1 tablespoon finely chopped onion
1 clove garlic, minced
3 tablespoons butter, melted
3 tablespoons all-purpose flour
1 cup half-and-half
Salt and freshly ground pepper to taste
⅛ teaspoon ground nutmeg
½ cup finely chopped proscuitto or cooked ham
½ cup soft breadcrumbs
2 tablespoons butter, melted

Cook noodles according to package directions; drain. Set aside.
Remove stems from spinach; wash leaves thoroughly, and tear into small pieces. Cook spinach in a small amount of boiling water 3 to 4 minutes. Drain; place on paper towels, and squeeze until barely moist. Place spinach in a medium bowl; add lemon juice, stirring well. Set aside.
Sauté onion and garlic in 3 tablespoons butter in a large skillet until tender. Add flour, stirring until smooth. Gradually add half-and-half; cook over medium heat, stirring constantly, until mixture is thickened and bubbly. Stir in salt, pepper, and nutmeg. Add spinach, stirring well.
Pour spinach mixture over noodles; add proscuitto, and toss well. Place in a buttered 13- x 9- x 2-inch baking dish. Combine breadcrumbs and 2 tablespoons butter; sprinkle over casserole. Cover and bake at 350° for 20 minutes. Yield: 6 to 8 servings.   Faye Reid

Calling All Cooks Two
The Telephone Pioneers of America
Birmingham, Alabama

Lemon Rice

1 cup sliced celery
1 small onion, chopped
¼ cup plus 2 tablespoons
  butter or margarine, melted
  and divided
2½ cups water
2 teaspoons grated lemon
  rind
¼ cup lemon juice

¼ teaspoon dried whole
  thyme
1 teaspoon salt
⅛ teaspoon pepper
1¼ cups uncooked long-grain
  rice
¾ pound fresh mushrooms,
  thinly sliced

Sauté sliced celery and chopped onion in 3 tablespoons melted butter in a large skillet. Stir in water, lemon rind, lemon juice, thyme, salt, and pepper; bring mixture to a boil. Add rice; cover, reduce heat, and simmer 20 minutes or until rice is tender and liquid is absorbed.

Sauté mushrooms in remaining 3 tablespoons butter in a small skillet until tender; drain. Add mushrooms to rice mixture; stir well. Yield: 10 servings.

Con Mucho Gusto
The Desert Club of Mesa, Arizona

Risotto with Asparagus and Pine Nuts

1 pound fresh asparagus
  spears
1 shallot, minced
2 tablespoons butter, melted
1 cup plus 2 tablespoons
  uncooked long-grain rice
½ cup Chablis or other dry
  white wine
3 to 3½ cups canned diluted
  chicken broth

¾ cup whipping cream
¼ cup plus 2 tablespoons
  freshly grated Parmesan
  cheese
2 cloves garlic, minced
½ teaspoon salt
½ teaspoon pepper
½ cup pine nuts, toasted

Snap off tough ends of asparagus. Remove scales from stalks with a knife or vegetable peeler, if desired. Cut off asparagus tips; set aside. Thinly slice stems; set aside.

Sauté shallot in butter in a large skillet over medium heat until tender; add rice. Stir in wine; cook, stirring constantly, until liquid evaporates. Add asparagus stems and ½ cup chicken broth; cook, stirring constantly, until liquid is absorbed. Continue adding broth, ½ cup at a time, stirring constantly until rice is tender and liquid is absorbed (about 30 minutes). Stir in whipping cream, Parmesan cheese, minced garlic, salt, and pepper; cook 3 minutes or until mixture is thickened. Add asparagus tips and pine nuts; stir well. Remove from heat, and let stand 5 minutes before serving. Yield: 8 to 10 servings.

Gourmet LA
The Junior League of Los Angeles, California

Baked Herb Rice with Pecans

1 cup sliced fresh
  mushrooms
½ cup chopped shallots
¼ cup plus 2 tablespoons
  butter, melted
1 cup uncooked long-grain
  rice
½ cup chopped pecans,
  toasted
1¼ cups canned undiluted
  chicken broth
1¼ cups water
1 (2-ounce) jar diced
  pimiento, drained

2 tablespoons chopped fresh
  parsley
1 tablespoon Worcestershire
  sauce
1 teaspoon dried whole
  thyme
1 teaspoon dried whole
  rosemary
2 bay leaves
Hot sauce to taste
Salt and freshly ground
  pepper to taste
Additional chopped toasted
  pecans

Sauté mushrooms and shallots in butter in a large Dutch oven until tender. Add rice and ½ cup pecans; stir well. Add chicken broth and remaining ingredients except additional pecans; bring to a boil. Remove from heat; cover and bake at 350° for 45 minutes to 1 hour or until rice is tender and liquid is absorbed. Remove and discard bay leaves before serving. Garnish with additional toasted pecans. Yield: 6 to 8 servings.

Delicious Decisions
The Junior League of San Diego, California

Pecan Pilaf

1 cup chopped pecans
½ cup butter or margarine,
   melted and divided
½ cup chopped onion
2 cups uncooked long-grain
   rice
4 cups canned diluted
   chicken broth
2 tablespoons chopped fresh
   parsley

½ teaspoon salt
¼ teaspoon dried whole
   thyme, crushed
⅛ teaspoon dried whole
   rosemary
⅛ teaspoon freshly ground
   pepper
1 cup grated carrot
1 tablespoon chopped fresh
   parsley

Sauté pecans in 3 tablespoons butter in a skillet until lightly browned. Remove pecans; set aside. Add remaining 5 tablespoons butter to skillet. Add onion, and sauté until tender. Add rice; stir well. Add broth and next 5 ingredients. Bring to a boil; cover, reduce heat, and simmer 20 minutes or until rice is tender and liquid is absorbed. Stir in pecans, carrot, and 1 tablespoon parsley. Fluff with a fork before serving. Yield: 12 to 14 servings.

Stir Crazy!
The Junior Welfare League of Florence, South Carolina

Two-Tone Greek Pilaf

6 green onions, finely
   chopped
½ cup butter, melted
¾ cup uncooked orzo
¾ cup uncooked long-grain
   rice

3 cups canned diluted
   chicken or beef broth
Salt and pepper to taste

Sauté onions in butter in a heavy saucepan until tender. Add orzo; sauté 2 minutes, stirring constantly. Add rice; sauté 2 minutes. Stir in broth, salt, and pepper. Bring to a boil; cover, reduce heat to low, and cook 30 to 35 minutes or until rice is tender and liquid is absorbed. Yield: 8 to 10 servings.

Burnt Offerings
Women's Auxiliary, Gales Ferry Volunteer Fire Company
Gales Ferry, Connecticut

Dirty Rice

2 cups uncooked long-grain
  rice
1 pound ground beef
½ pound ground pork
Salt and pepper to taste
¼ teaspoon hot sauce
½ pound chicken livers,
  chopped
½ pound chicken gizzards,
  chopped

2 medium onions, chopped
1 medium-size green pepper,
  chopped
¾ cup chopped green onions
¼ cup chopped fresh parsley
3 cloves garlic, minced
¾ cup Burgundy or other dry
  red wine
1 bay leaf
¼ teaspoon ground thyme

Cook rice according to package directions. Cook meat in a skillet until browned; stir to crumble. Drain. Stir in salt, pepper, and hot sauce. Add chopped liver and next 6 ingredients; stir well. Cook over medium-high heat 10 to 15 minutes. Add rice, wine, bay leaf, and thyme; stir well. Cover and simmer 30 minutes. Remove bay leaf before serving. Yield: 8 to 10 servings.   Mary G. Baham

The Bishop's Bounty
St. Mary's Training School for Retarded Children
Alexandria, Louisiana

Red Beans and Rice

1 to 1½ pounds hot smoked
  sausage, cut into ½-inch
  pieces
1 large onion, chopped
1 small green pepper,
  chopped (optional)

3 (16-ounce) cans red kidney
  beans, undrained
1½ cups catsup
1 clove garlic, crushed
Hot cooked rice

Cook sausage and onion in a large Dutch oven over medium-high heat until sausage is browned and onion is tender. Add green pepper, if desired. Add kidney beans, catsup, and garlic, stirring well. Bring to a boil; cover, reduce heat, and simmer 2 hours. Serve over rice. Yield: 8 servings.   Diane Rooker

The Share-Cropper
The Central Delta Academy Parent-Teacher Organization
Inverness, Mississippi

Wild Rice with Mushrooms and Almonds

1 cup uncooked wild rice
1 (8-ounce) can mushroom
   stems and pieces, drained
½ cup slivered blanched
   almonds
2 tablespoons chopped fresh
   chives or green onions

¼ cup butter or margarine,
   melted
3 cups canned diluted
   chicken broth

Wash rice in 3 changes of hot water; drain. Sauté rice, mushrooms, almonds, and chives in butter in a skillet 20 minutes or until almonds are golden. Place rice mixture in an ungreased 1½-quart casserole. Bring broth to a boil in a saucepan; stir into rice mixture. Cover and bake at 325° for 1½ hours or until rice is tender and liquid is absorbed. Yield: 4 to 6 servings.   Peggy Justice

Columbus Collection
Magnolia Homes Tour
Columbus, Texas

Brown Rice-Vegetable Casserole with Salsa

2 chicken-flavored bouillon
   cubes
2½ cups hot water
1 cup uncooked long-grain
   brown rice
¼ cup shredded carrot
¼ cup chopped green onions
½ teaspoon soy sauce
¼ cup mild green chili salsa
1 pound cauliflower, cut into
   1-inch pieces
1 pound broccoli, cut into
   1-inch pieces

2 medium-size yellow squash
   or zucchini, cut into 1-inch
   pieces
1 cup sliced fresh
   mushrooms
¼ cup chopped celery
20 cherry tomatoes, halved
¾ cup (3 ounces) shredded
   Monterey Jack cheese
¾ cup (3 ounces) shredded
   Cheddar cheese
3 tablespoons sunflower
   kernels, toasted

Dissolve bouillon cubes in hot water in a medium saucepan. Bring to a boil. Add rice; cover, reduce heat, and simmer 45 minutes or until rice is tender and liquid is absorbed. Add carrot, green onions, and soy sauce; stir well.

Spread rice mixture evenly in an ungreased 13- x 9- x 2-inch baking dish. Spoon salsa evenly over rice; set aside.

Arrange cauliflower and next 4 ingredients on a steaming rack. Place over boiling water; cover and steam 6 to 8 minutes or until crisp-tender.

Arrange steamed vegetables and tomatoes over rice. Sprinkle with cheeses. Bake, uncovered, at 350° for 15 to 20 minutes. Remove from oven; sprinkle with sunflower kernels. Yield: 8 servings.

From Scratch Cookbook
The Assistance League® of Glendale, California

Mixed Grain Pilaf

¼ cup butter or margarine
⅓ cup chopped almonds or walnuts (optional)
1 large onion, chopped
1 large carrot, scraped and shredded
⅓ cup chopped fresh parsley
1 clove garlic, minced
⅓ cup pearl barley
⅓ cup uncooked brown rice
⅓ cup uncooked bulgur wheat
2½ cups canned undiluted chicken or beef broth
¼ cup dry sherry or water
¾ teaspoon dried whole basil
¾ teaspoon dried whole oregano
Salt and pepper to taste

Melt butter in a large saucepan over medium heat. If desired, add almonds, and cook, stirring constantly, until almonds are lightly toasted. Remove almonds with a slotted spoon, and set aside.

Sauté onion, carrot, parsley, and garlic in butter in saucepan until vegetables are tender. Add barley, rice, and bulgur wheat; cook, stirring constantly, until lightly browned. Add broth and remaining ingredients; stir well. Bring to a boil; cover, reduce heat, and simmer 45 minutes or until rice is tender and liquid is absorbed. Remove from heat, and let stand, covered, 10 minutes. Garnish with almonds, if desired. Yield: 6 servings.   Barbara Hobe

A Taste of Salt Air and Island Kitchens
Ladies Auxiliary of the Block Island Volunteer Fire Department
Block Island, Rhode Island

Couscous with Pine Nuts and Currants

½ pound fresh mushrooms, sliced
¼ cup pine nuts
½ cup unsalted butter, melted and divided
1 cup chopped onion
½ cup chopped celery
½ cup chopped fresh parsley
2 cloves garlic, minced
¼ cup dried currants
½ teaspoon salt
½ teaspoon pepper
½ teaspoon herbes de Provence
3 cups canned diluted chicken broth
1 (16-ounce) package couscous

Sauté mushrooms and pine nuts in 2 tablespoons melted butter in a small skillet until mushrooms are tender. Remove from heat, and set aside.

Sauté onion, celery, parsley, and garlic in remaining ¼ cup plus 2 tablespoons butter in a large skillet until tender. Add reserved mushroom mixture, currants, and seasonings; stir well. Add chicken broth, and bring to a boil. Add couscous, stirring well. Cover, remove from heat, and let stand 10 minutes or until liquid is absorbed. Yield: 16 servings.   Iris Cosnow

Hemi-demi-semi Flavors
The Chamber Music Society of the North Shore
Glencoe, Illinois

Pies & Pastries

Courting couples once stopped under the roof of this "Kissing Bridge" in Old Sturbridge Village, Massachusetts, to make a wish. The roof and siding over the bridge protect the wooden timbers from the weather.

Meringue-Topped Apple "Cake"

1¾ cups all-purpose flour
½ cup ground blanched
  almonds
¼ cup sugar
1 teaspoon salt
¼ teaspoon ground cinnamon
½ cup butter
3 eggs, separated
½ cup firmly packed dark
  brown sugar
¼ cup plus 2 tablespoons
  apricot-flavored brandy,
  divided

1 tablespoon grated lemon
  rind
6 cups peeled, thinly sliced
  Granny Smith apples
1 cup apricot preserves
1 tablespoon lemon juice
⅛ teaspoon salt
2 tablespoons sugar
¼ cup sliced almonds

Combine flour, ground almonds, ¼ cup sugar, 1 teaspoon salt, and cinnamon in a large bowl; stir well. Cut in butter with a pastry blender until mixture resembles coarse meal. Reserve 1 cup flour mixture. Firmly press remaining flour mixture in bottom and up the sides of a 9-inch springform pan. Bake at 350° for 20 minutes or until golden brown. Set aside.

Combine egg yolks, brown sugar, 3 tablespoons brandy, and lemon rind in a large bowl, stirring until blended. Add apple slices, tossing gently. Spoon apple mixture into prepared crust; sprinkle reserved flour mixture over apples. Bake at 350° for 55 to 60 minutes or until lightly browned.

Combine remaining 3 tablespoons apricot brandy, apricot preserves, and lemon juice in a small bowl, and stir well. Pour brandy mixture over apple mixture.

Beat egg whites (at room temperature) and ⅛ teaspoon salt at high speed of an electric mixer just until foamy. Gradually add 2 tablespoons sugar, 1 tablespoon at a time, beating until stiff peaks form and sugar dissolves (2 to 4 minutes).

Spread meringue over hot filling, sealing to edge of pastry. Sprinkle sliced almonds evenly over meringue. Bake 15 minutes or until meringue is golden brown. Let cool completely. Carefully remove sides of springform pan before serving. Yield: 10 to 12 servings.
Billie Staats Heath

A Grand Heritage
The Heritage Academy
Columbus, Mississippi

Shredded Apple Pie

Pastry for double-crust 9-inch
  pie
1½ cups sugar
½ cup butter or margarine,
  melted
2 eggs, beaten
4 cups shredded, unpeeled
  cooking apples

1 tablespoon lemon juice
2 teaspoons ground cinnamon
1 teaspoon vanilla extract
¼ teaspoon salt
Whipped cream

Roll half of pastry to ⅛-inch thickness on a lightly floured surface. Place in a 9-inch pieplate; set aside.

Combine sugar, butter, and eggs in a large bowl. Beat at medium speed of an electric mixer until well blended. Add shredded apple and next 4 ingredients, stirring well. Pour apple mixture into prepared pastry shell.

Roll remaining pastry to ⅛-inch thickness; cut into ½-inch strips. Arrange strips, lattice fashion, across top of pie. Trim pastry even with edges; fold edges under and flute. Bake at 350° for 1 hour and 15 minutes. Garnish with whipped cream. Serve warm. Yield: one 9-inch pie.   Mary Grantham

Keeping the Feast
The Episcopal Church Women of St. Thomas Church
Abingdon, Virginia

Rhubarb-Raspberry Pie

Pastry for double-crust 9-inch
  pie
3 cups chopped rhubarb
1 cup frozen raspberries,
  thawed
1⅓ cups sugar

¼ cup all-purpose flour
⅛ teaspoon salt
½ teaspoon lemon juice
⅛ teaspoon almond extract
1 tablespoon butter or
  margarine

Roll half of pastry to ⅛-inch thickness on a lightly floured surface. Place in a 9-inch pieplate; set aside.

Combine chopped rhubarb, raspberries, sugar, flour, salt, lemon juice, and almond extract in a large bowl, stirring well. Cover and let stand 15 minutes. Pour rhubarb mixture into prepared pastry shell, and dot with butter.

Roll remaining pastry to ⅛-inch thickness; transfer to top of pie. Trim off excess pastry along edges. Fold edges under and flute. Cut slits in top crust for steam to escape. Bake at 400° for 40 minutes or until golden brown. Yield: one 9-inch pie.   Elmer Grindle

Bethany Christian Community, A Recipe Collection
Bethany Christian Community
Anchorage, Alaska

"Lovin' You" Butterscotch Pie

1¼ cups firmly packed brown sugar
¼ cup plus 2 tablespoons all-purpose flour
¼ teaspoon salt
2 cups milk
¼ cup plus 2 tablespoons butter or margarine

3 eggs, separated
1 teaspoon vanilla extract
1 baked 9-inch pastry shell
¼ teaspoon cream of tartar
½ cup sugar

Combine brown sugar, flour, and salt in top of a double boiler. Bring water to a boil; reduce heat to low. Gradually stir in milk; add butter. Cook until mixture thickens and comes to a boil. Boil 1 minute, stirring constantly. Remove from heat, and set aside.

Beat egg yolks at high speed of an electric mixer until thick and lemon colored. Gradually stir about one-fourth of hot mixture into yolks; add to remaining hot mixture, stirring constantly. Cook in top of double boiler over low heat, stirring constantly, 2 minutes or until mixture thickens. Remove from heat; stir in vanilla. Spoon into pastry shell.

Beat egg whites (at room temperature) and cream of tartar at high speed of electric mixer just until foamy. Gradually add ½ cup sugar, 1 tablespoon at a time, beating until stiff peaks form and sugar dissolves (2 to 4 minutes).

Spread meringue over hot filling, sealing to edge of pastry. Bake at 350° for 5 minutes or until meringue is lightly browned. Let cool completely. Yield: one 9-inch pie.

Elvis Fans Cookbook, Volume 3
The Elvis Presley Memorial Trauma Center
Memphis, Tennessee

Coconut Cream Pie

¾ cup sugar, divided
¼ cup cornstarch
½ teaspoon salt
2½ cups milk
3 eggs, separated

1 cup flaked coconut, divided
1 tablespoon butter or
  margarine, softened
1 teaspoon vanilla extract
1 baked 9-inch pastry shell

Combine ½ cup sugar, cornstarch, and salt in a medium saucepan. Stir in milk; cook over medium heat, stirring constantly, until mixture thickens slightly. Remove from heat, and set aside.

Beat egg yolks at high speed of an electric mixer until thick and lemon colored. Gradually stir about one-fourth of hot mixture into yolks; add to remaining hot mixture, stirring constantly. Cook over medium heat 2 to 3 minutes, stirring constantly . Remove from heat; add ¾ cup coconut, butter, and vanilla, stirring until butter melts. Spoon coconut mixture into pastry shell.

Beat egg whites (at room temperature) at high speed of electric mixer just until foamy. Gradually add remaining ¼ cup sugar, 1 tablespoon at a time, beating until stiff peaks form and sugar dissolves (2 to 4 minutes).

Spread meringue over filling, sealing to edge of pastry. Sprinkle with remaining ¼ cup coconut. Bake at 425° for 5 minutes or until meringue is lightly browned. Yield: one 9-inch pie.

Steeped in Tradition
The Junior Service League of DeLand, Florida

Lemon Meringue Pie

1¼ cups plus 2 tablespoons
  sugar, divided
¼ cup cornstarch
½ teaspoon salt
1 cup boiling water
2½ tablespoons grated lemon
  rind

½ cup lemon juice
4 eggs, separated
2 tablespoons butter
1 baked 9-inch pastry shell

Combine 1 cup sugar, cornstarch, salt, and water in a heavy saucepan. Cook over medium heat, stirring constantly, until mixture thickens and comes to a boil. Boil 1 minute, stirring constantly. Stir in lemon rind and juice; remove from heat.

Beat egg yolks at high speed of an electric mixer until thick and lemon colored. Gradually stir about one-fourth of hot mixture into yolks; add to remaining hot mixture, stirring constantly. Cook over medium heat, stirring constantly, 2 to 3 minutes or until thickened. Remove from heat; add butter, stirring until butter melts. Spoon into pastry shell.

Beat egg whites (at room temperature) at high speed of electric mixer just until foamy. Gradually add remaining ¼ cup plus 2 tablespoons sugar, 1 tablespoon at a time, beating until stiff peaks form and sugar dissolves (2 to 4 minutes).

Spread meringue over hot filling, sealing to edge of pastry. Bake at 325° for 15 minutes or until meringue is lightly browned. Let cool completely. Yield: one 9-inch pie.   Thelma B. Holmes

Calling All Cooks Two
The Telephone Pioneers of America
Birmingham, Alabama

Pecan-Cheese Pie

1 (8-ounce) package cream
  cheese, softened
⅓ cup sugar
1 egg
1 teaspoon vanilla extract
¼ teaspoon salt
1 unbaked 9-inch pastry
  shell

1½ cups chopped pecans
1 cup light corn syrup
¼ cup sugar
3 eggs, beaten
1 teaspoon vanilla extract

Combine cream cheese and ⅓ cup sugar in a large bowl; beat at high speed of an electric mixer until fluffy. Add 1 egg, 1 teaspoon vanilla, and salt; blend well. Pour into pastry shell; sprinkle with pecans. Set aside.

Combine corn syrup and remaining ingredients, stirring well. Pour over cream cheese mixture. Bake at 375° for 35 to 40 minutes or until set. Let cool completely. Chill until ready to serve. Yield: one 9-inch pie.

Second Round, Tea-Time at the Masters®
The Junior League of Augusta, Georgia

Shirley's Lime and Sour Cream Pie

¾ cup sugar
3 tablespoons cornstarch
2½ teaspoons grated lime
  rind
⅓ cup lime juice
1 cup half-and-half
¼ cup unsalted butter

1 (8-ounce) carton sour cream
1 (9-inch) graham cracker
  crust or baked pastry shell
1 cup whipping cream
1 to 2 tablespoons powdered
  sugar

Combine ¾ cup sugar, cornstarch, and lime rind in a medium saucepan. Add lime juice, stirring until smooth. Add half-and-half and butter; cook over medium heat, stirring constantly, until mixture thickens and comes to a boil. Remove from heat, and let cool. Add sour cream, stirring well. Pour lime mixture into crust.

Beat cream until foamy; gradually add powdered sugar, beating until soft peaks form. Spread whipped cream over pie. Let cool completely. Yield: one 9-inch pie.   Lyn Cain Zehner

VIP Cookbook, Volume VI
The American Cancer Society, Virginia Division
Vienna, Virginia

Lemon-Berry Pie

1 envelope unflavored gelatin
1 cup sugar, divided
½ teaspoon salt
4 eggs, separated
1¼ cups milk
1 (3-ounce) package cream
  cheese, softened

½ cup lemon juice, divided
1 baked 9-inch pastry shell
1 pint fresh strawberries,
  hulled

Combine gelatin, ¾ cup sugar, and salt in top of a double boiler. Lightly beat egg yolks with a wire whisk. Stir beaten egg yolks and milk into gelatin mixture; let stand one minute. Bring water to a boil; cook, stirring constantly, until gelatin mixture thickens and coats a metal spoon. Remove from heat; set aside, and let cool.

Pour about 1 cup gelatin mixture into a small bowl; add cream cheese, and beat at medium speed of an electric mixer until smooth. Stir in ¼ cup lemon juice. Cover and chill until cream cheese mixture thickens.

Pour remaining gelatin mixture into a bowl; stir in remaining ¼ cup lemon juice. Cover and chill until thickened.

Spoon cream cheese mixture into pastry shell; spread evenly. Reserve 6 to 8 whole strawberries for garnish; slice remaining strawberries, and arrange over cream cheese mixture.

Beat egg whites (at room temperature) at high speed just until foamy. Gradually add remaining ¼ cup sugar, 1 tablespoon at a time, beating until stiff peaks form and sugar dissolves (2 to 4 minutes). Gently fold beaten egg whites into chilled lemon mixture; spread evenly over strawberry slices. Chill until set. Garnish with whole strawberries. Yield: one 9-inch pie.

Company's Coming
The Junior League of Kansas City, Missouri

Margarita Pie

¾ cup pretzel crumbs
⅓ cup butter, melted
3 tablespoons sugar
1 envelope unflavored gelatin
½ cup lemon juice
4 eggs, separated

1 cup sugar, divided
1 teaspoon grated lemon rind
¼ teaspoon salt
⅓ cup tequila
3 tablespoons Triple Sec or other orange-flavored liqueur

Combine first 3 ingredients; stir well. Firmly press crumb mixture evenly in bottom and up the sides of a 9-inch pieplate. Chill. Sprinkle gelatin over lemon juice, and let stand 1 minute.

Place egg yolks in top of a double boiler; beat with a wire whisk. Add ½ cup sugar, lemon rind, and salt; beat well. Add gelatin mixture, stirring well; bring water to a boil. Reduce heat to low; cook, stirring constantly, until mixture thickens. Remove from heat, and stir in tequila and Triple Sec. Set aside, and let cool completely.

Beat egg whites (at room temperature) at high speed of an electric mixer just until foamy. Gradually add remaining ½ cup sugar, 1 tablespoon at a time, beating until stiff peaks form and sugar dissolves (2 to 4 minutes). Fold egg whites into yolk mixture; pour into prepared crust. Chill thoroughly. Yield: one 9-inch pie.

License to Cook New Mexico Style
New Mexico Federation of Business and Professional Women
Albuquerque, New Mexico

Pineapple-Glazed Apple Pie

1½ cups unsweetened pineapple juice, divided
¾ cup sugar
7 medium Granny Smith apples, peeled and cut into wedges
3 tablespoons cornstarch
1 tablespoon butter
½ teaspoon vanilla extract
¼ teaspoon salt
1 baked 9-inch pastry shell
Whipped cream
Chopped pecans or walnuts

Combine 1¼ cups pineapple juice and sugar in a saucepan. Bring to a boil over medium heat; add apple. Return to a boil; cover, reduce heat to medium low, and cook 6 to 8 minutes or just until apples are tender. Remove apples, using a slotted spoon; reserve juice mixture in saucepan. Set apples aside, and let cool.

Combine remaining ¼ cup pineapple juice and cornstarch; stir until smooth. Gradually stir cornstarch mixture into hot pineapple juice mixture. Cook over medium heat, stirring constantly, until mixture thickens and comes to a boil; cook 1 minute, stirring constantly. Remove from heat; add butter, vanilla, and salt, stirring until butter melts. Cover and let cool 30 minutes (do not stir).

Pour half of pineapple juice mixture into pastry shell; arrange apple wedges on top of mixture. Top with remaining pineapple juice mixture. Cover and chill 2 hours. Garnish with whipped cream and pecans. Yield: one 9-inch pie.   Mary Neavill

Mothers of Twins Cookbook
Twice as Nice, Mothers of Twins Club
Gillette, Wyoming

Frozen Lemon Pie

1½ cups graham cracker crumbs
½ cup butter, melted
1¼ cups sugar, divided
3 eggs, separated
½ teaspoon grated lemon rind
¼ cup lemon juice
⅛ teaspoon salt
1 cup whipping cream, whipped
Additional whipped cream (optional)
Lemon slices (optional)
Fresh mint sprigs (optional)

Combine crumbs, butter, and ¼ cup sugar; stir well. Firmly press crumb mixture evenly in bottom and up the sides of a 9-inch pieplate. Bake at 325° for 8 minutes. Remove from oven; let cool. Place egg yolks in top of a double boiler; beat well with a wire whisk. Add remaining 1 cup sugar, lemon rind, juice, and salt; stir well. Bring water to a boil; reduce heat to low, and cook until thickened, stirring constantly. Remove from heat; let cool.

Beat egg whites (at room temperature) at high speed of an electric mixer until stiff peaks form. Gently fold beaten egg whites into lemon mixture. Fold in whipped cream. Pour mixture into crust; freeze until firm. If desired, garnish with additional whipped cream, lemon slices, and fresh mint sprigs. Let stand at room temperature 5 minutes before serving. Yield: one 9-inch pie.

Simply Sensational
TWIGS, The Auxiliary of the Children's Medical Center
Dayton, Ohio

Frozen Lime Cream Pie

1¼ cups graham cracker crumbs
⅓ cup finely chopped pecans
¼ cup sugar
¼ teaspoon ground cinnamon
¼ cup plus 2 tablespoons butter, melted
3 eggs, separated

½ cup sugar, divided
1 tablespoon grated lime rind
¼ cup fresh lime juice
⅛ teaspoon salt
1 cup whipping cream, whipped

Combine first 4 ingredients; stir well. Add butter, stirring well. Firmly press crumb mixture evenly in bottom and up the sides of a 9-inch pieplate. Bake at 325° for 10 minutes; let cool. Combine egg yolks, ¼ cup sugar, rind, juice, and salt in top of a double boiler; stir well. Cook over medium-high heat, stirring until thickened and coats a metal spoon. Pour into a bowl; chill.

Beat egg whites (at room temperature) at high speed of an electric mixer just until foamy. Gradually add remaining ¼ cup sugar, 1 tablespoon at a time, beating until stiff peaks form and sugar dissolves (2 to 4 minutes). Fold beaten egg whites and whipped cream into lime mixture; pour into crust. Freeze at least 4 hours or until firm. Yield: one 9-inch pie.   Mary Jo Mason

Diamonds in the Desert
The Woman' League of Ozona, Texas

Frozen Crunchy Strawberry Pie

1 cup all-purpose flour
½ cup butter or margarine,
   softened
¼ cup firmly packed brown
   sugar
½ cup chopped pecans
2 cups fresh strawberries,
   mashed or 1 (10-ounce)
   package frozen strawberries,
   thawed

½ cup sugar
1 egg white
2 tablespoons lemon juice
½ cup whipping cream,
   whipped
Additional fresh strawberries

Combine first 3 ingredients in a medium bowl; beat at medium speed of an electric mixer until well blended. Stir in pecans. Spread mixture evenly in the bottom of a 13- x 9- x 2-inch baking pan. Bake at 400° for 12 minutes or until crumbly, stirring occasionally with a fork. Let cool. Reserve ½ cup crumb mixture for topping. Press remaining crumb mixture evenly in bottom and up the sides of a buttered 9-inch pieplate. Chill thoroughly.

Combine 2 cups strawberries, ½ cup sugar, egg white, and lemon juice in a large bowl; beat at high speed 5 minutes or until mixture thickens. Fold in whipped cream; pour into crust. Sprinkle reserved crumb mixture over pie. Freeze 3 hours or until firm. Garnish with fresh strawberries. Yield: one 9-inch pie.

Merrymeeting Merry Eating
The Regional Memorial Hospital Auxiliary
Brunswick, Maine

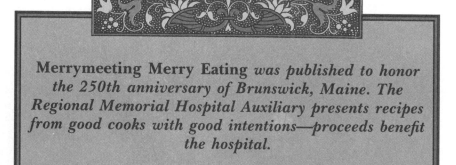

Merrymeeting Merry Eating *was published to honor the 250th anniversary of Brunswick, Maine. The Regional Memorial Hospital Auxiliary presents recipes from good cooks with good intentions—proceeds benefit the hospital.*

Lemon-Blueberry Tart

2 cups all-purpose flour
2 tablespoons sugar
⅛ teaspoon salt
1 teaspoon grated lemon rind
½ cup unsalted butter, cut
  into pieces

3 tablespoons shortening
1 tablespoon cognac
2 to 4 tablespoons ice water
Lemon Filling
4 cups fresh blueberries,
  raspberries, or blackberries

Combine flour, sugar, salt, and lemon rind in a large bowl; cut in butter and shortening with a pastry blender until mixture resembles coarse meal. Sprinkle cognac and ice water (1 tablespoon at a time) evenly over surface; stir with a fork just until dry ingredients are moistened.

Shape dough into a ball; flatten into a large circle. Cover and chill at least 1 hour.

Roll dough to a 12-inch circle. Fit into a greased 11-inch tart pan with removable sides; chill until firm. Prick bottom of pastry with a fork. Line with buttered parchment paper, and fill with dried beans or pie weights. Bake at 450° for 5 minutes. Reduce heat to 350°, and bake 10 minutes. Remove paper and beans; bake an additional 20 minutes or until lightly browned.

Spoon Lemon Filling into prepared crust. Garnish with fresh berries. Carefully remove sides of tart pan before serving. Yield: one 11-inch tart.

Lemon Filling

1½ cups sugar
½ cup unsalted butter, melted
1 to 2 tablespoons grated
  lemon rind

¼ cup plus 3 tablespoons
  fresh lemon juice
3 eggs, beaten
2 egg yolks, beaten

Combine all ingredients in a medium saucepan; cook over low heat, stirring frequently, 15 to 20 minutes or until mixture thickens. Remove saucepan from heat, and let mixture cool completely. Yield: about 3 cups.   Ginny Puryear Fleming

Sampler
The Women's Art Guild, Laguna Gloria Art Museum
Austin, Texas

Fresh Raspberry Tart

¾ cup plus 2 tablespoons
  butter, softened and divided
¼ cup plus 1 tablespoon
  sugar, divided
1 egg, beaten
1 teaspoon almond extract
½ teaspoon vanilla extract
½ cup finely chopped pecans
1⅓ cups all-purpose flour

2 egg yolks
2 tablespoons cornstarch
⅔ cup milk
4 cups fresh raspberries
1 cup red currant jelly
1 tablespoon brandy
1 cup whipping cream
¼ cup sifted powdered sugar

Cream ½ cup butter; gradually add 2½ tablespoons sugar, beating at medium speed of an electric mixer. Add egg; beat well. Stir in almond and vanilla extracts and chopped pecans. Stir in flour until mixture forms a dough.

Gently fit pastry into a buttered 11-inch tart pan. Cover and chill 30 minutes. Bake at 350° for 20 minutes or until golden brown. Let cool completely in pan on a wire rack.

Beat egg yolks at high speed of electric mixer until thick and lemon colored; gradually add remaining 2½ tablespoons sugar, beating well. Add cornstarch; beat well.

Place milk in a medium saucepan; cook over medium heat until thoroughly heated. Gradually add to egg mixture, beating until smooth. Pour into saucepan; cook over medium heat, stirring constantly with a wire whisk, until mixture thickens. Return mixture to mixing bowl, and beat until cool. Add remaining ¼ cup plus 2 tablespoons butter, 1 tablespoon at a time, beating until mixture is smooth. Cover and chill 4 hours.

Spoon chilled custard mixture into cooled tart shell, spreading evenly. Arrange fresh raspberries evenly over custard mixture. Set tart aside.

Place jelly in a small saucepan; cook over low heat until jelly melts, stirring occasionally. Remove from heat, and stir in brandy. Brush jelly mixture over raspberries. Chill 30 minutes.

Beat whipping cream until foamy; gradually add powdered sugar, beating until soft peaks form. Garnish tart with whipped cream. Yield: 12 servings.

South of the Fork
The Junior League of Dallas, Texas

Fresh Peach Crisp

8 medium-size fresh peaches
  (about 2½ pounds), peeled
  and sliced
1 cup all-purpose flour
1 cup sugar

2 tablespoons brown sugar
¼ teaspoon salt
½ teaspoon cinnamon
½ cup butter or margarine,
  softened

Place peach slices in a lightly greased 8-inch square baking dish. Set aside.

Combine flour, sugar, brown sugar, salt, and cinnamon in a medium bowl, stirring well. Cut in butter with a pastry blender until mixture resembles coarse meal. Sprinkle flour mixture evenly over peaches. Bake at 375° for 45 to 50 minutes or until crust is golden brown. Yield: 6 to 8 servings.   Mary Labay

Columbus Collection
Magnolia Homes Tour
Columbus, Texas

Gilded Lily Pear Crisp

5 ripe pears, peeled and
  sliced
2 tablespoons butter, melted
2 tablespoons brandy
½ cup all-purpose flour
½ cup firmly packed light
  brown sugar

¼ cup plus 2 tablespoons
  butter
½ cup coarsely chopped
  walnuts
¼ cup golden raisins
¼ cup semisweet chocolate
  morsels

Place pear slices in a 2-quart casserole. Combine 2 tablespoons melted butter and brandy; stir well. Pour over pears, and toss gently. Set aside.

Combine flour and brown sugar; cut in ¼ cup plus 2 tablespoons butter with a pastry blender until mixture resembles coarse meal. Add walnuts, raisins, and chocolate morsels, stirring gently to combine. Sprinkle mixture over pears. Bake at 350° for 30 to 35 minutes or until pears are tender and topping is lightly browned. Serve warm. Yield: 6 to 8 servings.

The Mystic Seaport All Seasons Cookbook
Mystic Seaport Museum Stores
Mystic, Connecticut

Christmas Pie
or Cranberry Goodin' Puddin'

2 cups fresh cranberries
1½ cups sugar, divided
1 cup chopped pecans
2 eggs
½ teaspoon vanilla extract

1 cup all-purpose flour
½ cup butter, melted
¼ cup shortening, melted
Whipped cream or vanilla ice
  cream

Spoon cranberries into bottom of a greased 10-inch pieplate. Sprinkle with ½ cup sugar and pecans. Set aside.

Beat eggs at high speed of an electric mixer; add remaining 1 cup sugar and vanilla, beating well. Add flour, butter, and shortening; beat well. Pour batter over cranberry mixture; bake at 325° for 50 minutes or until golden brown. Serve warm with whipped cream or ice cream. Yield: one 10-inch pie.

1838-1988 Out of Our Kitchens
Smith Mills Christian Congregational Church
North Dartmouth, Massachusetts

Rhubarb Cobbler

1 cup all-purpose flour
1 cup firmly packed brown
  sugar
¾ cup regular oats, uncooked
½ cup butter, melted
1 teaspoon ground cinnamon

1 cup sugar
1 cup water
3 tablespoons cornstarch
1 teaspoon vanilla extract
4 cups sliced rhubarb
Vanilla ice cream

Combine first 5 ingredients; stir well. Firmly press half the crumb mixture evenly in the bottom of an 8-inch square baking pan; set aside. Reserve remaining half of crumb mixture for topping.

Combine sugar, water, cornstarch, and vanilla in a saucepan. Cook over medium heat, stirring constantly, until thickened. Add rhubarb; stir well. Pour mixture into prepared crust. Top with reserved crumb mixture. Bake at 350° for 40 to 45 minutes or until rhubarb is tender. Serve warm with ice cream. Yield: 6 servings.

A Slice of Nantucket
St. Mary's Guild, St. Mary-Our Lady of the Isle Church
Nantucket, Massachusetts

Almond Pita (Pita od Badema)

1¼ cups butter, softened
1½ cups sugar, divided
3 cups all-purpose flour
¼ cup bourbon
7 eggs, separated
4 (1-ounce) squares
   unsweetened chocolate,
   melted

1¼ cups ground blanched
   almonds
1 teaspoon vanilla extract

Cream butter; gradually add ½ cup sugar, beating well. Stir in flour until mixture forms a soft dough. Stir in bourbon. Roll half of dough to ⅛-inch thickness on a lightly floured surface. Fit pastry into a 9-inch square baking pan; set aside.

Beat egg yolks until thick and lemon colored; gradually add remaining 1 cup sugar, beating well. Stir in melted chocolate. Stir in almonds and vanilla. Set aside.

Beat egg whites (at room temperature) until stiff peaks form. Fold egg whites into chocolate mixture. Pour filling into pastry. Roll remaining dough to ⅛-inch thickness; place over filling. Trim off excess pastry along edges. Fold edges under and flute. Bake at 400° for 5 minutes. Reduce heat to 325°, and bake for 1½ to 2 hours or until lightly browned. Yield: 9 servings.   Barbara Zelwer

St. George Women's Auxiliary Cookbook
St. George Women's Auxiliary
Oakland, California

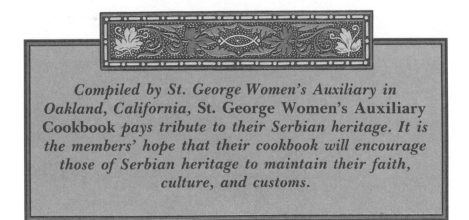

Compiled by St. George Women's Auxiliary in Oakland, California, St. George Women's Auxiliary Cookbook pays tribute to their Serbian heritage. It is the members' hope that their cookbook will encourage those of Serbian heritage to maintain their faith, culture, and customs.

Amaretto Cream Puffs with Raspberry Sauce

½ cup water
¼ cup unsalted butter
1 teaspoon sugar
½ cup all-purpose flour

2 eggs
Amaretto Filling
Raspberry Sauce

Combine water, butter, and sugar in a medium saucepan; bring to a boil. Add flour, all at once, stirring vigorously over medium-high heat until mixture leaves sides of pan and forms a smooth ball. Remove from heat, and let cool 4 to 5 minutes.

Add eggs, one at a time, beating thoroughly with a wooden spoon after each addition; beat until dough is smooth.

Drop pastry by rounded tablespoonfuls 3 inches apart on an ungreased baking sheet. Bake at 375° for 30 to 35 minutes or until puffed and golden brown. Let cream puffs cool completely on a wire rack.

Make a small opening in the bottom of each cream puff with a small knife. Spoon Amaretto Filling into decorating bag fitted with a No. 1 tip. Pipe filling into cream puffs until full. Serve with Raspberry Sauce. Yield: 10 servings.

Amaretto Filling

1 cup whipping cream
1 tablespoon plus 1 teaspoon
sugar

¼ cup amaretto

Beat whipping cream at high speed of an electric mixer until foamy; gradually add sugar, beating until soft peaks form. Fold in amaretto. Yield: 2 cups.

Raspberry Sauce

2 (10-ounce) packages frozen
raspberries in syrup,
thawed
1 tablespoon water

2 teaspoons cornstarch
1 tablespoon powdered sugar
(optional)

Place thawed raspberries in container of an electric blender or food processor and process 10 seconds or until raspberries are pureed. Press raspberry puree through a sieve; discard seeds. Set puree aside.

Combine water and cornstarch in a saucepan; stir until smooth. Add raspberry puree and, if desired, sugar, stirring well. Bring to a boil; remove from heat, and lct cool. Yield: 2⅓ cups.

Dining In
The Young Woman's League of Westport, Connecticut

Lemon Pastry Coffee Cakes

1 cup water
½ cup butter or margarine
1 teaspoon sugar
¼ teaspoon salt
1 cup all-purpose flour
4 eggs
2 tablespoons grated lemon
rind

Lemon Frosting
½ (1-ounce) square
unsweetened chocolate,
grated
¼ cup sliced almonds,
toasted

Combine water, butter, sugar, and salt in a medium saucepan; bring to a boil. Add flour, all at once, stirring vigorously over medium-high heat until mixture leaves sides of pan and forms a smooth ball. Remove from heat, and let cool 4 to 5 minutes.

Add eggs, one at a time, beating thoroughly with a wooden spoon after each addition; beat until dough is smooth. Stir in lemon rind. Spoon batter into two 15- x 2-inch strips, 4 inches apart, in a greased 15- x 10- x 1-inch jellyroll pan.

Bake at 400° for 35 minutes or until puffed and golden brown. Remove from oven, and let cool away from drafts. Spread Lemon Frosting over coffee cakes. Sprinkle with grated chocolate and sliced almonds. Yield: 12 servings.

Lemon Frosting

¾ cup sifted powdered sugar
1 tablespoon butter, melted
1 tablespoon milk

½ teaspoon vanilla extract
¼ teaspoon almond extract
¼ teaspoon lemon juice

Combine all ingredients; beat at medium speed of an electric mixer until smooth. Yield: ⅓ cup.   Deborah Head Siceloff

Taste of the Town—Second Serving
The Charity League of Lexington, North Carolina

Norwegian Kringler

2 cups all-purpose flour,
  divided
2 tablespoons sugar
¼ teaspoon salt
1 cup butter or margarine,
  divided
2 tablespoons cold water

1 cup water
4 eggs
½ teaspoon almond extract
Frosting (recipe follows)
¾ cup sliced almonds,
  toasted

Combine 1 cup flour, sugar, and salt; stir well. Cut in ½ cup butter with a pastry blender until mixture resembles coarse meal. Sprinkle 2 tablespoons cold water (1 tablespoon at a time) evenly over surface; stir with a fork until dry ingredients are moistened. Press pastry in the bottom of a 13- x 9- x 2-inch baking pan; set aside.

Combine 1 cup water and remaining ½ cup butter in a medium saucepan; bring to a boil. Add remaining 1 cup flour, all at once, stirring vigorously over medium-high heat until mixture leaves sides of pan and forms a smooth ball. Remove from heat, and let cool 4 to 5 minutes.

Add eggs, one at a time, beating thoroughly with a wooden spoon after each addition. Add almond extract, beating until dough is smooth. Spread mixture evenly over pastry. Bake at 425° for 30 minutes. Remove from oven, and let cool. Drizzle with frosting, and sprinkle with almonds. Yield: 12 to 15 servings.

Frosting

1 cup sifted powdered sugar
2 to 3 tablespoons milk

1 tablespoon butter, melted
½ teaspoon almond extract

Combine all ingredients in a small bowl. Beat at medium speed of an electric mixer until smooth. Yield: ½ cup.

Simply Sensational
TWIGS, The Auxiliary of the Children's Medical Center
Dayton, Ohio

Poultry

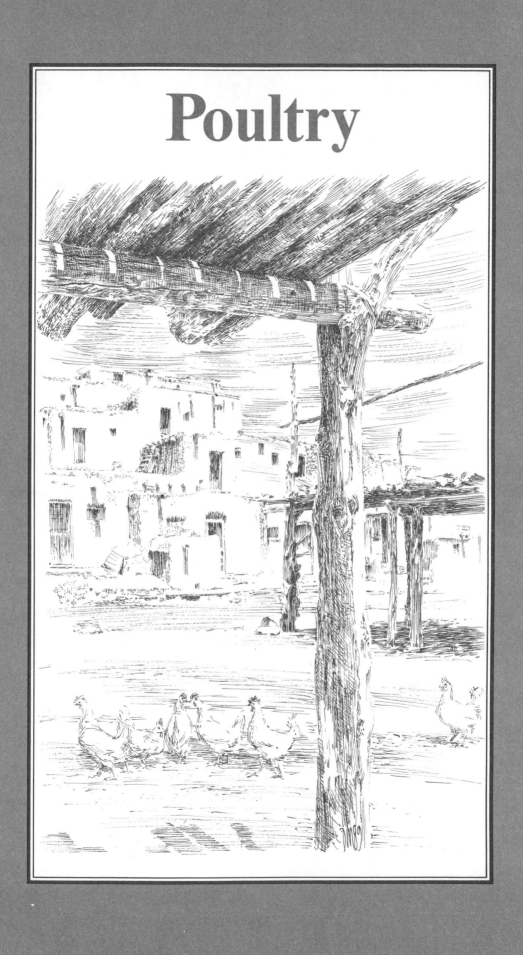

Simple adobe houses are scattered throughout sun-drenched Taos, New Mexico, an area well known for its Pueblo Indian fiestas and ceremonial dances. Once a trading post on the Santa Fe Trail, Taos has become a resort colony for writers and painters who are attracted by its old Spanish influence and beautiful scenery.

Herb Baked Chicken

1 (2½-pound) broiler-fryer
1 teaspoon garlic salt
2 teaspoons dried whole
  rosemary, crushed and
  divided
⅓ cup butter, melted
⅓ cup Chablis or other dry
  white wine

½ teaspoon dried whole basil,
  crushed
½ teaspoon salt
¼ teaspoon ground white
  pepper

Remove giblets and neck from chicken; reserve for use in other recipes. Sprinkle garlic salt and 1 teaspoon rosemary evenly in cavity of chicken. Truss chicken, and place breast side up in a shallow roasting pan.

Combine remaining 1 teaspoon rosemary, butter, and remaining ingredients in a small bowl; stir well. Brush chicken generously with herb mixture. Bake, uncovered, at 350° for 1½ hours or until chicken is done, basting occasionally with any remaining herb mixture. Yield: 6 servings.   Ann McBride Chilcutt

A Grand Heritage
The Heritage Academy
Columbus, Mississippi

Crispy Sesame Chicken

1 cup grated Parmesan
  cheese
½ cup fine, dry breadcrumbs
¼ cup plus 2 tablespoons
  sesame seeds

1 (3- to 3½-pound)
  broiler-fryer, cut up
½ cup butter, melted

Combine first 3 ingredients in a small bowl; stir well. Dip chicken in butter; dredge in breadcrumb mixture. Place chicken in a 13- x 9- x 2-inch baking dish. Bake at 350° for 1 hour or until done. Yield: 4 to 6 servings.

Please Cook with Children
The Please Touch Museum
Philadelphia, Pennsylvania

Gingered Pear Chicken

1 (16-ounce) can pear halves in syrup, undrained
2 whole chicken breasts
¼ teaspoon salt
3 tablespoons butter or margarine, melted
¾ cup ginger ale
¼ cup firmly packed brown sugar
3 tablespoons soy sauce
¼ teaspoon ground ginger
1 tablespoon cornstarch
¼ cup water
Chopped walnuts (optional)

Drain pears, reserving ¾ cup syrup. Slice pears lengthwise into wedges. Set aside. Sprinkle chicken breasts evenly with salt. Brown chicken in butter in a medium skillet over medium heat.

Combine reserved syrup, ginger ale, sugar, soy sauce, and ginger; stir well. Pour over chicken. Bring to a boil; cover, reduce heat, and simmer 25 minutes. Transfer chicken to a 9-inch square baking pan; reserve liquid in skillet. Arrange pears around chicken.

Combine cornstarch and water, stirring until well blended. Add to liquid in skillet, stirring well. Cook over medium heat, stirring constantly, until thickened. Pour over chicken and pears. Sprinkle with chopped walnuts, if desired. Bake, uncovered, at 350° for 10 minutes. Yield: 4 servings.   Bridget Guccione

Hudson Cooks
The Community Playground of Hudson, Ohio

Arroz con Pollo

1 large onion, finely chopped
2 large green peppers, finely chopped
2 large cloves garlic, minced
½ teaspoon threads of saffron, crushed
¼ cup olive oil
1 large tomato, seeded and chopped
1 teaspoon dried whole oregano
1 cup uncooked long-grain rice
2 (10¾-ounce) cans chicken broth, undiluted
1 (4-ounce) jar sliced pimiento, drained
½ teaspoon salt
½ teaspoon pepper
8 chicken breast halves, skinned and boned
⅓ cup pimiento-stuffed olives

Sauté onion, green pepper, garlic, and saffron in olive oil in a large skillet 10 minutes or until vegetables are tender. Add tomato and oregano; sauté 5 minutes. Stir in rice, broth, pimiento, salt, and pepper. Spoon into a 13- x 9- x 2-inch baking dish; arrange chicken on top of rice mixture. Bake, uncovered, at 350° for 55 minutes or until chicken is done, rice is tender, and liquid is absorbed. Sprinkle olives over chicken; bake an additional 5 minutes. Cover and let stand 15 minutes before serving. Yield: 8 servings.

Jackson Hole à la Carte
The Jackson Hole Alliance for Responsible Planning
Jackson, Wyoming

Three-Flavor Chinese Chicken

3 tablespoons sesame seeds, toasted
2 cloves garlic, crushed
¼ to ½ teaspoon crushed red pepper
¼ teaspoon ground ginger
⅓ cup soy sauce
¼ cup honey
¼ cup dry sherry
4 chicken breast halves, skinned and boned
1 large green pepper, cut into strips
1 tablespoon vegetable oil
6 lemon slices, halved
2 cups hot cooked rice

Combine sesame seeds, garlic, red pepper, and ginger; stir well. Add soy sauce, honey, and sherry; stir well. Place chicken in a shallow baking dish. Pour marinade mixture over chicken; cover and marinate in refrigerator 3 to 4 hours, turning occasionally.

Remove chicken from marinade, reserving marinade. Place chicken in a 9-inch square baking pan. Bake at 325° for 15 minutes, basting frequently with marinade. Turn chicken breasts, and bake an additional 10 minutes, basting frequently with marinade. Broil 6 inches from heat 2 to 3 minutes on each side or until done. Set aside, and keep warm.

Sauté green pepper in oil in a skillet until tender; set aside, and keep warm. Slice each chicken breast diagonally into 4 pieces. Alternate chicken slices and lemon slices on a serving platter. Arrange pepper strips and rice beside chicken on serving platter. Yield: 4 servings.   Kathy Hansen

Calvary Collections
Calvary Lutheran Church
Kalispell, Montana

Grilled Marinated Breast of Chicken with Fresh Tomato-Pepper Salsa

4 chicken breast halves, skinned and boned
⅓ cup rice wine vinegar
¼ cup plus 2 tablespoons fresh lime juice, divided
3 tablespoons chopped fresh rosemary, divided
8 fresh basil leaves, crushed and divided
8 Italian-style tomatoes, seeded, diced, and divided
1 cup olive oil, divided
Salt and freshly ground pepper to taste
1 small sweet onion, sliced
1 medium-size sweet red pepper, diced
2 medium-size sweet yellow peppers, diced
4 small jalapeño peppers, seeded and diced
¼ teaspoon salt
⅛ teaspoon pepper

Place each piece of chicken between 2 sheets of wax paper; flatten to ¼-inch thickness, using a meat mallet or rolling pin. Place chicken in an 11- x 7- x 2-inch baking dish.

Combine vinegar, ¼ cup lime juice, 2 tablespoons rosemary, 4 crushed basil leaves, ½ cup diced tomatoes, ¾ cup olive oil, and salt and pepper to taste in a jar; cover tightly, and shake vigorously. Pour marinade mixture over chicken. Cover and marinate in refrigerator 1 hour.

Remove chicken from marinade; discard marinade. Grill chicken over medium coals 2 to 3 minutes on each side or until done. Arrange on a serving platter; set aside, and keep warm.

Sauté onion in remaining ¼ cup olive oil in a large skillet 5 minutes. Add red and yellow peppers, jalapeño pepper, ¼ teaspoon salt, and ⅛ teaspoon pepper; sauté 2 to 4 minutes, stirring frequently. Add remaining 2 tablespoons lime juice, 1 tablespoon chopped fresh rosemary, 4 crushed basil leaves, and diced tomatoes, and sauté 2 to 3 minutes or until vegetables are crisp-tender.

Spoon vegetable mixture evenly over warm chicken on serving platter. Serve immediately. Yield: 4 servings.

You Can't Be Too Rich or Too Thin
Southampton Hospital
Southampton, New York

Chicken Florentine in Phyllo

1 (10-ounce) package frozen chopped spinach, thawed	2 teaspoons dried Italian seasoning
1 cup finely chopped onion	1/8 teaspoon salt
2 tablespoons butter or margarine, melted	1/8 teaspoon pepper
1 (16-ounce) carton ricotta cheese	16 sheets commercial frozen phyllo pastry, thawed
1 egg, lightly beaten	1/2 cup butter, melted
1/4 cup grated Parmesan cheese	8 chicken breast halves, skinned and boned
1/4 cup mayonnaise	1/3 cup grated Parmesan cheese

Drain spinach; press between paper towels to remove excess moisture. Set aside. Sauté onion in 2 tablespoons butter in a medium skillet until tender. Combine onion, spinach, ricotta cheese, and next 6 ingredients in a large bowl; stir well.

Place 2 sheets of phyllo on a flat surface (keep remaining phyllo covered); brush with butter. Place 1 chicken breast half in center of phyllo, 3 inches from bottom. Spoon about 1/3 cup spinach mixture over chicken. Fold bottom of phyllo over spinach mixture. Fold sides of phyllo over chicken, wrapping like a package; roll jellyroll fashion. Place seam side down in a 13- x 9- x 2-inch baking dish. Repeat with remaining phyllo, butter, chicken, and spinach mixture. Brush with melted butter. Sprinkle with 1/3 cup Parmesan cheese. Bake at 375° for 45 minutes or until done. Yield: 8 servings.

Albertina's II
The Albertina Kerr Centers for Children
Portland, Oregon

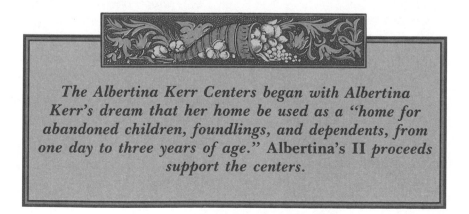

The Albertina Kerr Centers began with Albertina Kerr's dream that her home be used as a "home for abandoned children, foundlings, and dependents, from one day to three years of age." Albertina's II proceeds support the centers.

Chicken Breasts with Sesame Seeds

6 chicken breast halves,
  skinned and boned
¼ cup honey
2 tablespoons butter or
  margarine, melted

1 tablespoon soy sauce
1¼ teaspoons sesame seeds
¼ teaspoon salt

Place chicken between 2 sheets of wax paper; flatten to ¼-inch thickness, using a meat mallet. Place chicken in a greased 13- x 9- x 2-inch baking pan. Combine honey, butter, and soy sauce; stir well. Pour over chicken. Bake at 325° for 45 minutes, basting chicken every 15 minutes with pan drippings. Remove from oven; sprinkle chicken with sesame seeds and salt. Bake at 450° for 10 minutes. Yield: 6 servings.   Patricia L. Davis

A Cook's Book of Recipes from the Pacific Northwest
The Rosehill Community Center
Mukilteo, Washington

Crispy Chicken Rolls

6 chicken breast halves,
  skinned and boned
Salt and pepper to taste
½ cup butter, divided
3 (2-ounce) slices mozzarella
  or Swiss cheese, cut in half
  lengthwise
½ cup all-purpose flour
2 eggs, beaten
1 cup fine, dry breadcrumbs

1 teaspoon dried whole
  oregano
½ teaspoon dried whole
  rosemary, crushed
½ teaspoon dried parsley
  flakes
½ teaspoon dried whole
  thyme, crushed
½ cup Chablis or other dry
  white wine

Place chicken between 2 sheets of wax paper. Flatten to ¼-inch thickness, using a meat mallet. Sprinkle with salt and pepper; dot each piece of chicken with 1 teaspoon butter. Top each with a slice of cheese. Fold sides of chicken over cheese, and roll up; secure with wooden picks. Dredge rolls in flour; dip in egg, and coat with breadcrumbs. Place in a buttered 13- x 9- x 2-inch baking dish.

Melt remaining ¼ cup plus 2 tablespoons butter; pour over chicken. Combine herbs; stir well, and sprinkle over chicken. Bake at 350° for 20 minutes. Pour wine over chicken, and bake an additional 15 minutes or until chicken is done. Remove wooden picks before serving. Yield: 6 servings.   Ann Townsend

From the Grapevine
The Crossroads Guild of Indianapolis, Indiana

Mexican-Style Chicken Kiev

8 chicken breast halves, skinned and boned
1 (4-ounce) can whole green chiles, drained
½ cup fine, dry breadcrumbs
¼ cup grated Parmesan cheese
1 teaspoon chili powder
½ teaspoon garlic salt
¼ teaspoon ground cumin
¼ teaspoon pepper
4 ounces Monterey Jack cheese, cut into 1- x ½- x ½-inch pieces
¼ cup plus 2 tablespoons butter or margarine, melted
Spicy Tomato Sauce

Place chicken between wax paper; flatten to ¼-inch thickness, using a meat mallet. Set aside. Cut chiles in half lengthwise; remove seeds. Cut chiles into 8 equal pieces. Set aside. Combine breadcrumbs and next 5 ingredients; stir well. Set aside.

Top each chicken breast with a slice of chile and a piece of cheese. Fold long sides of chicken over chile and cheese; fold ends over, and secure with wooden picks. Dip chicken in butter; dredge in breadcrumb mixture. Place seam side down in a 13- x 9- x 2-inch baking dish. Drizzle with any remaining butter. Cover and chill 4 hours. Bake at 400° for 20 minutes or until done. Remove wooden picks; serve with Spicy Tomato Sauce. Yield: 8 servings.

Spicy Tomato Sauce

1 (15-ounce) can tomato sauce
⅓ cup chopped green onions
½ teaspoon ground cumin
½ teaspoon salt
½ teaspoon pepper

Combine all ingredients in a saucepan; stir well. Bring to a boil; reduce heat, and simmer 5 minutes. Yield: 1¾ cups.

License to Cook New Mexico Style
New Mexico Federation of Business and Professional Women
Albuquerque, New Mexico

Rolled Chicken Breasts

8 large chicken breast halves, skinned and boned
½ teaspoon salt
¼ teaspoon pepper
¼ teaspoon paprika
1 cup (4 ounces) shredded Gruyère cheese
1 (3-ounce) package cream cheese, softened
⅓ cup grated Parmesan cheese
¼ cup sour cream
4 green onions, minced
1 clove garlic, minced
2 shallots, minced
½ cup butter, melted and divided
¼ to ½ pound fresh mushrooms, sliced
8 slices prosciutto
3 tablespoons all-purpose flour
¾ cup dry sherry
Additional grated Parmesan cheese

Place chicken breast halves between 2 sheets of wax paper; flatten to ¼-inch thickness, using a meat mallet or rolling pin. Sprinkle chicken with salt, pepper, and paprika. Set aside.

Combine Gruyère cheese and next 5 ingredients in a small bowl; stir well. Set aside.

Sauté shallots in 2 tablespoons butter in a medium skillet until tender. Add mushrooms, and sauté until tender. Remove mushrooms and shallots, using a slotted spoon. Set aside.

Place one slice prosciutto on each chicken breast half. Spread reserved cheese mixture evenly over prosciutto. Fold sides of chicken breast over stuffing, roll up, and secure with wooden picks. Brown chicken in 3 tablespoons butter in a large skillet. Place chicken in a greased 11- x 7- x 2-inch baking dish. Bake at 350° for 15 minutes. Remove from oven; set aside, and keep warm.

Add remaining 3 tablespoons butter to skillet; stir in flour until smooth. Cook over medium heat until browned, stirring constantly. Gradually add sherry; cook, stirring constantly, until thickened and bubbly. Add mushrooms and shallots; stir well. Pour over chicken. Sprinkle with additional Parmesan cheese. Bake 5 minutes; remove wooden picks. Transfer chicken and mushrooms to a serving platter, using a slotted spoon. Yield: 8 servings.

Stanford University Medical Center Auxiliary Cookbook
Stanford University Medical Center Auxiliary
Palo Alto, California

Chicken Valencia

⅔ cup raisins, divided
½ cup dry sherry
¼ cup soft breadcrumbs
¼ cup chopped cooked ham
2 tablespoons butter, softened
1 tablespoon chopped fresh
  parsley
¼ teaspoon grated orange
  rind
6 large chicken breast halves,
  skinned and boned
2 tablespoons all-purpose
  flour

1 teaspoon paprika
½ teaspoon garlic salt
3 tablespoons shortening,
  melted
1 cup canned diluted chicken
  broth
½ cup orange juice
¼ cup chopped green onions
1 (3-inch) stick cinnamon
Salt and pepper to taste

Combine raisins and sherry in a small bowl. Let stand 30 minutes; drain, reserving liquid. Set aside ⅓ cup raisins; chop remaining ⅓ cup raisins. Combine chopped raisins, breadcrumbs, chopped ham, butter, chopped parsley, and orange rind in a small bowl; stir well. Set aside.

Place chicken between 2 sheets of wax paper; flatten to ¼-inch thickness, using a meat mallet or rolling pin.

Spoon stuffing evenly over center of each chicken breast half; roll up chicken, jellyroll fashion, starting with short end, and secure with wooden picks.

Combine flour, paprika, and garlic salt; stir well. Dredge chicken in flour mixture.

Brown chicken in shortening in a large skillet over medium-high heat. Discard pan drippings. Add reserved sherry, chicken broth, orange juice, green onions, cinnamon stick, and salt and pepper to taste. Bring to a boil; cover, reduce heat, and simmer 30 minutes or until chicken is done.

Add remaining ⅓ cup raisins; simmer 3 to 4 minutes. Remove and discard cinnamon stick. Remove wooden picks; transfer chicken to a serving platter. Yield: 6 servings.

Second Round, Tea-Time at the Masters®
The Junior League of Augusta, Georgia

Chicken Stuffed with Crab

8 chicken breast halves,
   skinned and boned
3 tablespoons butter
¼ cup all-purpose flour
¾ cup milk
¾ cup canned diluted
   chicken broth
⅓ cup Chablis or other dry
   white wine
¼ cup chopped onion
1 tablespoon butter, melted
7½ ounces fresh lump
   crabmeat, drained and
   flaked

1 (3-ounce) can sliced
   mushrooms, drained
10 saltine crackers, crushed
2 tablespoons chopped fresh
   parsley
½ teaspoon salt
½ teaspoon pepper
1 cup (4 ounces) shredded
   Swiss cheese
½ teaspoon paprika

Place chicken between 2 sheets of wax paper; flatten to ¼-inch thickness, using a meat mallet or rolling pin. Set aside.

Melt 3 tablespoons butter in a heavy saucepan over low heat; add flour, stirring until smooth. Cook 1 minute, stirring constantly. Gradually add milk, chicken broth, and wine; cook over medium heat, stirring constantly, until mixture is thickened and bubbly. Set sauce aside.

Sauté onion in 1 tablespoon butter in a large skillet until tender. Add crabmeat, sliced mushrooms, cracker crumbs, chopped fresh parsley, salt, and pepper; stir well. Add 2 tablespoons reserved sauce, stirring well.

Top each chicken breast half with ¼ cup crabmeat mixture. Fold long sides of chicken over crabmeat mixture; fold ends over, and secure with wooden picks.

Place chicken rolls, seam side down, in a 13- x 9- x 2-inch baking dish. Top with remaining sauce. Cover and bake at 350° for 1 hour or until chicken is done. Uncover and sprinkle chicken with shredded Swiss cheese and paprika. Bake an additional 2 minutes or until cheese melts. Remove wooden picks, and serve chicken immediately. Yield: 8 servings.

Jan Inman

More Memoirs of a Galley Slave
The Kodiak Fishermen's Wives Association
Kodiak, Alaska

Chicken Macadamia

2 eggs
½ cup all-purpose flour
½ cup cold water
¼ cup cornstarch
1 medium onion,
  grated
2 tablespoons brandy or
  cream sherry
2 tablespoons soy sauce
2 tablespoons peanut oil
2 teaspoons minced fresh
  ginger

1 teaspoon salt
½ teaspoon pepper
6 chicken breast halves,
  skinned, boned, and cut
  into 1-inch pieces
Peanut oil
Hot cooked rice
Sweet-and-Sour Sauce
1 (3½-ounce) jar macadamia
  nuts, chopped

Combine eggs, flour, cold water, cornstarch, grated onion, brandy, soy sauce, 2 tablespoons peanut oil, minced fresh ginger, salt, and pepper in container of an electric blender or food processor; process until mixture is smooth.

Place chicken in a large shallow dish. Pour marinade mixture over chicken. Cover and marinate in refrigerator 20 minutes.

Remove chicken from marinade, discarding marinade. Fry chicken in hot peanut oil (375°) in a large skillet until chicken is done. Drain on paper towels.

Place chicken over rice on individual serving plates. Top each serving with Sweet-and-Sour Sauce, and sprinkle with chopped macadamia nuts. Yield: 6 servings.

Sweet-and-Sour Sauce

½ cup firmly packed brown
  sugar
½ cup cold water

½ cup white vinegar
¼ cup cornstarch
¼ cup soy sauce

Combine all ingredients in a medium saucepan; stir well. Cook over medium heat, stirring constantly, until thickened. Yield: about 1¼ cups.   Marlyss Swallow

Secret Recipes II
4450th Tactical Group, Nellis Air Force Base
Las Vegas, Nevada

Walnut Chicken

¼ cup plus 1 tablespoon vegetable oil, divided
1 tablespoon plus 2 teaspoons soy sauce, divided
1 tablespoon cornstarch, divided
4 chicken breast halves, skinned, boned, and cut into 1-inch pieces
½ cup canned diluted chicken broth
½ teaspoon ground ginger
½ teaspoon crushed red pepper
1 sweet red pepper, cut into 1-inch pieces
1 medium onion, cut into 1-inch pieces
1 clove garlic, minced
½ pound broccoli, cut into 1-inch pieces
½ cup chopped walnuts
Hot cooked rice

Combine 1 tablespoon oil, 2 teaspoons soy sauce, and 1 teaspoon cornstarch; stir well. Add chicken; cover and marinate in refrigerator 30 minutes. Combine broth, ginger, remaining 1 tablespoon soy sauce, and remaining 2 teaspoons cornstarch; stir well. Pour remaining ¼ cup oil around top of preheated wok, coating sides; heat at medium high (325°) for 2 minutes. Add chicken mixture and crushed red pepper, and stir-fry 5 to 8 minutes. Remove chicken; set aside. Add sweet red pepper, onion, and garlic; stir-fry 1 minute. Add broccoli, and stir-fry 1 minute. Return chicken to wok; stir gently. Add broth mixture; cook until thickened, stirring constantly. Stir in walnuts. Serve over rice. Yield: 4 servings.

Con Mucho Gusto
Desert Club of Mesa, Arizona

The Desert Club of Mesa has been meeting the social, civic, and cultural needs of their community since 1946. Through money raised from the sale of Con Mucho Gusto, *members are able to help fund numerous community programs.*

The Big Grill—Chicken Kabobs with Mustard Dipping Sauce

½ cup olive oil, divided
¼ cup lime juice
2 cloves garlic, minced
2 tablespoons chopped onion
1 teaspoon hot sauce
3 lime slices
6 chicken breast halves, skinned, boned, and cut into 1-inch pieces
2 cloves garlic, crushed
1 medium-size green pepper, cut into 1-inch pieces

1 sweet red pepper, cut into 1-inch pieces
1 sweet yellow pepper, cut into 1-inch pieces
2 small purple onions, cut into wedges
12 small red potatoes
12 medium-size fresh mushrooms
12 cherry tomatoes
Mustard Dipping Sauce

Combine ¼ cup olive oil and next 5 ingredients in a medium bowl; add chicken. Cover and marinate in refrigerator 8 hours.

Combine remaining ¼ cup olive oil and crushed garlic in a small bowl, stirring well; brush over vegetables. Remove chicken from marinade, discarding marinade.

Alternate chicken and vegetables on six 12-inch metal skewers. Grill kabobs over hot coals 5 minutes on each side or until chicken is done and vegetables are crisp-tender. Serve kabobs with Mustard Dipping Sauce. Yield: 6 servings.

Mustard Dipping Sauce

1 cup sour cream
3 tablespoons Dijon mustard
2 teaspoons Worcestershire sauce
1 teaspoon fresh lemon juice

½ teaspoon hot sauce
¼ teaspoon pepper
2 tablespoons chopped green onions
1 clove garlic, minced

Combine all ingredients in a small bowl, and stir until well combined. Yield: 1¼ cups.   Barbara Beach

Hudson Cooks
The Community Playground of Hudson, Ohio

Honey-Glazed Chicken Kabobs

4 large chicken breast halves, skinned, boned, and cut into 1-inch pieces
1 large zucchini, cut into 1-inch pieces
1 large yellow squash, cut into 1-inch pieces
2 medium-size sweet red peppers, cut into 1-inch pieces
¼ pound fresh mushrooms, halved
Honey-Mustard Glaze

Alternate chicken and vegetable pieces on eight 12-inch metal skewers. Grill kabobs about 6 inches from medium-hot coals 10 to 20 minutes or until chicken is done and vegetables are crisp-tender, turning and basting kabobs often with Honey-Mustard Glaze. Yield: 4 servings.

Honey-Mustard Glaze

¾ cup honey
½ cup spicy brown mustard
2 tablespoons soy sauce
1 tablespoon cider vinegar
2 tablespoons cornstarch
¼ cup water

Combine first 4 ingredients in a medium saucepan. Bring mixture to a boil over medium-high heat, and boil 1 minute. Combine cornstarch and water in a small bowl, stirring until smooth. Gradually stir cornstarch mixture into honey mixture. Return to a boil, stirring constantly. Boil 1 minute or until mixture is thickened. Yield: 1½ cups.   Mark May

Cooking with the Skins
The National Multiple Sclerosis Society/National Capital Chapter
Washington, DC

Breast of Chicken with Fontina
(Petti di Pollo alla Modena)

4 chicken breast halves, skinned and boned
Salt and pepper
½ cup all-purpose flour
¼ cup butter or margarine, melted
¼ cup olive oil
12 slices prosciutto
12 (1-ounce) slices fontina cheese
½ cup grated Parmesan cheese

Slice each chicken breast half lengthwise into 3 pieces; sprinkle with salt and pepper. Dredge chicken in flour. Brown chicken in butter and oil in a large skillet over medium-high heat.

Place chicken in a 13- x 9- x 2-inch baking dish. Place prosciutto slices over chicken. Top with slices of fontina cheese, and sprinkle with Parmesan cheese. Bake, uncovered, at 350° for 15 to 20 minutes or until hot and bubbly. Yield: 4 servings.

Celebrated Seasons
The Junior League of Minneapolis, Minnesota

Artichoke-Chicken Stroganoff

4 (6-ounce) jars marinated artichoke hearts, undrained
8 chicken breast halves, skinned, boned, and cut into strips
1 cup chopped onion
2 cloves garlic, minced
4 chicken-flavored bouillon cubes
1½ cups boiling water
¼ cup all-purpose flour
1 teaspoon dry mustard
1 teaspoon dried whole dillweed
1 (8-ounce) carton sour cream
¼ teaspoon salt
Hot cooked rice or noodles

Drain artichoke hearts, reserving marinade. Set artichoke hearts and marinade aside.

Sauté chicken, onion, and garlic in ¼ cup reserved marinade in a large skillet until chicken is lightly browned and onion is tender.

Dissolve bouillon cubes in boiling water; pour over chicken.

Combine flour, dry mustard, and dillweed in a small bowl; stir well. Add flour mixture to remaining artichoke marinade; stir until smooth. Pour over chicken. Bring mixture to a boil; cover, reduce heat, and simmer 4 to 5 minutes or until chicken is done. Remove from heat.

Stir in reserved artichoke hearts, sour cream, and salt. Serve over rice. Yield: 8 servings.   Lawrence R. Miller

Capital Connoisseur
The Lawrence Center Independence House
Schenectady, New York

Sunshine Chicken with Poached Oranges

½ cup soy sauce
½ cup catsup
¼ cup vegetable oil
¼ cup honey
2 cloves garlic, crushed
8 broiler-fryer leg quarters, separated

1 teaspoon salt
1 teaspoon dried whole basil
¼ teaspoon freshly ground pepper
Poached Oranges

Combine soy sauce, catsup, vegetable oil, honey, and garlic in a medium bowl; beat with a wire whisk until mixture is well blended. Set sauce aside.

Sprinkle chicken pieces evenly with salt, basil, and pepper. Place chicken in a 13- x 9- x 2-inch baking pan, and baste with sauce. Bake, uncovered, at 350° for 50 minutes or until chicken is done. Remove chicken to a serving platter, and keep warm. Garnish with Poached Oranges.

Combine any remaining basting sauce with syrup from Poached Oranges in a heavy saucepan. Bring to a boil; boil 5 minutes. Serve with chicken. Yield: 6 to 8 servings.

Poached Oranges

1½ cups sugar
3 tablespoons orange rind strips
¾ cup water
6 oranges, peeled and sectioned

2 tablespoons Grand Marnier or other orange-flavored liqueur

Combine sugar, orange rind strips, and water in a heavy saucepan; cook over medium heat 8 to 10 minutes or until mixture is slightly thickened, stirring occasionally. Add orange sections to syrup. Reduce heat, and simmer until orange sections are thoroughly heated. Remove from heat, and let mixture cool 15 minutes. Stir in Grand Marnier. Cover and chill thoroughly. Yield: 2 cups.

Biscayne Bights and Breezes
The Villagers, Inc.
Coral Gables, Florida

Chicken Livers in Wine

¾ cup all-purpose flour
1 teaspoon salt
¼ teaspoon pepper
1 pound chicken livers
3 tablespoons vegetable oil, divided
½ pound fresh mushrooms, sliced
¼ cup chopped onion
¾ cup Chablis or other dry white wine
¾ cup canned diluted chicken broth
Hot cooked rice

Combine first 3 ingredients; stir well. Dredge livers in flour mixture, and brown in 2 tablespoons oil in a skillet. Set livers aside. Reserve pan drippings. Add remaining 1 tablespoon oil to pan drippings. Add mushrooms and onion, and sauté until tender. Return livers to skillet. Add wine and chicken broth. Bring to a boil; cover, reduce heat, and simmer 8 to 10 minutes or until livers are tender. Serve over rice. Yield: 4 servings.   Gladys Lazarus

A Rainbow of Kosher Cuisine
The Baltimore Chapter of Hadassah
Baltimore, Maryland

Turkey Sweet-and-Sour

1 cup turkey broth
½ cup firmly packed brown sugar
⅓ cup cider vinegar
¼ cup soy sauce
¼ cup catsup
2 tablespoons cornstarch
¾ cup diced carrots
2 tablespoons vegetable oil
¾ cup diced green pepper
¾ cup pineapple chunks
4 cups cubed cooked turkey
Hot cooked rice

Combine first 6 ingredients in a saucepan. Cook over medium heat, stirring until thickened. Remove from heat. Sauté carrots in oil in a skillet 1 minute. Add pepper, pineapple, and turkey; cook over medium heat 5 minutes. Add sauce, and cook until thoroughly heated. Serve over rice. Yield: 6 to 8 servings.   Aileen Curtis

Pioneers of Alaska Cookbook
The Pioneers of Alaska Auxiliary #4
Anchorage, Alaska

Turkey Piccata

1 pound boneless turkey
  breast slices
¾ cup all-purpose flour
½ cup plus 2 tablespoons
  butter, divided
2 tablespoons fresh lemon
  juice, divided

16 medium-size fresh
  mushrooms, sliced
1 cup Chablis or other dry
  white wine
Lemon slices

Cut turkey slices in half crosswise; dredge in flour. Place between 2 sheets of wax paper; flatten to ¼-inch thickness, using a meat mallet or rolling pin. Dredge again in flour.

Melt ¼ cup plus 2 tablespoons butter in a large skillet over medium heat. Stir in 1 tablespoon lemon juice. Sauté turkey slices in butter mixture until lightly browned, adding remaining ¼ cup butter and 1 tablespoon lemon juice as needed. Remove turkey to a serving platter, and keep warm.

Sauté mushrooms in pan drippings until tender. Add wine, and cook, stirring constantly, until mixture comes to a boil. Add turkey slices to mushroom mixture. Arrange lemon slices over turkey. Reduce heat, and simmer, uncovered, 5 minutes. Serve immediately. Yield: 4 servings.

Crème de LA Coast
Small World Guild-Childrens Hospital of Orange County,
California

Grilled Turkey Tenderloins

¼ cup butter or margarine,
  melted and divided
2 cloves garlic, crushed
4 turkey tenderloins (about
  1¼ to 1½ pounds)
Salt and pepper

4 shallots, sliced
½ pound fresh mushrooms,
  sliced
¼ cup chopped fresh
  parsley

Combine 2 tablespoons butter and garlic, stirring well. Brush turkey tenderloins lightly with butter mixture, reserving any remaining butter mixture. Sprinkle with salt and pepper. Grill turkey over hot coals 5 to 6 minutes on each side or until done, basting with butter mixture. Transfer to a serving platter, and keep warm.

Sauté shallots in remaining 2 tablespoons butter in a large skillet until tender. Add mushrooms, and sauté 2 to 3 minutes. Reduce heat, and cook until liquid is absorbed. Spoon mushroom mixture over turkey tenderloins; sprinkle with chopped fresh parsley. Yield: 4 servings.

Only in California
The Children's Home Society of California
Los Angeles, California

Cornish Hens with Wild Rice and Grape Dressing

8 (1- to 1½-pound) Cornish hens
2 cups cooked wild rice
2 cups cooked brown rice
1 cup seedless green grapes, halved
⅓ cup slivered blanched almonds

1½ cups butter, melted
½ cup bourbon
1½ teaspoons salt
¼ teaspoon ground white pepper
½ cup red currant jelly

Remove giblets from hens; reserve giblets for use in other recipes. Rinse hens with cold water, and pat dry.

Combine wild rice, brown rice, grape halves, and slivered almonds in a large bowl; stir well. Stuff hens with rice mixture, and close cavities. Secure with wooden picks; truss. Place hens, breast side up, in a shallow roasting pan.

Combine butter, bourbon, salt, and pepper; stir well. Brush hens generously with butter mixture. Bake at 350° for 1 hour and 15 minutes, basting hens frequently with butter mixture.

Place currant jelly in a small saucepan; cook over medium heat 5 minutes or until melted, stirring occasionally. Brush hens with melted currant jelly, and bake an additional 15 to 20 minutes or until done. Yield: 8 servings.   Mary Coneway

Sampler
The Women's Art Guild, Laguna Gloria Art Museum
Austin, Texas

Southern Quail with Wild Rice, Orange, and Almond Stuffing

1 cup Chablis or other dry white wine
¼ cup raisins
3 whole cloves
⅔ cup cooked wild rice
½ cup whole blanched almonds, coarsely chopped

1 tablespoon grated orange rind
¼ teaspoon ground ginger
¼ cup butter, melted and divided
6 quail, dressed
¼ cup orange juice

Combine wine, raisins, and cloves in a small saucepan. Bring mixture to a boil; reduce heat, and simmer 5 minutes. Remove and discard whole cloves. Drain raisins, reserving liquid; set raisins and liquid aside.

Combine raisins, wild rice, chopped almonds, orange rind, and ginger in a small bowl; stir well. Add 2 tablespoons melted butter, and stir well.

Spoon rice mixture into body cavities of quail; brush with remaining 2 tablespoons butter. Tie legs together with cord. Place quail on a rack in a roasting pan.

Combine reserved liquid and orange juice in a small bowl; stir well. Bake quail at 450° for 10 minutes; reduce heat to 325°, and bake 25 to 30 minutes, basting frequently with orange juice mixture. Yield: 3 servings.

Libretto
The Opera Society of Fort Lauderdale, Florida

Salads & Salad Dressings

The restoration of Colonial Williamsburg in Virginia began in 1926. Since then, nearly 150 buildings and their grounds, such as this house and garden, have been restored or reconstructed to appear as they did in colonial times. Hostesses, craftsmen, and militiamen dressed in the style of the day add to the atmosphere of living history.

Tomato Aspic

2 envelopes unflavored
  gelatin
4 cups vegetable juice
  cocktail, divided
1 small onion, thinly sliced
3 stalks celery with leaves,
  coarsely chopped
2 tablespoons white vinegar
1 tablespoon sugar

1 bay leaf
6 black peppercorns
1 teaspoon salt
1 teaspoon Worcestershire
  sauce
Dash of ground allspice
½ cup sliced pimiento-stuffed
  olives or small cooked
  shrimp

Sprinkle gelatin over ½ cup juice in a saucepan; let stand 1
minute. Cook over medium heat, stirring until gelatin dissolves.
Add remaining 3½ cups juice, onion, and next 8 ingredients; stir
well. Bring to a boil; reduce heat, and simmer 10 minutes. Strain;
pour into a 4-cup ring mold. Chill until partially set; stir in olives.
Chill 8 hours. Unmold onto a serving plate. Yield: 8 to 10 servings.

Steeped in Tradition
The Junior Service League of DeLand, Florida

Apricot Bavarian Salad

2 (12-ounce) cans apricot
  nectar, divided
1 cup sugar
3 envelopes unflavored
  gelatin
Dash of salt

⅓ cup lemon juice
1 egg white
1 cup whipping cream,
  whipped
Fresh mint sprigs

Bring 12 ounces apricot nectar to a boil in a saucepan. Remove
from heat. Add sugar, gelatin, and salt; stir until gelatin dissolves.
Stir in remaining 12 ounces apricot nectar and lemon juice. Pour ¾
cup gelatin mixture into an oiled 6-cup mold. Chill until firm.

Let remaining gelatin mixture cool to room temperature. Stir in
egg white. Chill until slightly thickened; beat until light and fluffy.
Fold in whipped cream; pour over mixture in mold. Chill until firm.
Unmold onto a serving plate; garnish with mint. Yield: 12 servings.

The Gathering
The Blue Bird Circle
Houston, Texas

Apple Salad
with Honey-Yogurt Dressing

3 Granny Smith apples,
  unpeeled and diced
2 stalks celery, thinly sliced
1 large carrot, scraped and
  shredded

½ cup golden raisins
½ cup coarsely chopped
  pecans, toasted
Honey-Yogurt Dressing
Lettuce leaves

Combine apple, celery, carrot, raisins, and pecans in a large bowl. Pour Honey-Yogurt Dressing over apple mixture; toss gently to combine. Cover and chill 2 to 3 hours. Serve salad in a lettuce-lined salad bowl. Yield: 6 to 8 servings.

Honey-Yogurt Dressing

½ cup plain yogurt
2 tablespoons vegetable oil
2 tablespoons honey
1 tablespoon white wine
  vinegar

1½ teaspoons Dijon mustard
⅛ teaspoon salt
⅛ teaspoon pepper

Combine all ingredients in a small bowl, and stir well with a wire whisk. Yield: about ¾ cup.

Jackson Hole à la Carte
The Jackson Hole Alliance for Responsible Planning
Jackson, Wyoming

Mandarin Orange and Almond Salad

¼ cup whole blanched
  almonds
¼ cup sugar, divided
1 small head iceberg lettuce,
  shredded
1 cup chopped celery
1 (11-ounce) can mandarin
  oranges, drained
2 green onions, chopped

1 tablespoon minced fresh
  parsley
¼ cup vegetable oil
2 tablespoons white
  vinegar
½ teaspoon salt
¼ teaspoon pepper
⅛ teaspoon hot sauce

Cut almonds in half crosswise. Combine almonds and 2 tablespoons sugar in a heavy saucepan; place over medium heat. Cook, stirring constantly, until sugar melts and coats almonds. Remove from heat, and let cool completely.

Combine lettuce, chopped celery, mandarin oranges, green onions, and minced parsley in a large bowl; toss well.

Combine remaining 2 tablespoons sugar, vegetable oil, white vinegar, salt, pepper, and hot sauce in a jar. Cover tightly, and shake vigorously.

Combine lettuce mixture, dressing, and almonds; toss gently. Yield: 6 to 8 servings.   Edna Schwab

Thou Preparest a Table Before Me
East Avenue United Methodist Church Women
York, Nebraska

Orange-Kiwifruit Salad

1 head romaine lettuce, torn
3 kiwifruit, peeled and sliced
1 (11-ounce) can mandarin
   oranges, drained
1 large purple onion, sliced
Dressing (recipe follows)

3 ounces blue cheese,
   crumbled
⅓ cup chopped walnuts or
   pecans
Commercial croutons

Combine lettuce, sliced kiwifruit, mandarin oranges, and sliced onion in a large bowl, toss gently. Pour dressing over salad; toss gently. Top salad with blue cheese, chopped walnuts, and croutons. Yield: 6 servings.

Dressing

½ cup extra virgin olive oil
⅓ cup fresh lime juice
3 tablespoons red wine
   vinegar
3 tablespoons orange
   marmalade

1 teaspoon salt
1 teaspoon freshly ground
   pepper

Combine all ingredients in a jar. Cover tightly, and shake vigorously. Yield: 1⅓ cups.

Second Round, Tea-Time at the Masters®
The Junior League of Augusta, Georgia

Saundra's Cabbage Salad

1 large cabbage, shredded
1 medium-size green pepper, thinly sliced
2 medium onions, thinly sliced and separated into rings
1 (4-ounce) jar sliced pimiento, drained

1 cup sugar
1 cup vegetable oil
¾ cup vinegar
1½ teaspoons salt
1 teaspoon celery seeds

Layer cabbage, green pepper, onion rings, and pimiento in a large container. (Do not stir.)

Combine sugar and remaining ingredients in a small saucepan. Bring to a boil; reduce heat, and simmer 2 minutes.

Pour hot dressing over layered vegetables. Cover and chill at least 4 hours. Yield: 16 to 18 servings.   Bettye White

Southern Secrets
SouthTrust Corporation
Birmingham, Alabama

Crunchy Vegetable Salad

1 medium cauliflower, broken into flowerets
3 cups broccoli flowerets
2 cups chopped celery
1 cup sliced carrot
1 cup chopped green onions
1 (8-ounce) carton sour cream
1 cup mayonnaise

1 tablespoon sugar
1 tablespoon white vinegar
1 teaspoon celery seeds
1 teaspoon dried whole dillweed
½ teaspoon salt
½ teaspoon garlic salt

Combine cauliflower, broccoli, celery, carrot, and green onions in a large bowl.

Combine sour cream and remaining ingredients; stir well. Pour sour cream mixture over vegetables; toss gently. Cover and chill thoroughly. Yield: 10 to 12 servings.   Betty Erickson Johnson

One Hundred Years of Sharing
Calvary Covenant Church Women
Evansville, Minnesota

Corn Slaw

½ cup sour cream
½ cup mayonnaise
¼ cup sugar
¼ cup white vinegar
Salt and pepper to taste
1 (16-ounce) can whole kernel
  corn, drained

3 to 4 carrots, scraped and
  chopped
1 green pepper, chopped
1 small onion, chopped

Combine first 5 ingredients in a large bowl; stir well. Add vegetables; toss gently. Cover and chill 2 hours. Use a slotted spoon to serve slaw. Yield: 6 servings.   Ruth Z. Peters

The Thresher Table
The Bethel College Women's Association
North Newton, Kansas

Schuette Potato Salad

5 pounds red potatoes
1 pound bacon
2½ cups chopped onion
2 cups cider vinegar
1½ cups sugar
⅓ cup all-purpose flour

1 cup water
1 tablespoon salt
½ teaspoon pepper
12 hard-cooked eggs, sliced
½ cup chopped fresh parsley

Cook potatoes in boiling water to cover 15 minutes or until tender. Drain and let cool slightly. Peel and slice potatoes. Set aside.

Cook bacon in a large skillet until crisp. Remove bacon, reserving ½ cup drippings in skillet. Crumble bacon, and set aside.

Sauté onion in pan drippings until tender. Add vinegar and sugar, stirring until sugar dissolves. Combine flour and water, beating with a wire whisk until smooth. Add to onion mixture, stirring constantly. Cook over medium heat until slightly thickened. Stir in salt and pepper. Remove from heat, and set aside.

Layer one-third each of potatoes, eggs, sauce, bacon, and parsley in a large serving bowl. Repeat layers twice. Serve salad warm. Yield: 18 to 20 servings.   Fred, Silvia, and Paula Schuette

200th Anniversary Year Cookbook
Christ Evangelical Lutheran Church
Jeffersontown, Kentucky

Potato Salad with Feta, Olives, and Red Pepper

1½ pounds red potatoes, cut into ¾-inch cubes
¼ cup fresh lemon juice, divided
¼ teaspoon salt
1 sweet red pepper, cut into julienne strips
½ cup pitted ripe olives

3 green onions, minced
4 ounces feta cheese, crumbled
¾ teaspoon dried whole oregano
½ cup olive oil
Salt and pepper to taste

Cook potatoes in boiling water to cover 15 minutes or until tender; drain. Combine potatoes, 2 tablespoons lemon juice, and ¼ teaspoon salt, tossing gently.

Cook red pepper strips in a small amount of boiling water 1 to 2 minutes; drain.

Combine potatoes, red pepper strips, olives, green onions, and feta cheese; toss gently.

Combine remaining 2 tablespoons lemon juice and oregano in a small bowl; add oil in a thin, steady stream, beating well with a wire whisk. Pour dressing over salad; toss gently. Add salt and pepper to taste. Yield: 4 to 6 servings.   Pat Deane

Black-Eyed Susan Country
The Saint Agnes Hospital Auxiliary
Baltimore, Maryland

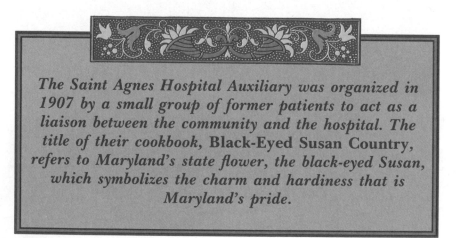

The Saint Agnes Hospital Auxiliary was organized in 1907 by a small group of former patients to act as a liaison between the community and the hospital. The title of their cookbook, Black-Eyed Susan Country, *refers to Maryland's state flower, the black-eyed Susan, which symbolizes the charm and hardiness that is Maryland's pride.*

Chinese Chicken Salad

1 (2½- to 3-pound) broiler-fryer
3½ tablespoons soy sauce, divided
3 tablespoons vegetable oil, divided
1 tablespoon dry sherry
1 clove garlic, crushed
¼ teaspoon ground ginger
¼ teaspoon Chinese Five-Spice powder
½ pound fresh snow pea pods
2 cups shredded lettuce

1 cup cashews, peanuts, or slivered blanched almonds, toasted
3 green onions, thinly sliced
½ pound fresh bean sprouts
½ cup sunflower kernels
½ cup sesame seeds, toasted
2 tablespoons lemon juice
1½ tablespoons white vinegar
3 cloves garlic, crushed
2 teaspoons grated fresh ginger
2 teaspoons sugar

Remove giblets and neck from chicken; reserve for use in other recipes. Rinse chicken, and pat dry. Place chicken, breast side up, on a rack in a roasting pan.

Combine 2 tablespoons soy sauce, 1 tablespoon oil, sherry, 1 crushed garlic clove, ground ginger, and Chinese Five-Spice powder in a small bowl; stir well.

Bake chicken at 375° for 1½ hours, basting with marinade mixture every 30 minutes. Remove chicken from oven, and let cool. Skin and bone chicken; shred meat.

Trim ends from snow peas. Place snow peas in a steaming rack over boiling water; cover and steam 2 to 3 minutes or until tender. Let cool. Combine snow peas, shredded lettuce, cashews, green onions, bean sprouts, sunflower kernels, and toasted sesame seeds in a large bowl; add shredded chicken, and toss well.

Combine remaining 2 tablespoons oil, lemon juice, remaining 1½ tablespoons soy sauce, vinegar, 3 crushed garlic cloves, grated ginger, and sugar; stir well. Pour dressing over salad, and toss gently. Cover and chill. Yield: 8 to 10 servings.   Kathy Lickiss

Crème de la Congregation
Our Saviors Lutheran Church
Lafayette, California

Pasta, Chicken, and Pesto Salad

1 (16-ounce) package
  medium-size seashell
  macaroni
5 cups cubed cooked chicken
  breast
1½ cups diced zucchini
1 cup seeded and diced
  tomatoes
1 cup diced celery
1 (8-ounce) carton sour cream

1 cup mayonnaise
⅓ cup pine nuts
¼ cup minced fresh parsley
3 tablespoons dried whole
  basil
1 tablespoon lemon juice
2 teaspoons dried whole
  oregano
1½ teaspoons salt
¼ teaspoon pepper

Cook macaroni according to package directions; drain. Rinse with cold water; drain. Combine pasta, chicken, zucchini, tomato, and celery; toss well. Cover and chill thoroughly.

Combine sour cream and remaining ingredients in container of an electric blender or food processor; process until smooth. Chill at least 1 hour. Pour chilled dressing over pasta mixture, tossing to coat well. Yield: 14 cups.   Jeanne C. Scott

Chestnut Hill Cookbook
The Chestnut Hill Senior Services Center
Philadelphia, Pennsylvania

Provençal Beef Salad
with Anchovy Vinaigrette

3 pounds new potatoes
Anchovy Vinaigrette
4 cups cooked beef
  tenderloin, sirloin tip roast,
  or roast beef, cut into
  ½-inch cubes
2 cups sliced green onions

1 (3¼-ounce) jar capers,
  drained
1 pint cherry tomatoes,
  halved
⅓ cup minced fresh parsley
Romaine lettuce leaves

Cook potatoes in boiling water to cover 15 minutes or until tender; drain carefully, leaving skins intact. Cube potatoes. Pour Anchovy Vinaigrette over potatoes, tossing gently. Cover and chill 8 hours. Add beef and next 4 ingredients; toss gently. Serve on a bed of romaine lettuce leaves. Yield: 12 to 14 servings.

Anchovy Vinaigrette

1½ cups vegetable oil
½ cup white vinegar
¼ cup minced fresh parsley
2 cloves garlic, minced

1½ teaspoons salt
1 teaspoon sugar
1 teaspoon pepper
1 teaspoon anchovy paste

Combine all ingredients in a medium bowl; beat with a wire whisk until blended. Yield: about 2 cups.

Palm Country Cuisine
The Junior League of Greater Lakeland, Florida

Warm Salad of Scallops, Peppers, and Arugula

⅓ pound arugula
1 medium-size sweet red pepper, cut into julienne strips
1 medium-size sweet yellow pepper, cut into julienne strips

Sherry Vinaigrette Dressing
1 pound bay scallops, rinsed and drained
1 small clove garlic, minced
¼ cup butter, melted
Fresh Italian parsley sprigs

Combine arugula, peppers, and 1 tablespoon Sherry Vinaigrette Dressing; toss well. Divide evenly among 6 salad plates. Sauté scallops and garlic in butter 2 minutes or until scallops are done. Remove scallops; divide evenly among salads. Garnish with parsley. Add remaining Sherry Vinaigrette Dressing to skillet; cook until thoroughly heated. Serve with salads. Yield: 6 servings.

Sherry Vinaigrette Dressing

1 tablespoon sherry wine vinegar
1 teaspoon fresh lemon juice
1 tablespoon walnut oil

⅓ cup extra virgin olive oil
⅛ teaspoon salt
Dash of freshly ground pepper

Combine vinegar and juice. Add oils in a slow, steady stream, beating until blended. Add salt and pepper, stirring well. Yield: about ⅓ cup.

One Magnificent Cookbook
The Junior League of Chicago, Illinois

Cold Seafood Rice Salad

3 cups cooked rice
2 cups cooked, peeled, and
   deveined shrimp or lobster
½ pound fresh mushrooms,
   sliced
1 cup sliced water chestnuts
1 cup chopped green pepper
3 pimientos, thinly sliced or
   1 (4-ounce) jar sliced
   roasted peppers, drained

¼ cup chopped fresh parsley
¼ cup chopped fresh chives
1 cup olive oil
3 tablespoons white vinegar
3 tablespoons soy sauce
2 teaspoons Dijon mustard
½ teaspoon hot sauce
Salt and pepper to taste

Combine rice, shrimp, sliced mushrooms, water chestnuts, green pepper, pimiento, parsley, and chives in a large bowl; toss gently.

Combine olive oil, vinegar, soy sauce, mustard, and hot sauce in a small bowl; stir well.

Pour dressing over rice mixture; toss gently. Add salt and pepper to taste. Cover and chill at least 1 hour. Yield: 6 servings.

Off the Hook
The Junior League of Stamford-Norwalk
Darien, Connecticut

Couscous Salad

1 cup canned diluted chicken
   broth
¾ cup uncooked
   couscous
1 large tomato, diced
1 medium-size sweet red,
   yellow, or green pepper,
   diced
3 green onions, chopped
2 carrots, scraped and thinly
   sliced

1 stalk celery, thinly sliced
3 or 4 Greek olives, pitted
   and chopped
½ cup torn Bibb lettuce
3 tablespoons lemon juice
1 tablespoon olive oil
1 tablespoon pine nuts,
   toasted
Bibb lettuce leaves

Bring chicken broth to a boil in a medium saucepan; stir in couscous. Remove from heat; cover and let stand 5 minutes or until liquid is absorbed. Let cool completely.

Combine tomato and next 9 ingredients; stir well. Add couscous; toss gently to combine. Serve salad on a bed of lettuce leaves. Yield: 4 to 6 servings.   Phyllis Holmes

The Less Fat Cookbook
The Cancer Education and Prevention Center
Oakland, California

French Dressing

½ cup vegetable oil
1 tablespoon lemon juice
¼ cup sugar
1 teaspoon salt
1 teaspoon grated onion

1 clove garlic, crushed
¼ cup white vinegar
⅓ cup catsup
1 teaspoon paprika

Combine first 6 ingredients in a small bowl; beat at medium speed of an electric mixer until smooth. Stir in vinegar, catsup, and paprika. Serve over salad greens. Yield: 1 cup.   Elsie Coats

Pioneers of Alaska Cookbook
The Pioneers of Alaska Auxiliary #4
Anchorage, Alaska

Garlic-Honey Salad Dressing

2 cups mayonnaise
⅓ cup vegetable oil
¼ cup buttermilk
¼ cup sour cream
3 tablespoons honey

1 tablespoon lemon juice
1 tablespoon white wine
  vinegar
1 large clove garlic, crushed
¾ teaspoon dry mustard

Combine all ingredients in container of an electric blender; process until mixture is blended. Serve dressing over salad greens. Yield: 3¼ cups.   Stephanie Parrish

The Florida Cooking Adventure
The Florida Federation of Women's Clubs
Lakeland, Florida

Herbed Buttermilk Dressing

1 cup buttermilk
2 tablespoons instant minced onion
2 tablespoons chopped fresh parsley
¼ teaspoon dried whole basil
¼ teaspoon dried whole rosemary
¼ teaspoon dried whole oregano
¼ teaspoon dried whole savory
1 clove garlic, crushed
1 cup mayonnaise
Salt and pepper to taste
1 cup crumbled Roquefort cheese

Combine first 8 ingredients in a small bowl; stir well, and let stand 5 minutes. Add mayonnaise; stir well. Add salt and pepper to taste. Cover and chill thoroughly. Stir in cheese just before serving. Serve dressing over salad greens. Yield: 2⅔ cups.

Con Mucho Gusto
The Desert Club of Mesa, Arizona

Green Goddess Dressing

1 cup mayonnaise
½ cup sour cream
¼ cup minced fresh parsley
2 tablespoons minced fresh chives
2 tablespoons chopped green onions
1 tablespoon lemon juice
1 tablespoon tarragon vinegar
½ teaspoon salt
½ teaspoon pepper
⅛ teaspoon minced garlic

Combine all ingredients in a small bowl; stir well. Cover and chill thoroughly. Serve dressing over salad greens. Yield: 1¾ cups.

The Farmer's Daughters
The National Multiple Sclerosis Society
St. Charles, Arkansas

Sauces & Condiments

An autumn scene of cornstalks, pumpkins, and a scarecrow in a farmer's field in Manchester, Vermont, brings to mind crisp fall weather and Halloween. Manchester is a year-round resort community, with skiers flocking to nearby Snow Valley, Bromley, and Stratton mountains.

Brandied Apricot Sauce

1 (16-ounce) jar apricot
  preserves
¼ cup plus 2 tablespoons
  butter or margarine

1 cup brandy
¼ cup raisins

Cook preserves and butter over medium heat, stirring until butter melts. Remove from heat; stir in brandy and raisins. Serve warm over ice cream or cheesecake. Yield: 3 cups.

Celebrated Seasons
The Junior League of Minneapolis, Minnesota

Lemon Sauce

½ cup sugar
1 egg, beaten
½ cup butter
3 tablespoons hot water

1 tablespoon grated lemon
  rind
3 tablespoons lemon juice
⅛ teaspoon salt

Combine sugar and egg in top of a double boiler; stir well. Add butter and remaining ingredients, stirring well; bring water to a boil. Reduce heat to low; cook, stirring constantly, until smooth and thickened. Serve warm over pound cake. Yield: 1⅓ cups.

Only in California
The Children's Home Society of California
Los Angeles, California

Orange Sauce

⅔ cup sugar
4 egg yolks, beaten
2 tablespoons grated orange rind

⅓ cup orange juice
1 cup whipping cream,
  whipped

Combine first 4 ingredients in a saucepan; bring to a boil. Cook, stirring until thickened. Remove from heat; let cool completely. Fold in whipped cream. Serve over pound cake. Yield: 2 cups.

Food for Thought—Just Desserts
The Shipley School
Bryn Mawr, Pennsylvania

Praline Sauce

1¼ cups firmly packed brown
sugar
1 cup half-and-half
16 large marshmallows

Dash of salt
⅓ cup chopped pecans
¼ cup butter
1 teaspoon vanilla extract

Combine brown sugar, half-and-half, marshmallows, and salt in a saucepan; bring mixture to a boil over medium heat. Cook, stirring occasionally, 8 to 10 minutes or until mixture reaches 204°. Remove from heat, and let cool slightly. Add pecans, butter, and vanilla, stirring until butter melts. Serve warm Praline Sauce immediately over ice cream. Yield: 2⅓ cups.   Nancy Hieta

Crème de la Congregation
Our Saviors Lutheran Church
Lafayette, California

Peanut Butter-Fudge Sauce

1 (6-ounce) package
semisweet chocolate
morsels
⅓ cup creamy peanut butter

⅓ cup milk
¼ cup corn syrup
½ teaspoon vanilla extract

Combine first 4 ingredients in a saucepan; cook over medium heat, stirring constantly, until mixture comes to a boil. Remove from heat, and add vanilla, stirring well. Serve sauce warm over ice cream. Yield: 1⅓ cups.   Judy Welcher

Lorimor Centennial Cookbook, Volume II
The Centennial Committee
Lorimor, Iowa

Toffee Bar Sauce

¾ cup sugar
½ cup whipping cream
¼ cup light corn syrup
2 tablespoons butter

5 (1.2-ounce) English
toffee-flavored candy
bars, frozen and
crushed

Combine first 4 ingredients in a saucepan, stirring well. Bring mixture to a boil; boil 2 minutes, stirring constantly. Remove from heat, and add crushed candy bars, stirring well. Serve Toffee Bar Sauce warm over ice cream or fruit. Yield: 1⅔ cups.

Very Innovative Parties
The Loma Linda University School of Dentistry Auxiliary
Loma Linda, California

Café Maple Syrup

2 cups sugar
1 cup hot coffee

Dash of salt
½ teaspoon maple flavoring

Combine sugar, coffee, and salt in a small saucepan; bring mixture to a boil over medium heat, stirring constantly. Boil mixture 1 minute or until sugar dissolves, stirring constantly. Remove from heat, and stir in maple flavoring. Let mixture cool. Cover and chill. Serve Café Maple Syrup over waffles, French toast, or pancakes. Yield: about 2 cups.   Claire Blanchard

State Hospital Cooks
Patient/Staff Advocacy Committee, Vermont State Hospital
Waterbury, Vermont

State Hospital Cooks, *sponsored by the patient/staff advocacy committee of Vermont State Hospital, was created in an effort to raise money for the Patient Benefit Fund. The fund sponsors special trips and outings for patients to places such as the zoo, Spider Web Farm, a wildflower farm, and the beach.*

Western Weekend Marinade for Shish Kabobs

1½ cups vegetable oil
¾ cup soy sauce
½ cup white wine vinegar
⅓ cup fresh lemon juice
¼ cup Worcestershire sauce
2 tablespoons dry mustard
1 tablespoon freshly ground pepper
1½ teaspoons dried parsley flakes
1 clove garlic, crushed

Combine all ingredients in container of an electric blender; process 30 seconds or until well blended. Store in an airtight container in the refrigerator up to 10 days. Use as a marinade for beef, fish, or chicken before cooking and as a basting sauce during cooking. Yield: 3⅓ cups.   Gail Stern Cooney

Home on the Range
West Marin Health Project and Dance Palace Community Center
Point Reyes, California

Birmingham Barbecue Sauce

1 (17-ounce) bottle catsup
½ cup firmly packed brown sugar
1 small onion, finely chopped
⅓ cup olive oil
¼ cup plus 1 tablespoon white vinegar
2 tablespoons Worcestershire sauce
2 cloves garlic, minced
1½ teaspoons dry mustard
2 beef-flavored bouillon cubes
1 bay leaf
1 teaspoon salt
1 teaspoon black pepper
½ teaspoon ground red pepper

Combine all ingredients in a medium saucepan; stir well. Bring to a boil over medium heat; reduce heat, and simmer 45 minutes to 1 hour. Remove and discard bay leaf. Store in an airtight container in the refrigerator. Use as a basting sauce for chicken or pork during cooking. Yield: 3 cups.

Our Favorite Recipes
The Azara Club of St. George Melkite Greek-Catholic Church
Birmingham, Alabama

Tartar Sauce

1½ cups mayonnaise
5 gherkin pickles, minced
1 tablespoon chopped fresh
  parsley
1 clove garlic, minced

1 teaspoon capers, chopped
½ teaspoon tarragon vinegar
¼ teaspoon ground white
  pepper

Combine all ingredients in a small bowl; stir well. Cover and chill. Serve with fish. Yield: 1⅔ cups.　　　　Marcelle Phillips

Pioneers of Alaska Cookbook
The Pioneers of Alaska Auxiliary #4
Anchorage, Alaska

Whipped Cream-Horseradish Sauce

¼ cup prepared horseradish,
  drained
1 tablespoon white wine vinegar
1 teaspoon sugar
½ teaspoon salt

½ teaspoon ground white
  pepper
¼ teaspoon dry mustard
½ cup whipping cream,
  whipped

Combine first 6 ingredients in a small bowl; stir well. Fold in whipped cream. Cover and chill. Serve with beef. Yield: 1¼ cups.

Finely Tuned Foods
The Symphony League of Leawood, Kansas

Swedish-Style Mustard

4 eggs, beaten
½ cup firmly packed light
  brown sugar
½ cup dry mustard
½ cup honey

½ cup apple cider
½ cup cider vinegar
1 tablespoon all-purpose flour
½ teaspoon ground cardamom
⅛ teaspoon ground cloves

Combine all ingredients in a saucepan; stir well. Cook over low heat, stirring constantly, until thickened. Cover and chill. Use as a spread for meats or sandwiches. Yield: 2 cups.　　Pat Ouderkirk

As You Like It
St. Bernard's School
New York, New York

Shrimp Butter

1 (8-ounce) package frozen
  cooked shrimp, thawed,
  drained, and chopped
1 (8-ounce) package cream
  cheese, softened
¼ cup butter, softened
¼ cup lemon juice

2 tablespoons minced green
  onions
¼ teaspoon salt
¼ teaspoon dried whole
  dillweed
⅛ teaspoon hot sauce

Combine all ingredients in a medium bowl, stirring well. Cover
tightly, and chill 24 hours. Let Shrimp Butter stand at room temperature 1 hour before serving. Serve with party white or rye bread.
Yield: 2 cups.

Spokane Cooks!
The Community Centers Foundation of Spokane, Washington

Pumpkin Butter

2½ cups cooked, mashed
  pumpkin
¾ cup sugar
¼ cup apple cider or orange
  juice

½ teaspoon ground cinnamon
½ teaspoon ground cloves
¼ teaspoon ground allspice
¼ teaspoon ground nutmeg

Combine all ingredients in a heavy saucepan. Bring to a boil;
reduce heat, and simmer, uncovered, 10 minutes or until mixture
thickens. Cover and chill. Serve Pumpkin Butter with muffins or
toast. Yield: 3 cups.   Elizabeth Collier

The Heart of Adirondack Cooking
Women's Fellowship
Warrensburg, New York

Rosemary-Sherry Jelly

1 (25.4-ounce) bottle cream
  sherry
7 cups sugar
¼ cup lemon juice

3 large fresh rosemary sprigs
2 (3-ounce) packages liquid
  pectin
9 small fresh rosemary sprigs

Combine first 4 ingredients in a saucepan; bring to a boil, stirring occasionally. Boil 1 minute, stirring constantly. Add liquid pectin; boil 1 minute, stirring constantly. Remove from heat. Quickly pour hot jelly through a sieve into hot sterilized jars, leaving ¼-inch headspace; wipe jar rims. Place a small rosemary sprig in each jar. Cover at once with metal lids, and screw on bands. Process in boiling-water bath 5 minutes. Serve with lamb. Yield: 9 half pints.

Parishables
St. Paul's Episcopal Church
Cleveland Heights, Ohio

Aunt Margaret's Cranberry Jelly

4 cups fresh cranberries   **2 cups sugar**
1 cup water

Wash cranberries, and drain. Combine cranberries and water in a saucepan. Bring to a boil; reduce heat, and simmer 6 to 8 minutes or until skins pop. Press cranberries through a sieve; discard skins. Return cranberries to saucepan; bring to a boil. Remove from heat; add sugar, stirring until dissolved. Pour hot jelly into hot sterilized jars, leaving ¼-inch headspace; wipe jar rims. Cover at once with metal lids, and screw on bands; process in boiling-water bath 5 minutes. Yield: 2 half pints.   Elizabeth Upham

Diamonds in the Desert
The Woman's League of Ozona, Texas

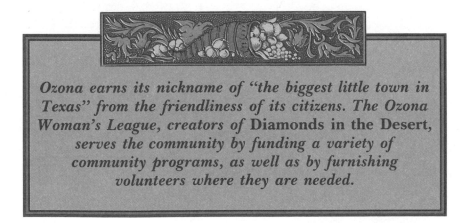

Ozona earns its nickname of "the biggest little town in Texas" from the friendliness of its citizens. The Ozona Woman's League, creators of **Diamonds in the Desert,** *serves the community by funding a variety of community programs, as well as by furnishing volunteers where they are needed.*

Cranberry-Orange Chutney

4 cups fresh cranberries	½ cup raisins
2 cups sugar	¼ cup chopped walnuts
2 cups water	¼ cup orange juice
1 cup unpecled, chopped apple	1 tablespoon white vinegar (5% acidity)
2 oranges, peeled and sectioned	½ teaspoon ground cinnamon
	½ teaspoon ground ginger

Wash cranberries, and drain. Combine all ingredients in a large saucepan. Bring to a boil; reduce heat, and simmer 10 to 15 minutes or until cranberry skins pop.

Quickly spoon hot chutney into hot sterilized jars, leaving ¼-inch headspace; wipe jar rims. Cover jars at once with metal lids, and screw on metal bands. Process chutney in boiling-water bath 15 minutes. Yield: 4 pints.   Patsy Major

Gingerbread . . . and all the trimmings
The Junior Service League of Waxahachie, Texas

Chutney

1 (8-ounce) can pineapple tidbits, undrained	½ cup sliced blanched almonds
1 cup firmly packed brown sugar	½ cup golden raisins
½ cup white wine vinegar	½ cup chopped green pepper
1 clove garlic, minced	2 tablespoons chopped crystallized ginger
½ teaspoon salt	2 teaspoons cornstarch

Drain pineapple, reserving ½ cup juice; set pineapple aside. Combine ½ cup pineapple juice, brown sugar, vinegar, garlic, and salt in a medium saucepan; stir well. Cook, uncovered, over medium heat 15 minutes, stirring occasionally. Add pineapple tidbits, almonds, and remaining ingredients, stirring well; cook until green pepper is tender. Serve Chutney with curried chicken or lamb. Yield: 2 cups.   Mamie Lark Henry

Educated Taste
The LaGrange College Alumni Association
LaGrange, Georgia

Blueberry Relish

2 cups sugar
1 cup water
6 cups fresh blueberries
10 whole cloves
2 (3-inch) sticks cinnamon,
  broken into pieces

1 teaspoon whole allspice
½ teaspoon coriander seeds
1 cup cider vinegar
3 tablespoons grated orange
  rind

Combine sugar and water in a large Dutch oven. Bring to a boil over medium heat, stirring until sugar dissolves. Add blueberries; reduce heat, and simmer until blueberry skins pop. Remove blueberries with a slotted spoon, and set aside.

Combine cloves, cinnamon, allspice, and coriander seeds in a cheesecloth bag. Add spice bag, vinegar, and orange rind to syrup in Dutch oven. Bring to a boil; reduce heat, and simmer 30 minutes or until syrup is reduced by half and begins to jell. Add reserved blueberries, and cook until thickened.

Spoon hot relish into jars; cover and chill. Serve with chicken or pork. Yield: 3 half pints.

Flavors of Cape Cod
The Thornton W. Burgess Society
Sandwich, Massachusetts

Fresh Vegetable Relish

5 medium tomatoes, peeled
  and diced
1 medium-size green pepper,
  diced
1 small onion, diced
½ cup diced celery

⅓ cup water
2 tablespoons sugar
2 tablespoons white vinegar
1½ teaspoons salt
⅛ teaspoon pepper

Combine all ingredients in a medium bowl; stir well. Cover and chill before serving. Yield: 3½ cups.   Darlene Duerksen Goertz

The Thresher Table
The Bethel College Women's Association
North Newton, Kansas

Hog Dog Relish

5 medium onions, minced
  (about 4 cups)
1 small cabbage, minced
  (about 4 cups)
4 large green tomatoes,
  minced (about 2 cups)
4 large tomatoes, minced
  (about 2 cups)
6 large green peppers,
  minced (about 4 cups)

6 sweet red peppers, minced
  (about 4 cups)
½ cup salt
6 cups sugar
4 cups white vinegar (5%
  acidity)
1 cup water
2 tablespoons mustard seeds
1 tablespoon celery seeds
1½ teaspoons ground turmeric

Combine first 6 ingredients in a large bowl; stir well. Sprinkle with salt, and let stand at room temperature 8 hours. Drain well.

Combine sugar and remaining ingredients in a large saucepan; bring mixture to a boil. Add vegetable mixture, stirring well; reduce heat, and simmer 3 minutes. Using a slotted spoon, quickly spoon hot relish into hot sterilized jars, leaving ¼-inch headspace. Remove air bubbles; wipe jar rims. Cover at once with metal lids, and screw on bands. Process relish in boiling-water bath 10 minutes. Yield: 11 half pints.   Alice R. Widmeyer

Mountain Memories
The American Cancer Society, West Virginia Division, Inc.
Charleston, West Virginia

Disappearing Pickles

12 (5-inch) pickling
   cucumbers
4 large onions, sliced
4 cups sugar
4 cups cider vinegar

½ cup salt
1¼ teaspoons ground
   turmeric
1¼ teaspoons celery salt
1¼ teaspoons mustard seeds

Wash cucumbers, and cut into ¼-inch slices. Layer cucumber and onion slices in a 1-gallon jar. Combine sugar and remaining ingredients; stir well. Pour vinegar mixture over layered cucumber and onion. Cover and chill at least 24 hours. Yield: 1 gallon.

Palm Country Cuisine
The Junior League of Greater Lakeland, Florida

Soups & Stews

Chimney Rock in southwestern Nebraska marked the end of the easiest portion of the trail west. During the first half of the nineteenth century, Nebraska served primarily as a water and land route to the rich trapping country that lay to its north and west.

Chilled Minted Cantaloupe Soup

2½ cups cubed cantaloupe
1½ tablespoons sugar
1½ teaspoons chopped fresh
   mint

¼ cup Chablis or other dry
   white wine
3 tablespoons plain yogurt
Fresh mint sprigs

Combine cantaloupe, sugar, and chopped fresh mint in container of an electric blender or food processor; process until mixture is smooth. Transfer mixture to a medium bowl. Add wine and yogurt, stirring with a wire whisk until smooth. Cover and chill at least 2 hours. Ladle into individual soup bowls. Garnish each serving with a fresh mint sprig. Yield: 2 cups.   Eloise Meigs

An Apple a Day
The Auxiliary to the Boyd County Medical Society
Ashland, Kentucky

Summertime Cherry Soup

1 (16-ounce) can pitted sweet
   red cherries, undrained
1 cup water
¼ cup sugar
1 (2-inch) stick cinnamon
⅛ teaspoon ground cloves
⅛ teaspoon ground nutmeg

1 tablespoon cornstarch
2 tablespoons water
½ cup Burgundy or other dry
   red wine
2 tablespoons lemon juice
1 (8-ounce) carton sour cream

Drain cherries, reserving syrup. Set cherries aside. Combine syrup, 1 cup water, sugar, cinnamon stick, cloves, and nutmeg in a saucepan. Bring mixture to a boil; reduce heat, and simmer 5 minutes. Remove and discard cinnamon stick.

Combine cornstarch and 2 tablespoons water in a small bowl, stirring until smooth. Stir cornstarch mixture into syrup mixture; cook, stirring constantly, until slightly thickened. Remove from heat; add wine and lemon juice, stirring well. Let cool completely. Add sour cream, stirring well with a wire whisk. Add reserved cherries; stir well. Cover and chill thoroughly. Yield: 4 cups.

Make It Miami
The Guild of the Museum of Science, Inc.
Miami, Florida

Chilled Strawberry Soup

2 quarts strawberries, washed
and hulled
3 tablespoons fresh lemon
juice
3 cups water

1 cup sugar
2 tablespoons quick-cooking
tapioca
1 cup Sauterne or other sweet
white wine

Place strawberries in container of an electric blender or food processor; process until smooth.

Combine strawberry puree and next 4 ingredients in a medium saucepan. Bring mixture to a boil; cook 15 minutes, stirring occasionally. Remove from heat; stir in wine. Cover and chill 8 hours. Yield: 10 cups.   Carolyn Monfort Bernard

Educated Taste
The LaGrange College Alumni Association
LaGrange, Georgia

Carrot Vichyssoise

3 leeks
5 cups canned diluted
chicken broth
2 cups peeled, diced potatoes
1½ cups scraped, sliced
carrots

1 cup half-and-half
1 teaspoon salt
Dash of ground white pepper
Sour cream
Chopped fresh chives

Trim leeks to 3 inches in length, reserving remainder for other uses. Wash leeks; cut in half, and slice thin. Combine leeks, chicken broth, potatoes, and carrots in a large saucepan. Bring to a boil; reduce heat, and simmer 25 minutes or until vegetables are tender.

Pour half of vegetable mixture into container of an electric blender; process until smooth. Transfer to a large bowl. Repeat procedure with remaining vegetable mixture.

Add half-and-half, salt, and pepper; stir well. Cover and chill at least 4 hours. Garnish each serving with a dollop of sour cream and chopped fresh chives. Yield: 7½ cups.

Knollwood Cooks II
Christian Women's Guild, Knollwood United Methodist Church
Granada Hills, California

Iced Tomato Soup

6 large tomatoes, peeled, seeded, and chopped	2 tablespoons all-purpose flour
1 cup finely chopped onion	1 tablespoon tomato paste
¼ cup water	½ teaspoon sugar
½ teaspoon salt	1 cup whipping cream
⅛ teaspoon pepper	2 medium tomatoes, peeled and chopped
2 cups canned diluted chicken broth, divided	Fresh dillweed
	Fresh chives

Combine first 5 ingredients in a large Dutch oven. Bring to a boil; cover and boil 5 to 10 minutes or until onion is tender.

Combine ¼ cup chicken broth, flour, and tomato paste in a small bowl; stir well. Add to tomato mixture; cook, stirring constantly, until thickened. Remove from heat.

Transfer tomato mixture in batches to container of an electric blender or food processor; process until smooth. Return tomato mixture to Dutch oven. Stir in remaining 1¾ cups chicken broth and sugar. Cover and chill thoroughly.

Just before serving, stir in whipping cream and 2 chopped tomatoes. Ladle into individual soup bowls. Garnish with fresh dillweed and chives. Yield: 9 cups.   Carol Fields

Keeping the Feast
The Episcopal Church Women of St. Thomas Church
Abingdon, Virginia

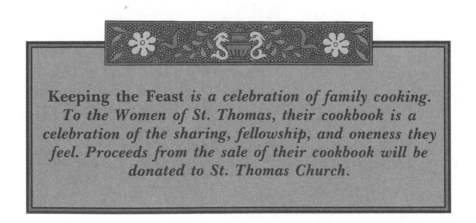

Keeping the Feast *is a celebration of family cooking. To the Women of St. Thomas, their cookbook is a celebration of the sharing, fellowship, and oneness they feel. Proceeds from the sale of their cookbook will be donated to St. Thomas Church.*

Summer Essence Soup

1 cup unpeeled, thinly sliced new potatoes
1 cup chopped green onions
¼ cup butter, melted
2 (14½-ounce) cans chicken broth, undiluted
1 large cucumber, peeled and diced
2 cups shredded lettuce
1 teaspoon chopped fresh dillweed
1 teaspoon salt
⅛ teaspoon ground white pepper
1 (8-ounce) carton plain yogurt
3 tablespoons fresh lemon juice
Radish slices

Sauté potato and green onions in melted butter in a medium saucepan 5 minutes. Stir in chicken broth, cucumber, shredded lettuce, chopped dillweed, salt, and white pepper. Bring mixture to a boil; cover, reduce heat, and simmer 15 minutes. Remove from heat, and stir in yogurt and lemon juice.

Pour half of vegetable mixture into container of an electric blender or food processor; process until smooth. Transfer to a large bowl. Repeat procedure with remaining vegetable mixture. Cover and chill. Ladle into individual soup bowls; garnish with radish slices. Yield: 7 cups.

CordonBluegrass
The Junior League of Louisville, Kentucky

Celery-Shrimp Bisque

2 cups peeled, diced potatoes
2 cups chopped celery
2 cups water
½ cup chopped onion
1 teaspoon salt
1 teaspoon pepper
4 cups half-and-half
¼ cup all-purpose flour
¾ pound medium-size fresh shrimp, peeled and deveined
½ cup chopped fresh parsley
¼ cup butter
½ teaspoon celery salt
½ teaspoon dried whole thyme, crushed
¼ cup dry sherry
10 medium-size fresh shrimp, cooked, peeled and deveined
Fresh celery leaves

Combine diced potato, chopped celery, water, chopped onion, salt, and pepper in a large Dutch oven. Bring vegetable mixture to a boil; cover, reduce heat, and simmer 10 minutes or until potatoes are tender.

Combine half-and-half and flour in a small bowl; stir until well blended. Add to potato mixture. Add ¾ pound shrimp, parsley, butter, celery salt, and thyme; cook over medium-high heat until thickened and bubbly. Stir in sherry.

Ladle into individual soup bowls. Garnish each serving with 1 shrimp and fresh celery leaves. Yield: 10 cups.   Jane Kreiner

Black-Eyed Susan Country
The Saint Agnes Hospital Auxiliary
Baltimore, Maryland

Velvety Brie Soup

1 (6-ounce) round
  fully-ripened Brie
2 medium carrots, scraped
  and finely chopped
¾ cup finely chopped celery
½ cup finely chopped onion
½ cup butter, melted
½ cup all-purpose flour
2 (15-ounce) cans chicken
  broth, diluted

1 teaspoon dried whole
  thyme
1 bay leaf
½ cup whipping cream
Commercial seasoned
  croutons
Chopped pimiento
Chopped fresh parsley

Remove and discard rind from cheese. Cut cheese into ½-inch cubes, and set aside.

Sauté carrot, celery, and onion in butter in a large saucepan until tender. Sprinkle flour over vegetable mixture; stir until well blended. Stir in chicken broth; cook until thickened and bubbly. Add thyme and bay leaf. Gradually add cubed cheese, stirring until cheese melts. Reduce heat to low, stir in whipping cream, and cook until thoroughly heated. Remove and discard bay leaf.

Ladle into individual soup bowls. Garnish each serving with croutons, pimiento, and parsley. Yield: 6 cups.

Hearts and Flours
The Junior League of Waco, Texas

Jarlsberg Vegetable Soup

3 tablespoons butter
3 tablespoons all-purpose flour
4 cups canned diluted
   chicken broth
2 cups coarsely chopped
   broccoli
¾ cup shredded carrot
½ cup chopped celery
1 small onion, chopped

1 small clove garlic, minced
¼ teaspoon dried whole
   thyme, crushed
½ teaspoon salt
⅛ teaspoon pepper
1 cup half-and-half
1 egg yolk, beaten
1½ cups (6 ounces) shredded
   Jarlsberg cheese

Melt butter in a saucepan over low heat; add flour, stirring until smooth. Cook 1 minute, stirring constantly. Add broth; cook over medium heat, stirring constantly, until thickened and bubbly. Add broccoli and next 7 ingredients; stir well. Cover, reduce heat, and simmer 20 to 25 minutes or until vegetables are tender. Combine half-and-half and egg yolk; stir well. Stir about one-fourth of hot mixture into yolk mixture; add to remaining hot mixture, stirring until thickened. Add cheese; stir until melted. Yield: 6 cups.

Albertina's II
The Albertina Kerr Centers for Children
Portland, Oregon

Zesty Zucchini Soup

3 cups water
7 chicken-flavored bouillon
   cubes
6 zucchini, sliced
2 carrots, scraped and sliced

1 small onion, sliced
1 (8-ounce) package cream
   cheese, cubed and softened
Salt and pepper to taste
Hot sauce to taste

Bring water to a boil in a Dutch oven; add bouillon cubes, stirring until dissolved. Add vegetables; reduce heat, and simmer 20 minutes or until tender. Pour into container of an electric blender; process until smooth. Return mixture to Dutch oven; stir in cream cheese, salt, pepper, and hot sauce. Cook over low heat, stirring until thoroughly heated. Serve hot or chilled. Yield: 8 cups.

South of the Fork
The Junior League of Dallas, Texas

Fresh Leek Soup

1½ cups finely chopped leeks
  with tops
1 cup chopped onion
1 clove garlic, minced
¼ cup plus 1 tablespoon
  butter, melted
4 cups canned diluted
  chicken broth

2 cups peeled, diced potatoes
1 cup half-and-half
Salt and pepper to taste
Chopped fresh parsley
  (optional)
Chopped green onions
  (optional)

Sauté leeks, onion, and garlic in butter in a large Dutch oven over medium-high heat until tender. Add chicken broth and potato; reduce heat, and simmer 20 minutes. Add half-and-half and salt and pepper to taste; stir well. Serve soup warm or chilled. If desired, garnish each serving with chopped fresh parsley or green onions. Yield: 5½ cups.   Patricia Pate

Sampler
The Women's Art Guild, Laguna Gloria Art Museum
Austin, Texas

Cream of Mushroom Soup

1 pound fresh mushrooms,
  sliced
1 medium onion, finely
  chopped
3 tablespoons butter, melted
¼ cup all-purpose flour
4 cups canned diluted
  chicken broth
2 cups whipping cream

¼ cup Chablis or other dry
  white wine
1½ teaspoons salt
1 teaspoon ground sage
1 teaspoon dried whole
  tarragon
¼ teaspoon freshly ground
  pepper
¼ teaspoon hot sauce

Sauté mushrooms and onion in butter in a large skillet over medium heat until tender; add flour, stirring until smooth. Cook 1 minute, stirring constantly. Add chicken broth and remaining ingredients. Bring mixture to a boil; reduce heat, and simmer 20 minutes. Yield: 8 cups.   Cheri Adams

Our Town Cookbook
The Historical Society of Peterborough, New Hampshire

Hearty Lentil Soup

8 cups water
5 chicken-flavored bouillon
  cubes
3 carrots, scraped
1 (28-ounce) can tomatoes,
  undrained and chopped
1½ cups dried lentils, washed
  and sorted
1 cup uncooked brown rice
1 onion, chopped
½ cup chopped celery

3 cloves garlic, minced
1 bay leaf
½ teaspoon dried whole basil
½ teaspoon dried whole
  oregano
¼ teaspoon dried whole
  thyme
½ cup minced fresh parsley
2 tablespoons cider vinegar
1 teaspoon salt
½ teaspoon pepper

Bring water to a boil in a large Dutch oven; add bouillon cubes, stirring until dissolved.

Cut carrots in half lengthwise; cut diagonally into ¼-inch slices. Add carrot and next 10 ingredients to Dutch oven; stir well. Bring to a boil; cover, reduce heat, and simmer 45 minutes. Stir in parsley, vinegar, salt, and pepper. Remove and discard bay leaf before serving. Yield: 14 cups.

Crème de la Congregation
Our Saviors Lutheran Church
Lafayette, California

Brazilian Black Bean Soup

2 cups dried black beans
3½ cups canned diluted
  chicken broth
2 teaspoons salt
1 cup chopped onion
1 cup chopped green pepper
1 stalk celery, chopped
1 large carrot, scraped and
  chopped
3 cloves garlic, crushed
2 tablespoons vegetable oil
3 tablespoons water

1½ teaspoons ground cumin
1 teaspoon ground coriander
2 oranges, peeled and
  sectioned
½ cup orange juice
1 tablespoon dry sherry
½ teaspoon fresh lemon
  juice
¼ teaspoon ground red
  pepper
¼ teaspoon pepper
Sour cream or plain yogurt

Sort and wash beans; place in a large Dutch oven. Cover with water 2 inches above beans; let soak 20 to 24 hours. Drain beans, and return to Dutch oven. Add chicken broth and salt. Bring to a boil; cover, reduce heat, and simmer 1½ hours.

Sauté onion, green pepper, celery, carrot, and garlic in oil in a skillet over medium heat until tender. Stir in 3 tablespoons water. Add cumin and coriander, stirring well; cook 5 minutes. Add vegetable mixture to beans; simmer 10 minutes. Add orange and next 5 ingredients; stir well. Cover and simmer 10 minutes. Ladle into individual soup bowls. Top each serving with a dollop of sour cream. Yield: 8 cups.   Beverly Boyd

From the Hills
The Lutheran Church of Vestavia Hills, Alabama

Chicken-Rice Soup

1 (2-pound) broiler-fryer
5½ cups water
1 onion, quartered
12 (2-inch) celery stalk tops
  with leaves
6 sprigs fresh parsley
1 bay leaf
2 (14½-ounce) cans tomatoes,
  undrained and chopped
1 cup diced carrot

1 cup diced onion
1 cup diced green pepper
1 cup peeled, diced potato
½ cup uncooked long-grain
  rice
2 (.19-ounce) packages instant
  chicken broth
1 tablespoon salt
½ teaspoon pepper

Combine first 6 ingredients in a large Dutch oven. Bring to a boil; cover, reduce heat, and simmer 1 hour or until chicken is tender. Strain; reserve broth. Remove and discard onion, celery, parsley, and bay leaf. Remove and discard skin from chicken. Bone chicken, and finely chop meat; set aside. Combine chicken broth, tomatoes, and remaining ingredients in Dutch oven. Bring to a boil; cover, reduce heat, and simmer 30 minutes. Add chicken; cover and cook over medium heat 15 minutes or until vegetables are tender. Yield: 12 cups.   Isabel C. Massei

The Oaks Cookbook
Colonel Timothy Bigelow Chapter, DAR
Worcester, Massachusetts

Corn Off the Cob Chowder

1 cup chopped onion
2 tablespoons butter, melted
½ cup chopped green
  pepper
½ cup chopped sweet red
  pepper
4 cups fresh cut corn (5 or 6
  ears)
½ teaspoon salt

½ teaspoon dried whole basil
¼ teaspoon dried whole
  thyme
¼ teaspoon freshly ground
  pepper
1 cup canned diluted chicken
  broth
1 cup evaporated milk

Sauté chopped onion in melted butter in a heavy saucepan until tender. Add green pepper and next 6 ingredients, stirring well. Cover, reduce heat, and simmer 5 minutes. Add chicken broth, and simmer 10 minutes.

Place half of vegetable mixture in container of an electric blender or food processor, and process until mixture is smooth. Return puree to saucepan; stir well. Add milk, and cook just until thoroughly heated. Yield: 5 cups.

License to Cook New Mexico Style
New Mexico Federation of Business and Professional Women
Albuquerque, New Mexico

Puerto Penasco Fish Chowder

¼ cup butter or vegetable oil
2 medium onions, chopped
1 clove garlic, minced
½ pound fresh mushrooms,
  sliced
1 medium-size green pepper,
  cut into julienne strips
1 sweet red pepper, cut into
  julienne strips
1 tablespoon lemon juice
2 (10¾-ounce) cans chicken
  broth, undiluted
1 (28-ounce) can whole tomatoes,
  undrained and chopped

2 potatoes, peeled and
  cubed
¾ cup clam juice
½ cup Chablis or other dry
  white wine
2 pounds sole or other fish
  fillets, cut into 1-inch
  pieces
1 (6½-ounce) can chopped
  clams, drained
½ cup minced fresh parsley
Salt and pepper to taste
Grated Parmesan cheese
Lemon wedges

Melt butter in a large Dutch oven. Add onion, garlic, mushrooms, peppers, and lemon juice; cook over medium-high heat, stirring frequently, 5 minutes or until vegetables are tender. Add chicken broth, tomatoes, potatoes, clam juice, and wine; bring mixture to a boil. Cover, reduce heat, and simmer 15 minutes or until potatoes are tender.

Add fish, clams, and minced fresh parsley to vegetable mixture; stir well. Return to a boil; cover, reduce heat, and simmer 5 minutes or until fish flakes easily when tested with a fork. Add salt and pepper to taste. Ladle chowder into individual soup bowls. Sprinkle each serving with Parmesan cheese. Serve with lemon wedges. Yield: 14 cups.

Palm Country Cuisine
The Junior League of Greater Lakeland, Florida

Firehouse Chowder

1 cup chopped onion
1 cup chopped celery
1 cup chopped green pepper
1 cup peeled, diced potato
1 cup scraped, diced carrot
1 clove garlic, minced
3 tablespoons butter or margarine
2 (10¾-ounce) cans chicken broth, undiluted
1 (17-ounce) can cream-style corn
1 (6½-ounce) can salmon, drained
1 (6½-ounce) can chopped clams, drained
¼ teaspoon dried whole thyme
1½ teaspoons salt
⅛ teaspoon pepper
1 (12-ounce) can evaporated milk

Combine all ingredients except evaporated milk in a large Dutch oven; stir well. Bring to a boil; cover, reduce heat to medium, and cook 1 to 1½ hours or until potatoes are tender.

Add evaporated milk to chowder, stirring well; cook just until thoroughly heated (do not boil). Ladle chowder into individual soup bowls. Yield: 9 cups.   The Family of Elizabeth Ewing

Symphony of Tastes
The Youth Symphony of Anchorage, Alaska

Seafood Chowder

6 cups peeled, diced potatoes
1½ pounds cod or halibut
  fillets
2 quarts milk, divided
1 pound bacon
2 cups finely chopped onions
2 cups finely chopped celery
½ cup chopped sweet red
  pepper

½ cup chopped green pepper
¼ cup chopped fresh parsley
2 tablespoons butter
2 teaspoons salt
½ teaspoon garlic salt
½ teaspoon pepper
⅛ teaspoon ground red
  pepper

Cook potatoes in boiling water to cover just until tender; drain well. Set aside.

Place fish in a single layer in a large skillet; add 1 quart milk. Cook over medium heat just until milk begins to simmer. Cover and simmer 8 minutes or until fish flakes easily when tested with a fork. Remove from heat, and set aside.

Cook bacon in skillet over medium-high heat until crisp. Drain, reserving ¼ cup drippings in pan. Crumble bacon; set aside.

Sauté chopped onion, chopped celery, chopped red and green peppers, and chopped parsley in reserved bacon drippings in skillet until vegetables are tender. Transfer sautéed vegetable mixture to a large Dutch oven. Add cooked potato, fish mixture, crumbled bacon, remaining 1 quart milk, butter, and remaining ingredients; stir well. Simmer 20 minutes. Ladle chowder into individual soup bowls. Yield: 19 cups.   Marie and Charles Jones

Chestnut Hill Cookbook
The Chestnut Hill Senior Services Center
Philadelphia, Pennsylvania

Oyster Chowder

½ cup chopped carrot
½ cup chopped celery
½ cup chopped onion
½ cup peeled, diced potato
3 tablespoons unsalted butter,
  melted
1 (12-ounce) container
  Standard oysters, drained

2 cups whipping
  cream
¼ teaspoon dried whole
  tarragon
Dash of hot sauce
Salt and pepper to taste
Chopped fresh parsley
  (optional)

Sauté carrot, celery, onion, and potato in melted butter in a large saucepan over medium heat. Add oysters; cook until edges of oysters begin to curl. Stir in whipping cream; bring mixture just to a boil. Add tarragon; reduce heat, and simmer, uncovered, 30 seconds. Add hot sauce and salt and pepper to taste; stir well. Ladle chowder into individual soup bowls. Sprinkle each serving with chopped fresh parsley, if desired. Yield: 4 cups.

Spokane Cooks!
The Community Centers Foundation of Spokane, Washington

Louisiana Shrimp and Corn Gumbo

¼ cup plus 1 tablespoon olive oil
¼ cup plus 1 tablespoon all-purpose flour
2 cups finely chopped onions
1 medium-size green pepper, finely chopped
4 shallots, chopped
2 tablespoons minced fresh parsley
1 tablespoon dried whole basil
1 teaspoon Cajun seasoning
⅛ teaspoon ground red pepper
⅛ teaspoon hot pepper sauce
⅛ teaspoon Worcestershire sauce
Salt and pepper to taste
3 cups canned diluted chicken broth
1 (16-ounce) package frozen whole kernel corn, thawed
1 (14½-ounce) can tomatoes, undrained and chopped
2 pounds medium-size fresh shrimp, peeled

Combine olive oil and flour in a large Dutch oven; cook over medium heat, stirring constantly, until mixture is caramel colored. Stir in onion, green pepper, shallots, and parsley; cook over low heat 10 minutes or until onion is tender. Add basil, Cajun seasoning, ground red pepper, hot pepper sauce, Worcestershire sauce, and salt and pepper to taste, stirring well; simmer, uncovered, 5 minutes. Add chicken broth, corn, and tomatoes; stir well. Cover and simmer 1 hour and 15 minutes. Stir in shrimp; cover and cook 10 minutes or until shrimp turn pink. Yield: 10 cups.

Celebrations on the Bayou
The Junior League of Monroe, Louisiana

Old-Time Beef Stew

2 pounds beef stew meat
2 tablespoons vegetable oil
3 cups water
1 teaspoon Worcestershire sauce
1 medium onion, sliced
1 tablespoon salt
1 clove garlic
1 or 2 bay leaves
1 teaspoon sugar
½ teaspoon paprika

¼ teaspoon pepper
Dash of ground allspice or ground cloves
6 medium carrots, scraped and quartered
5 medium potatoes, peeled and quartered
1 pound pearl onions, peeled
¼ cup water
2 tablespoons all-purpose flour

Brown beef on all sides in hot oil in a Dutch oven. Add 3 cups water and next 9 ingredients. Bring to a boil; cover, reduce heat, and simmer 1½ hours, stirring occasionally. Remove and discard garlic clove and bay leaves. Add vegetables; cover and simmer 30 to 45 minutes or until vegetables are tender. Remove beef and vegetables with a slotted spoon; set aside, and keep warm. Drain off fat from drippings; reserve 1¾ cups drippings in Dutch oven. Combine ¼ cup water and flour; stir until smooth. Add to reserved drippings, stirring constantly. Cook over medium heat 3 minutes or until thickened, stirring occasionally. Return meat and vegetables to Dutch oven; stir to combine. Yield: 9 cups.   Pam Holley

The Florida Cooking Adventure
The Florida Federation of Women's Clubs
Lakeland, Florida

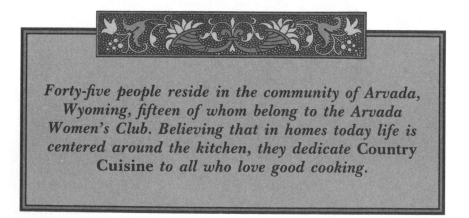

Forty-five people reside in the community of Arvada, Wyoming, fifteen of whom belong to the Arvada Women's Club. Believing that in homes today life is centered around the kitchen, they dedicate Country Cuisine *to all who love good cooking.*

Spiced Kettle of Beef and Vegetables

1 whole clove
1 teaspoon mixed pickling
  spices
½ cup all-purpose flour
1 tablespoon salt
1 tablespoon pepper
½ teaspoon paprika
2 pounds boneless beef
  chuck, cut into 1-inch
  cubes
2 tablespoons olive oil
1 cup chopped onion
1 clove garlic, minced
6¼ cups water, divided
3 (16-ounce) cans whole
  tomatoes, drained
3 cups peeled, diced
  potatoes

2 cups diced carrots
1 cup sliced celery
1 cup frozen English peas,
  thawed
2 tablespoons chopped fresh
  chives
1 tablespoon soy sauce
1 tablespoon Worcestershire
  sauce
1 teaspoon sugar
¼ teaspoon pepper
⅛ teaspoon dried whole basil
⅛ teaspoon dried whole
  thyme
1 bay leaf
3 tablespoons cornstarch

Place whole clove and pickling spices on a piece of cheesecloth; tie ends securely. Set spice bag aside.

Combine flour, salt, pepper, and paprika in a medium bowl; dredge beef cubes in flour mixture. Brown beef in hot olive oil in a large Dutch oven. Add chopped onion, minced garlic, and 6 cups water. Bring beef mixture to a boil; cover, reduce heat, and simmer 30 minutes.

Add spice bag, tomatoes, potato, carrot, celery, peas, chives, soy sauce, Worcestershire sauce, sugar, ¼ teaspoon pepper, basil, thyme, and bay leaf; stir well. Simmer 1½ hours or until meat is tender. Remove and discard spice bag and bay leaf. Remove 1 cup broth from stew. Combine broth, remaining ¼ cup water, and cornstarch in a small bowl; stir until blended. Add cornstarch mixture to stew, stirring well. Simmer stew until slightly thickened and thoroughly heated. Yield: 12 cups.   Sherry Angerhofer

Country Cuisine
The Women's Club of Arvada, Wyoming

Veal Marengo

3 pounds boneless veal, cut
  into 1-inch cubes
2 tablespoons vegetable oil
2 tablespoons olive oil
2 tablespoons all-purpose
  flour
Salt and pepper to taste
2 cups canned diluted
  chicken broth
1 cup Chablis or other dry
  white wine
3 tablespoons tomato paste
1 clove garlic, minced
2 fresh parsley sprigs
1 bay leaf
2 to 3 teaspoons chopped
  fresh thyme

2 tablespoons butter or
  margarine
20 pearl onions, peeled
1 tablespoon sugar
1 pound fresh mushrooms,
  sliced
2 medium carrots, scraped
  and sliced
1 (14-ounce) can whole
  tomatoes, undrained and
  chopped
1 tablespoon minced fresh
  parsley
Hot cooked rice

Brown veal in vegetable and olive oils in a large Dutch oven. Add flour and salt and pepper to taste, stirring well; cook 3 minutes. Add chicken broth and next 6 ingredients; stir well. Bring to a boil; cover, reduce heat, and simmer 1 hour, stirring occasionally.

Melt butter in a large skillet. Add onions and sugar, and cook until onions are lightly browned. Add mushrooms, and cook until lightly browned. Add onion mixture and carrot to veal mixture; simmer 30 to 45 minutes or until carrot is almost tender. Stir in tomatoes, and simmer 15 minutes or until carrot is tender. Remove and discard parsley sprigs and bay leaf.

Sprinkle minced fresh parsley over hot cooked rice. Serve stew over rice. Yield: 8 cups.   Debbie Drake

The Cooks' Book
The Nightingale-Bamford School
New York, New York

Vegetables

A farmer transports a profusion of fresh vegetables from a field in Dover, New Hampshire. Dover, located at the falls of the Coheco River near its junction with the Piscataqua River, was originally settled in 1623 by fishermen and traders. It was first known as Bristol.

Asparagus Flans

3 slices white bread, toasted
¾ cup fresh tiny English
  peas
18 large fresh asparagus
  spears (about 1½ pounds)
2 quarts water
3 eggs
2⅓ cups crème fraîche,
  divided

Salt and freshly ground
  pepper to taste
2 tablespoons chopped onion
¼ cup unsalted butter, melted
  and divided
⅛ teaspoon curry powder

Lightly butter six (6-ounce) custard cups; set aside.

Remove crust from toast, reserve for other uses. Cut each slice of toast into 2 triangles; set aside.

Cook peas in a small amount of boiling water 10 to 12 minutes or until tender; drain and set aside.

Snap off tough ends of asparagus. Remove scales from stalks with a knife or vegetable peeler, if desired. Bring 2 quarts water to a boil in the bottom of a double boiler. Tie asparagus spears in a bunch with cord. Place asparagus upright in top of double boiler. Cover and cook 6 to 8 minutes or until tender. Drain well. Cut off tips of asparagus; set tips aside.

Position knife blade in food processor bowl. Combine asparagus stalks, eggs, and 1 cup crème fraîche in processor bowl; process 1 minute or until smooth. Press mixture through a sieve; discard pulp. Add salt and pepper to taste. Pour into prepared custard cups. Place cups in a large shallow baking dish. Pour hot water to a depth of 1 inch into dish. Bake at 325° for 30 minutes or until a knife inserted near center comes out clean. Set aside, and keep warm.

Sauté chopped onion in 2 tablespoons melted butter in a skillet until tender. Add remaining 1⅓ cups crème fraîche and curry powder; simmer 3 minutes.

Combine onion mixture, peas, and remaining 2 tablespoons melted butter in processor bowl; process 30 seconds or until smooth. Divide sauce evenly among 6 individual salad plates.

To serve, loosen edges of flans with a spatula; invert onto salad plates. Top each flan with 3 asparagus tips. Place a toast triangle beside each flan. Serve immediately. Yield: 6 servings.

One Magnificent Cookbook
The Junior League of Chicago, Illinois

Green Beans with Almonds and Basil

1 pound fresh green beans
3 tablespoons slivered
blanched almonds
3 tablespoons butter,
melted

1½ tablespoons minced
fresh parsley
1 teaspoon minced fresh
basil

Wash beans and remove strings. Cover and cook in a small amount of boiling water 10 to 12 minutes or until crisp-tender. Drain well.

Sauté almonds in butter in a small skillet until lightly browned. Stir in fresh parsley and basil. Pour over green beans, tossing gently. Yield: 4 servings.   Mary Jo Mason

Diamonds in the Desert
The Woman's League of Ozona, Texas

Those Good Green Beans

2 (9-ounce) packages frozen
French-style green beans
½ cup chopped onion
2 tablespoons butter, melted
2 tablespoons all-purpose
flour

1 teaspoon salt
¼ teaspoon pepper
1 (8-ounce) carton sour cream
1½ cups (6 ounces) shredded
sharp Cheddar cheese

Cook green beans according to package directions; drain well, and set aside.

Sauté onion in butter in a large skillet until tender. Stir in flour, salt, and pepper. Add sour cream; stir well. Cook over medium heat, stirring constantly, until thickened and bubbly (do not boil). Remove from heat; stir in green beans.

Pour green bean mixture into a buttered 2-quart casserole. Sprinkle with cheese, and bake at 350° for 30 minutes or until hot and bubbly. Yield: 6 servings.

Make It Miami
The Guild of the Museum of Science, Inc.
Miami, Florida

Beans Breton with Tomatoes

1 pound dried navy beans
8 cups water
Salt and pepper to taste
2 whole cloves
1 onion, peeled
1 carrot, scraped
2 sprigs fresh parsley
1 clove garlic
1 bay leaf

1 cup finely chopped onion
1 tablespoon minced garlic
¼ cup butter, melted
2 cups crushed Italian-style
   tomatoes
1 teaspoon chopped fresh
   thyme
¼ cup chopped fresh parsley

Sort and wash beans; place in a large Dutch oven. Cover with water 2 inches above beans; let soak 8 hours. Drain and return to Dutch oven. Add 8 cups water and salt and pepper to taste; stir well. Insert whole cloves into onion; add onion to beans. Add carrot, parsley sprigs, 1 garlic clove, and bay leaf; stir well. Bring to a boil; cover, reduce heat, and simmer 1 hour or until beans are tender. Drain beans, reserving 1 cup liquid. Remove and discard vegetables, parsley sprigs, garlic clove, and bay leaf. Set beans aside.

Sauté chopped onion and minced garlic in butter in a skillet until tender. Stir in tomatoes and thyme. Bring to a boil; cover, reduce heat, and simmer 15 minutes. Add reserved liquid and beans. Bring to a boil; cover, reduce heat, and simmer 15 minutes. Sprinkle with chopped parsley. Yield: 6 to 8 servings.   Elizabeth Leete

The Ashfield Cookbook
The Ladies' Circle of the First Congregational Church
Ashfield, Massachusetts

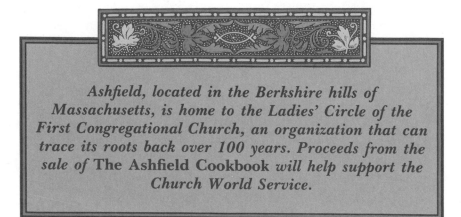

Ashfield, located in the Berkshire hills of Massachusetts, is home to the Ladies' Circle of the First Congregational Church, an organization that can trace its roots back over 100 years. Proceeds from the sale of **The Ashfield Cookbook** *will help support the Church World Service.*

Broccoli with Lemon Sauce and Pecans

1½ pounds fresh broccoli
⅓ cup chopped pecans
1 tablespoon butter, melted
½ cup canned diluted
  chicken broth
1 tablespoon sugar

1 tablespoon grated lemon
  rind
¼ cup lemon juice
2 teaspoons cornstarch
¼ teaspoon pepper

Trim off large leaves of broccoli, and remove tough ends of lower stalks. Wash broccoli thoroughly, and cut into spears. Cook in a small amount of boiling water 10 to 12 minutes or until crisp-tender. Drain. Transfer broccoli to a serving bowl, and keep warm.

Sauté pecans in butter until lightly browned. Remove from heat, and set aside.

Combine broth and remaining ingredients in a saucepan; stir well. Bring to a boil over medium heat, and cook until thickened. Pour sauce over broccoli; sprinkle with pecans. Serve immediately. Yield: 4 to 6 servings.   Carolyn Monfort Bernard

Educated Taste
The LaGrange College Alumni Association
LaGrange, Georgia

Sweet-and-Sour Brussels Sprouts

4 slices bacon, diced
2 (10-ounce) packages frozen
  brussels sprouts, thawed
¼ cup diced onion
¼ cup white vinegar

2 tablespoons sugar
1 teaspoon salt
1 teaspoon pepper
¼ teaspoon dry mustard

Fry bacon in a skillet until crisp. Drain bacon, and set aside, reserving drippings in skillet. Add brussels sprouts and remaining ingredients to drippings in skillet. Cover and cook over medium heat, stirring occasionally, 10 minutes or until brussels sprouts are crisp-tender. Stir in bacon. Yield: 6 servings.   Phyllis Siler

A Cook's Book of Recipes from the Pacific Northwest
The Rosehill Community Center
Mukilteo, Washington

Red Cabbage

2½ pounds red cabbage,
  shredded
3 large cooking apples,
  peeled and sliced
2 large onions, sliced
¾ cup boiling water
½ cup red currant jelly
¼ cup firmly packed brown
  sugar

1 tablespoon butter
1 bay leaf
2 teaspoons salt
¼ teaspoon pepper
¼ cup white vinegar
1½ tablespoons all-purpose
  flour

Combine cabbage and cold water to cover in a Dutch oven. Let stand 15 minutes; drain. Add apple and next 8 ingredients; bring to a boil over medium heat. Combine vinegar and flour, stirring until smooth; gradually stir into cabbage mixture. Cook, stirring constantly, until slightly thickened. Reduce heat, and simmer, uncovered, 2 hours. Remove bay leaf. Yield: 8 to 10 servings.

Libretto
The Opera Society of Fort Lauderdale, Florida

Carrots with Herbs

1 tablespoon minced onion
½ clove garlic, minced
1½ tablespoons butter, melted
1 tablespoon olive oil
1 pound carrots, scraped and
  thinly sliced
½ cup Chablis or other dry
  white wine
1 bay leaf

1½ tablespoons chopped
  fresh parsley
1½ tablespoons chopped
  fresh basil
½ teaspoon salt
⅛ teaspoon freshly ground
  pepper
⅛ teaspoon freshly grated
  nutmeg

Sauté onion and garlic in butter and oil until tender. Add carrot; sauté 5 minutes. Add wine and bay leaf; cover, reduce heat to medium, and simmer 10 minutes. Add parsley and remaining ingredients. Cook, uncovered, until carrots are crisp-tender. Remove bay leaf. Yield: 6 servings.

Keeping the Feast
The Episcopal Church Women of St. Thomas Church
Abingdon, Virginia

Carrots in Mustard Sauce

1 (12-ounce) package baby
  carrots, scraped
1 tablespoon butter
1 tablespoon all-purpose flour
1 cup milk or half-and-half

1 teaspoon prepared mustard
½ teaspoon salt
⅛ teaspoon pepper
1 tablespoon chopped fresh
  chives

Cook carrots in a small amount of boiling salted water 10 to 12 minutes or until crisp-tender. Drain well; set aside. Melt butter in a saucepan over low heat; add flour, stirring until smooth. Cook 1 minute, stirring constantly. Gradually add milk; cook over medium heat, stirring constantly, until thickened and bubbly. Stir in mustard, salt, and pepper. Pour over carrots; toss gently. Sprinkle with chives. Yield: 4 servings.   Shirley Barfield

Columbus Collection
Magnolia Homes Tour
Columbus, Texas

Cauliflower Gratin with Chiles and Cheese

1 large cauliflower
2 tablespoons butter
1½ cups (6 ounces) shredded
  Monterey Jack cheese
1 (8-ounce) carton sour cream
1 (4-ounce) can chopped
  green chiles, drained

½ cup diced onion
1 teaspoon salt
¼ teaspoon pepper
2 tablespoons butter, melted
½ cup fine, dry breadcrumbs

Remove large outer leaves and stalk of cauliflower. Break cauliflower into flowerets. Cover and cook in a small amount of boiling water 10 to 12 minutes or until tender; drain. Combine next 7 ingredients; stir well. Add cauliflower, tossing gently. Spoon into a buttered 2-quart baking dish. Combine melted butter and breadcrumbs; stir well. Sprinkle over casserole. Bake at 350° for 25 to 30 minutes or until lightly browned. Yield: 6 to 8 servings.

Jackson Hole à la Carte
The Jackson Hole Alliance for Responsible Planning
Jackson, Wyoming

Crusty-Topped Cauliflower

1 large cauliflower
½ cup mayonnaise
2 tablespoons Dijon
  mustard

¾ cup (3 ounces) shredded
  Cheddar cheese

Remove large outer leaves and stalk of cauliflower, leaving head whole. Wash cauliflower.

Place cauliflower in a large saucepan. Cover and cook in a small amount of boiling water 15 to 20 minutes or until tender; drain well. Place cauliflower in a 9-inch square baking pan.

Combine mayonnaise and mustard in a small bowl; stir well. Spread mayonnaise mixture evenly over cauliflower, and sprinkle with shredded cheese. Bake at 350° for 10 minutes or until cheese melts. Yield: 6 servings. Rikki Morrow

Gingerbread . . . and all the trimmings
The Junior Service League of Waxahachie, Texas

Celery Amandine

2 (2-ounce) packages slivered
  blanched almonds
¼ cup plus 2 tablespoons
  butter, melted and divided
4 cups diagonally sliced
  celery

1 clove garlic, crushed
2 tablespoons grated onion
2 tablespoons chopped green
  onions
2 tablespoons Chablis or
  other dry white wine

Sauté slivered almonds in 2 tablespoons melted butter in a small skillet until almonds are golden brown. Set aside, and keep warm.

Sauté celery in remaining ¼ cup melted butter in a large skillet over medium-high heat until crisp-tender. Add garlic, grated onion, chopped green onions, and wine; stir well. Cover, reduce heat, and simmer 10 minutes.

Add sautéed almonds to celery mixture, stirring well. Serve immediately. Yield: 4 to 6 servings.

The Gathering
The Blue Bird Circle
Houston, Texas

Maque Choux

4 large ears fresh corn
6 slices bacon
1 tablespoon vegetable oil
1 large onion, chopped
1 medium-size green pepper,
  chopped
1 clove garlic, minced
5 large ripe tomatoes, peeled
  and chopped

½ cup tomato juice
½ teaspoon salt
½ teaspoon pepper
½ teaspoon hot sauce
¼ cup water
3 yellow squash, sliced

Cut corn from cobs, scraping cobs well to remove milk. Set corn aside. Fry bacon in a skillet until crisp; drain bacon, reserving 3 tablespoons drippings in skillet. Crumble bacon, and set aside.

Add oil to drippings, and sauté onion, green pepper, and garlic until tender. Add tomato and next 4 ingredients; stir well. Bring to a boil; cover, reduce heat to medium, and simmer 30 minutes. Add corn and water. Cook, uncovered, 15 minutes, stirring occasionally. Add squash, and cook 12 to 15 minutes or until squash is tender. Stir in bacon. Yield: 10 to 12 servings.   Venita Scott

The Bishop's Bounty
St. Mary's Training School for Retarded Children
Alexandria, Louisiana

Grilled Corn with Chili Butter

½ cup butter, softened
1 teaspoon chili powder

4 ears fresh corn

Position knife blade in food processor bowl. Add butter and chili powder; process until smooth. Pull back husks from corn, leaving husks attached at base of cob; remove silks. Rinse corn, and pat dry. Spread 1 tablespoon Chili Butter over each ear; pull husks up over corn. Place each ear on a piece of heavy-duty aluminum foil; wrap tightly. Grill foil-wrapped ears of corn over hot coals 40 minutes or until tender, turning frequently. Serve corn with remaining Chili Butter. Yield: 4 servings.

South of the Fork
The Junior League of Dallas, Texas

Stuffed Eggplant

1 large eggplant
1 cup water
½ teaspoon salt
1 cup chopped fresh
  mushrooms
3 tablespoons chopped onion
1 clove garlic, minced
3 tablespoons butter, melted

Salt and pepper to taste
½ cup whipping cream
2 tablespoons fine, dry
  breadcrumbs or cracker
  crumbs
2 slices bacon, diced
  (optional)

Wash eggplant; cut in half lengthwise. Remove pulp, leaving a ¼-inch shell. Chop pulp, and set aside. Place eggplant shells in a 2-quart baking dish; set aside.

Combine chopped eggplant pulp, water, and ½ teaspoon salt in a saucepan. Bring to a boil; cover, reduce heat, and simmer 10 minutes or until eggplant is tender. Drain well, and set aside.

Sauté mushrooms, onion, and garlic in butter in a medium skillet until tender. Add eggplant, salt and pepper to taste, and whipping cream; stir well. Spoon into shells; sprinkle with breadcrumbs and, if desired, diced bacon. Bake at 350° for 45 minutes or until thoroughly heated. Yield: 4 servings.   Mary Conway

Sampler
The Women's Art Guild, Laguna Gloria Art Museum
Austin, Texas

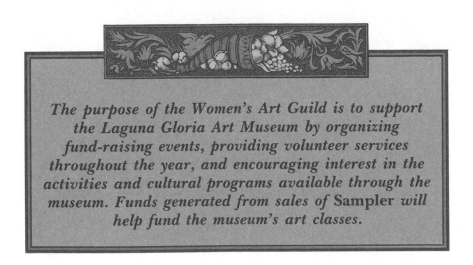

The purpose of the Women's Art Guild is to support the Laguna Gloria Art Museum by organizing fund-raising events, providing volunteer services throughout the year, and encouraging interest in the activities and cultural programs available through the museum. Funds generated from sales of Sampler *will help fund the museum's art classes.*

Elegant Onions

4 pounds boiling onions,
  quartered
½ cup plus 2 tablespoons
  butter
¼ cup plus 2 tablespoons
  all-purpose flour
2 cups canned diluted beef or
  chicken broth

2 tablespoons brown sugar
2 teaspoons Worcestershire
  sauce
Dash of pepper
½ teaspoon paprika
¼ cup slivered blanched
  almonds, toasted

Cook onions in boiling salted water 12 to 15 minutes or until tender. Drain well. Place onions in a 3-quart baking dish.

Melt butter in a heavy saucepan over low heat; add flour, stirring until smooth. Cook 1 minute, stirring constantly. Gradually add broth; cook over medium heat, stirring constantly, until mixture is thickened and bubbly. Stir in brown sugar, Worcestershire sauce, and pepper. Pour sauce over onions. Sprinkle evenly with paprika. Cover and bake at 375° for 20 to 25 minutes or until casserole is hot and bubbly. Sprinkle top evenly with toasted almonds. Yield: 6 to 8 servings.

Only in California
The Children's Home Society of California
Los Angeles, California

Parsnips with Almonds

1½ pounds fresh parsnips,
  scraped and sliced
1 egg, lightly beaten
3 tablespoons butter or
  margarine

¼ teaspoon ground nutmeg
⅛ teaspoon pepper
¼ cup slivered blanched
  almonds, toasted

Cook parsnips in boiling salted water 10 minutes or until tender. Drain well, and mash. Add egg, butter, nutmeg, and pepper, and stir well. Spoon parsnip mixture into an ungreased 1-quart casserole. Sprinkle top evenly with toasted almonds. Bake at 325° for 30 minutes. Yield: 4 servings.   Elizabeth Porter

Our Town Cookbook
The Historical Society of Peterborough, New Hampshire

Potatoes with Three Peppers

3 pounds potatoes, peeled
and cut into ½-inch cubes
3 tablespoons vegetable oil
⅓ cup cubed sweet yellow
pepper
⅓ cup cubed sweet red
pepper

⅓ cup cubed green pepper
⅓ cup chopped green onions
½ teaspoon salt
¼ teaspoon freshly ground
pepper
1 tablespoon butter

Blanch potatoes in boiling water to cover 3 to 5 minutes; drain well. Sauté potato in oil in a large skillet over medium-high heat 10 minutes. Add sweet yellow pepper and next 5 ingredients; sauté 3 minutes, stirring gently. Add butter, and sauté 2 minutes or until peppers are crisp-tender and potatoes are lightly browned. Serve immediately. Yield: 10 to 12 servings.

The Little Gourmet Cookbook for Children
The Auxiliary of the Children's Hospital of Philadelphia,
Pennsylvania

Golden Potato Squares

5 pounds potatoes
1½ cups chopped onions
⅔ cup butter, melted
1 cup evaporated milk
4 eggs, lightly beaten

2½ teaspoons salt
¼ teaspoon pepper
1½ cups (6 ounces) shredded
Cheddar cheese, divided
¼ cup chopped fresh parsley

Peel and shred potatoes. Place in a bowl with cold water to cover; set aside. Sauté onion in butter in a skillet until tender. Add evaporated milk, and cook just until mixture begins to simmer. Remove from heat, and set aside.

Combine eggs, salt, and pepper; stir well. Drain potatoes; add to egg mixture, stirring well. Add 1 cup cheese and parsley; stir well. Stir in milk mixture. Pour into a 13- x 9- x 2-inch baking dish. Bake at 350° for 1 hour. Sprinkle with remaining ½ cup cheese. Bake an additional 30 minutes or until potatoes are tender. Cut into squares. Yield: 12 servings.   St. Aloysius, Lisbon

Heritage Cookbook
The Catholic Diocese of Fargo, North Dakota

Mashed Potato Casserole

10 medium-size red potatoes,
    peeled and quartered
1 (8-ounce) package cream
    cheese, softened
¼ cup sour cream

¼ cup milk
Salt and pepper to taste
2 to 3 tablespoons butter or
    margarine, melted

Cook potatoes in boiling water to cover 15 minutes or until tender. Drain well, and mash. Add cream cheese, sour cream, milk, and salt and pepper to taste; beat at medium speed of an electric mixer just until smooth.

Spoon potato mixture into a greased 13- x 9- x 2-inch baking dish. Drizzle top evenly with melted butter. Bake at 350° for 30 minutes or until potatoes are lightly browned. Serve immediately. Yield: 8 to 10 servings.   Bonnie L. Jones

Shamrock Specialties
The Trinity High School Foundation
Louisville, Kentucky

Tasty Yams

4 medium yams or sweet
    potatoes, peeled and
    sliced
2 cooking apples, peeled
    and sliced
¼ cup firmly packed dark
    brown sugar

⅛ teaspoon ground nutmeg
⅛ teaspoon ground cinnamon
¼ cup dry or sweet sherry
¼ cup maple-flavored syrup

Layer half each of yam and apple slices in a greased 2-quart baking dish; repeat layers.

Combine brown sugar, nutmeg, and cinnamon in a small bowl; stir well. Add sherry and syrup, stirring well.

Pour syrup mixture evenly over layers of yams and apples. Cover and bake at 350° for 1 hour or until yams and apples are tender. Yield: 6 to 8 servings.   Bev Treadway

Burnt Offerings
Women's Auxiliary, Gales Ferry Volunteer Fire Company
Gales Ferry, Connecticut

Jalapeño Spinach

2 (10-ounce) packages frozen
  chopped spinach
¼ cup butter
2 tablespoons all-purpose flour
2 tablespoons chopped onion
½ cup milk
1 (8-ounce) package cream
  cheese, cubed

1 to 3 jalapeño peppers,
  seeded and diced
1 clove garlic, crushed
1 teaspoon Worcestershire
  sauce
Salt and pepper to taste
¼ cup fine, dry breadcrumbs

Cook spinach according to package directions. Drain well, reserving ½ cup liquid. Set spinach and liquid aside.

Melt butter in a heavy saucepan over low heat; add flour, stirring until smooth. Cook 1 minute, stirring constantly. Add onion; stir well. Gradually add milk and reserved spinach liquid; cook over medium heat, stirring constantly, until thickened and bubbly. Add cream cheese and next 4 ingredients; stir until smooth. Add spinach; stir well. Pour into a greased 2-quart casserole. Top with breadcrumbs, and bake at 375° for 20 to 30 minutes or until hot and bubbly. Yield: 4 to 6 servings.   Kate Cadiz Alling

Home on the Range
West Marin Health Project and Dance Palace Community Center
Point Reyes, California

Sour Cream Pattypan

¼ cup butter
2 tablespoons water
1 clove garlic, crushed
½ teaspoon dried whole basil
Salt and pepper to taste

2 pounds pattypan squash,
  coarsely shredded
1 tablespoon all-purpose flour
1 (8-ounce) carton sour cream

Combine first 5 ingredients in a skillet. Bring to a boil; reduce heat to medium. Add squash; cover and cook until tender. Add flour; stir well. Cook until hot and bubbly. Remove from heat; stir in sour cream. Yield: 6 to 8 servings.   Bernice Coulsting

The Delaware Heritage Cookbook
The Delaware Heritage Commission
Wilmington, Delaware

Baked Butternut Squash

1 large butternut squash
3 tablespoons brown sugar
2 teaspoons anise seeds,
 crushed
½ teaspoon salt
½ teaspoon pepper

⅛ teaspoon ground
 cardamom
½ cup butter, melted
2 tablespoons fresh lemon
 juice

Peel squash; cut in half lengthwise, and remove seeds. Cut squash into 1-inch pieces. Place squash in a greased 2-quart baking dish.

Combine brown sugar, crushed anise seeds, salt, pepper, and cardamom in a small bowl; stir well, and sprinkle over squash. Combine melted butter and lemon juice in a small bowl; drizzle over squash mixture. Bake at 350° for 35 to 45 minutes or until squash is tender. Yield: 4 to 6 servings.

Feed My People
Carter-Westminster United Presbyterian Church
Skokie, Illinois

Squash Casserole

2 pounds yellow squash,
 sliced
¾ cup chopped onion
½ cup butter or margarine,
 melted
2 cups Italian-seasoned
 breadcrumbs

1 cup (4 ounces) shredded
 sharp Cheddar cheese
2 eggs, beaten
½ teaspoon hot sauce
Salt and pepper to taste

Cook squash in boiling water to cover until tender. Drain well, and set aside.

Sauté onion in butter until tender. Add squash, breadcrumbs, and remaining ingredients; stir well.

Pour squash mixture into a greased 2-quart casserole. Bake at 350° for 30 to 35 minutes or until thoroughly heated. Yield: 6 servings.

Debbie Smith

What's Cooking?
The Sisterhood of Temple Shalom
Succasunna, New Jersey

Broiled Curried Tomatoes

¾ cup minced onion
½ teaspoon salt
¼ teaspoon sugar
¼ teaspoon curry powder

6 medium tomatoes, halved
¼ cup butter, divided
2 tablespoons chopped fresh
  parsley

Combine minced onion, salt, sugar, and curry powder in a small bowl; stir well. Spread onion mixture evenly over tomato halves. Top each half with 1 teaspoon butter.

Place tomatoes on rack of a broiler pan. Broil 6 inches from heat 8 to 10 minutes or until tomatoes are tender. Transfer tomatoes to a serving platter, and sprinkle with parsley. Yield: 12 servings.

Biscayne Bights and Breezes
The Villagers, Inc.
Coral Gables, Florida

Broccoli-Stuffed Tomatoes

6 medium tomatoes
Salt and pepper
1 (10-ounce) package frozen
  chopped broccoli
1 cup soft breadcrumbs
½ cup (2 ounces) shredded
  Swiss cheese

¼ cup mayonnaise
2 tablespoons chopped onion
2 tablespoons grated
  Parmesan cheese

Cut ½-inch slice off top of each tomato; reserve for other uses. Carefully scoop out pulp, leaving shells intact. Reserve pulp for other uses. Sprinkle inside of tomato shells with salt and pepper, and invert on paper towels to drain.

Cook broccoli according to package directions, omitting salt. Combine broccoli and next 4 ingredients in a large bowl; stir well. Spoon ⅓ cup broccoli mixture into each tomato shell. Place stuffed tomatoes in a lightly greased 11- x 7- x 2-inch baking dish. Sprinkle with Parmesan cheese. Bake at 350° for 30 minutes or until tomatoes are tender. Yield: 6 servings.   Nan L. Martin

Elvis Fans Cookbook, Volume 3
The Elvis Presley Memorial Trauma Center
Memphis, Tennessee

Italian Stuffed Tomatoes

6 large tomatoes
1 (10-ounce) package frozen
  chopped spinach, thawed
½ cup chopped sweet onion
3 tablespoons olive oil
½ cup Italian-seasoned
  breadcrumbs

¼ teaspoon salt
Dash of pepper
2 to 3 tablespoons grated
  Parmesan or Romano
  cheese

Cut ½-inch slice off top of each tomato; reserve for other uses. Carefully scoop out pulp, leaving shells intact. Chop pulp, and set aside. Invert tomato shells on paper towels to drain.

Press spinach between paper towels to remove excess moisture. Set aside. Sauté onion in olive oil in a large skillet 2 minutes. Add tomato pulp, spinach, breadcrumbs, salt, and pepper; stir well. Cook over medium-high heat until thoroughly heated.

Spoon spinach mixture evenly into tomato shells; sprinkle with cheese. Place stuffed tomatoes in a greased 8-inch square baking pan. Bake at 375° for 15 to 20 minutes or until tomatoes are tender. Yield: 6 servings.

Sharon Meyer

From the Hills
The Lutheran of Church of Vestavia Hills, Alabama

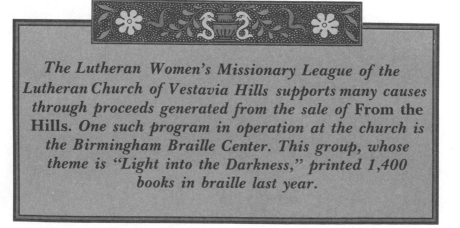

The Lutheran Women's Missionary League of the Lutheran Church of Vestavia Hills supports many causes through proceeds generated from the sale of From the Hills. *One such program in operation at the church is the Birmingham Braille Center. This group, whose theme is "Light into the Darkness," printed 1,400 books in braille last year.*

Shrimp Zucchini Boats

4 large zucchini
¾ pound unpeeled
  medium-size fresh shrimp
1 cup sliced fresh
  mushrooms
1 cup chopped celery
½ cup chopped green
  onions
3 tablespoons butter, melted
¼ cup plus 2 tablespoons
  all-purpose flour
½ teaspoon salt
½ teaspoon dried whole
  oregano

¼ teaspoon freshly ground
  pepper
2 cups (8 ounces) shredded
  Muenster cheese
½ cup chopped water
  chestnuts
1 (2-ounce) jar diced
  pimiento, drained
2 tablespoons grated
  Parmesan cheese
4 slices bacon, cooked and
  crumbled (optional)

Cut a ¼-inch-thick lengthwise slice from top of each zucchini; carefully scoop out pulp, leaving ¼-inch-thick shells. Chop zucchini pulp. Set pulp and shells aside.

Peel and devein shrimp; cut in half crosswise, and set aside.

Sauté mushrooms, celery, and green onions in melted butter in a large skillet 1 minute. Stir in flour, salt, oregano, and freshly ground pepper; remove from heat.

Add reserved chopped zucchini pulp and shrimp to vegetable mixture; stir well. Add Muenster cheese, chopped water chestnuts, and diced pimiento; stir well.

Place one-fourth of zucchini mixture in each zucchini shell. Place stuffed zucchini shells in a buttered 11- x 7- x 2-inch baking dish. Bake at 325° for 20 minutes. Sprinkle top of stuffing evenly with Parmesan cheese and, if desired, crumbled bacon. Bake stuffed zucchini an additional 5 to 10 minutes or until cheese melts. Yield: 4 servings.

Gourmet by the Bay
The Dolphin Circle of the King's Daughters and Sons
Virginia Beach, Virginia

Acknowledgments

Special thanks to Dot Gibson and Ellen Rolfes for their support of this program and for their continuing efforts to promote the sale of community cookbooks throughout America. While each of the cookbooks listed below is represented by recipes appearing in *America's Best Recipes 1990*, the editors also included descriptions of several of these fund-raising volumes to give a sampling of the diverse nature of the books and organizations represented. Unless otherwise noted, the copyright is held by the sponsoring organization whose mailing address is included below.

1838-1988 Out of Our Kitchens, Smith Mills Christian Congregational Church, 11 Anderson Way, North Dartmouth, MA 02747

200th Anniversary Year Cookbook, Christ Evangelical Lutheran Church, 9212 Taylorsville Rd., Jeffersontown, KY 40299

Academic Apron, Middlesex School, 1200 Lowell Rd., Concord, MA 01742

Albertina's II, Albertina Kerr Centers for Children, 424 N.E. 22nd Ave., Portland, OR 97232

Always in Good Taste, St. Anthony of Padua Church, 2456 Kewanee Ln., Cincinnati, OH 45230

Angel Fare, St. Michael and All Angels Episcopal Church, 1704 N.E. 43rd Ave., Portland, OR 97213

Another Taste of Palm Springs, Tiempo de Los Niños, P.O. Box 195, Palm Springs, CA 92263

An Apple a Day, Auxiliary to the Boyd County Medical Society, P.O. Box 1717, Ashland, KY 41105

The Ashfield Cookbook, Ladies' Circle of the First Congregational Church, Main St., Ashfield, MA 01330

As You Like It, St. Bernard's School, 4 East 98th St., New York, NY 10029

The Belle Grove Plantation Cookbook, Belle Grove, Inc., P.O. Box 137, Middletown, VA 22645

Bethany Christian Community, A Recipe Collection, Bethany Christian Community, 2824 E. 18th Ave., Anchorage, AK 99508

Biscayne Bights and Breezes, The Villagers, Inc., P.O. Box 14-1843, Coral Gables, FL 33114

The Bishop's Bounty, St. Mary's Training School for Retarded Children, P.O. Drawer 7768, Alexandria, LA 71306

Black-Eyed Susan Country, Saint Agnes Hospital Auxiliary, 900 Caton Ave., Baltimore, MD 21229

A Book of Favorite Recipes, Sisterhood of the Dormition of the Theotokos, SS. Cyril and Methodius Orthodox Church, 34 Fairview Ave., Terryville, CT 06782

Bound to Please, Junior League of Boise, P.O. Box 6126, Boise, ID 83707

Breaking Bread Together, Circle of Serbian Sisters, St. Stevan Serbian Orthodox Church, 240 N. Cassady Rd., Columbus, OH 43219

Burnt Offerings, Women's Auxiliary, Gales Ferry Volunteer Fire Co., Rt. 12, P.O. Box 307, Gales Ferry, CT 06335

Calling All Cooks Two, Telephone Pioneers of America, 3196 Hwy. 280 S., Room 301-NA, Birmingham, AL 35243

Cal Poly Pomona 50th Anniversary, Home Economics Alumni Association, 3801 W. Temple Ave., Pomona, CA 91768

Calvary Collections, Nurture Committee of Calvary Lutheran Church, 2200 Hwy. 2 East, Kalispell, MT 59901

Capital Connoisseur, Lawrence Center Independence House, 2660 Albany St., Schenectady, NY 12304

Celebrated Seasons, Junior League of Minneapolis, 428 Oak Grove St., Minneapolis, MN 55403

Celebrations on the Bayou, Junior League of Monroe, 2811 Cameron, Monroe, LA 71201

Central Texas Style, Junior Service League of Killeen, P.O. Box 1106, Killeen, TX 76540

Chestnut Hill Cookbook, Chestnut Hill Senior Services Center, 8700 Germantown Ave., Philadelphia, PA 19118

A Collection of Recipes, Worcester Country School Development Office, 508 S. Main St., Berlin, MD 21811

Columbus Collection, Magnolia Homes Tour, Inc., P.O. Box 817, Columbus, TX 78934

Company's Coming, Junior League of Kansas City, 4651 Roanoke Parkway, Kansas City, MO 64112

Con Mucho Gusto, Desert Club of Mesa, Inc., 331 E. Hackamore, Mesa, AZ 85201

Cook 'em Horns: The Quickbook, Ex-Students Association of the University of Texas, P.O. Box 7278, Austin, TX 78713

Cooking with the Skins, National Multiple Sclerosis Society/National Capital Chapter, 2021 K St., N.W., #100, Washington, DC 20006

Cookin' with the Lion, Penn State Alumni Association, 105 Old Main, University Park, PA 16802

A Cook's Book of Recipes from the Pacific Northwest, Rosehill Community Center, P.O. Box 81, Mukilteo, WA 98275

The Cooks' Book, Nightingale-Bamford School, 20 East 92nd St., New York, NY 10028

CordonBluegrass, Junior League of Louisville, 627 W. Main St., Dept. R99, Louisville, KY 40202

Country Cuisine, Arvada Women's Club, Box 133, Arvada, WY 82831

Crème de LA Coast, Small World Guild-Childrens Hospital of Orange County, 10 Jamestown, Irvine, CA 92720

Crème de la Congregation, Our Saviors Lutheran Church, 1035 Carol Ln., Lafayette, CA 94549

Critics' Choice, Corinth Theatre Arts Guild, P.O. Box 435, Corinth, MS 38834

The Delaware Heritage Cookbook, Delaware Heritage Commission, 820 N. French St., Wilmington, DE 19801

Delicious Decisions, Junior League of San Diego, 210 Maple St., San Diego, CA 92103

Diamonds in the Desert, Woman's League of Ozona, P.O. Box 1552, Ozona, TX 76943

Dining In, Young Woman's League of Westport, 10 Bay St., Suite 87, Westport, CT 06880

Dobar Tek, Yugoslav Women's Club, 4214 S. Holly St., Seattle, WA 98118

Educated Taste, LaGrange College Alumni Association, 601 Broad St., Box 17, LaGrange, GA 30240

Elizabeth H. Brown Humane Society Cookbook, Elizabeth H. Brown Humane Society, Inc., P.O. Box 102, Orleans, VT 05820

Elvis Fans Cookbook, Volume 3, Elvis Presley Memorial Trauma Center of Memphis, P.O. Box 238, Welcome, NC 27374

Exclusively Rhubarb Cookbook, Charity Cookbook Fund, 200 Broad Way, Coventry, CT 06238

The Farmer's Daughters, National Multiple Sclerosis Society, #1 Jefferson St., P.O. Box 365, St. Charles, AR 72140

Favorite Italian Recipes, St. Theresa Guild of Holy Rosary Church, 365 E. Washington Ave., Bridgeport, CT 06604

Favorite Recipes, Sponsor's Club, Robert Louis Stevenson School, P.O. Box 657, Pebble Beach, CA 93953

Favorite Recipes from Friends, Town Hill School, Interlaken Rd., Lakeville, CT 06039

Favorite Recipes from St. Paul's, St. Paul's Episcopal Church, Main St., Millis, MA 02054

Feed My People, Carter-Westminster United Presbyterian Church, 4950 Pratt, Skokie, IL 60077

Finely Tuned Foods, Symphony League, 9009 High Dr., Leawood, KS 66206

Flavors of Cape Cod, Thornton W. Burgess Society, P.O. Box 972, Sandwich, MA 02563

The Florida Cooking Adventure, Florida Federation of Women's Clubs, 215 E. Lime St., Lakeland, FL 33801

Food for Thought—Just Desserts, The Shipley School, Yarrow Street, Brownell House, Bryn Mawr, PA 19010

From Scratch Cookbook, Assistance League® of Glendale, 1305 California, Glendale, CA 91206

From the Grapevine, Crossroads Guild of Indianapolis, 3242 Sutherland Ave., Indianapolis, IN 46205

From the Hills, Lutheran Church of Vestavia Hills, 201 S. Montgomery Hwy., Vestavia Hills, AL 35216

The Gathering, Blue Bird Circle, 615 W. Alabama, Houston, TX 77006

Gatherings, Junior League of Milwaukee, 626 N. Broadway, Milwaukee, WI 53202

Georgia on My Menu, Junior League of Cobb-Marietta, Inc., P.O. Box 727, Marietta, GA 30060

Gingerbread . . . and all the trimmings, Junior Service League of Waxahachie, P.O. Box 294, Waxahachie, TX 75165

The Golden Apple Collection, White Plains Auxiliary of the White Plains Hospital Center, P.O. Box 8, Gedney Station, White Plains, NY 10605

Gourmet by the Bay, Dolphin Circle, International Order of the King's Daughters and Sons, P.O. Box 8335, Virginia Beach, VA 23450

Gourmet LA, Junior League of Los Angeles, Farmers' Market, 3rd and Fairfax, Los Angeles, CA 90036

A Grand Heritage, Heritage Academy, P.O. Box 9251, Columbus, MS 39701

The Heart of Adirondack Cooking, Women's Fellowship, 2 Stewart Farrar St., Warrensburg, NY 12885

Hearts and Flours, Junior League of Waco, 6801 Sanger, Suite 160B, Waco, TX 76710

Hemi-demi-semi Flavors, Chamber Music Society of the North Shore, 670 Longwood, Glencoe, IL 60022

Heritage Cookbook, Catholic Diocese of Fargo, 1310 Bdwy, Box 1750, Fargo, ND 58102

Home on the Range, West Marin Health Project and Dance Palace Community Center, P.O. Box 867, Point Reyes, CA 94956

Hudson Cooks, Hudson Community Playground, P.O. Box 2201, Hudson, OH 44236

Jackson Hole à la Carte, Jackson Hole Alliance for Responsible Planning, P.O. Box 2728, Jackson, WY 83001

Keeping the Feast, Episcopal Church Women of St. Thomas Church, P.O. Box 627, Abingdon, VA 24210

The Kentucky Derby Museum Cookbook, Kentucky Derby Museum, 704 Central Ave., Louisville, KY 40208

Knollwood Cooks II, Christian Women's Guild, Knollwood United Methodist Church, 12121 Balboa Blvd., Granada Hills, CA 91344

Korn Brew, Durham Elementary Parent Organization, Frances E. Korn School, Maiden Ln., Durham, CT 06422

Land of Cotton, John T. Morgan Academy, P.O. Drawer P, Selma, AL 36702

La Salette's Favorite Recipes, La Salette Shrine, 947 Park St., Attleboro, MA 02703

Lasting Impressions, Saint Joseph's Hospital of Atlanta Auxiliary, 5665 Peachtree Dunwoody Rd., N.E., Atlanta, GA 30342

The Less Fat Cookbook, Cancer Education and Prevention Center, 380-34th St., Oakland, CA 94610

Libretto, Opera Society of Fort Lauderdale, 333 Southwest 2nd St., Fort Lauderdale, FL 33312

License to Cook New Mexico Style, New Mexico Federation of Business and Professional Women, Penfield Press, 215 Brown St., Iowa City, IA 52245

The Little Gourmet Cookbook for Children, Auxiliary of the Children's Hospital of Philadelphia, 34th and Civic Center Blvd., Philadelphia, PA 19104

Lorimor Centennial Cookbook, Volume II, Centennial Committee, Box 125, Rt. 2, Lorimor, IA 50149

M.A.E.H. Cook Book, Michigan Association of Extension Homemakers, 301 S. Michigan Ave., Hastings, MI 49058

Make It Miami, Guild of the Museum of Science, Inc., 3280 S. Miami Ave., Miami, FL 33129

Merrymeeting Merry Eating, Regional Memorial Hospital Auxiliary, 58 Baribeau Dr., Brunswick, ME 04011

The Minnesota Ethnic Food Book, Minnesota Historical Society, 690 Cedar St., St. Paul, MN 55101

More Memoirs of a Galley Slave, Kodiak Fishermen's Wives Association, P.O. Box 467, Kodiak, AK 99615

. . . More Than Cookies!, Northwest Georgia Girl Scout Council, Inc., 100 Edgewood Ave. N.E., Suite 1100, Atlanta, GA 30335

Mothers of Twins Cookbook, Twice as Nice, Mothers of Twins Club, 4508 Hi-Line Rd., Gillette, WY 82716

Mountain Memories, American Cancer Society, West Virginia Division, Inc., 2428 Kanawha Blvd. E., Charleston, WV 25311

Movers & Shakers Cookbook, Lake County Public Library, 1919 W. 81st Ave., Merrillville, IN 46410

The Mystic Seaport All Seasons Cookbook, Mystic Seaport Museum Stores, 39 Greenmanville Ave., Mystic, CT 06355

The Oaks Cookbook, Colonel Timothy Bigelow Chapter, DAR, 140 Lincoln St., Worcester, MA 01605

Off the Hook, Junior League of Stamford-Norwalk, 748 Post Rd., Darien, CT 06820

One Hundred Years of Sharing, Calvary Covenant Church Women, 404 Meeker St., Evansville, MN 56326

One Magnificent Cookbook, Junior League of Chicago, Inc., 1447 N. Astor St., Chicago, IL 60601

Only in California, Children's Home Society of California, 2727 W. 6th St., Los Angeles, CA 90057

Our Favorite Recipes, Azara Club of St. George Melkite Greek-Catholic Church, 425 16th Ave. S., Birmingham, AL 35205

Our Favorite Recipes, St. Edmond's Church, 2130 S. 21st St., Philadelphia, PA 19145

Our Town Cookbook, Peterborough Historical Society, 19 Grove St., Peterborough, NH 03458

Palm Country Cuisine, Junior League of Greater Lakeland, Inc., 2020 Crystal Grove Dr., Lakeland, FL 33801

Parishables, St. Paul's Episcopal Church, 2747 Fairmount Blvd., Cleveland Heights, OH 44106

Parker's Blue Ribbon Recipes, Parker Ward Relief Society, Rt. 2, Box 27-A, St. Anthony, ID 83445

Pegasus Presents, Pegasus of Germantown, Inc., P.O. Box 382113, Germantown, TN 38138

Pesach Potpourri, Sinai Akiba Academy, 10400 Wilshire Blvd., Los Angeles, CA 90024

A Pinch of Salt Lake, Junior League of Salt Lake City, P.O. Box 6163, Salt Lake City, UT 84106

Pioneers of Alaska Cookbook, Pioneers of Alaska Auxiliary #4, Box 101547, Anchorage, AK 99510

Please Cook with Children, Please Touch Museum, 210 N. 21st St., Philadelphia, PA 19103

Port's Galley, Port Council of Port of Portland, P.O. Box 3529, Portland, OR 97208

Pot Luck, Village Green, P.O. Box 210, Temple, NH 03084

Quiltie Ladies Scrapbook, Variable Star Quilters, 16 Harbor Pl., Souderton, PA 18964

A Rainbow of Kosher Cuisine, Baltimore Chapter of Hadassah, 4000 Glengyle Ave., Baltimore, MD 21215

Rave Revues, Lakewood Center Associates, Lakewood Center for the Arts, P.O. Box 274, Lake Oswego, OR 97034

Recipes and Remembrances, Upsala Area Historical Society, Box 35, Upsala, MN 56384

Recipes Begged, Borrowed, Stolen, Highland Grange #48, Park St., Huntington, MA 01050

Recipes to Cherish, Women's Missionary and Service Commission, Harrisonburg Mennonite Church, 1552 S. High St., Harrisonburg, VA 22801

RSVP—Recipes Shared Very Proudly, First Church of Christ, 689 Hopmeadow St., Simsbury, CT 06092

St. George Women's Auxiliary Cookbook, St. George Women's Auxiliary, 94-9th Street, Oakland, CA 94607

A Samford Celebration Cookbook, Samford University Auxiliary, S.U. Box 2302, Birmingham, AL 35229

Sampler, Women's Art Guild, Laguna Gloria Art Museum, P.O. Box 5705, Austin, TX 78763

Savannah Style, Junior League of Savannah, P.O. Box 1864, Savannah, GA 31402

The Scott & White Collection, Scott and White Memorial Hospital Auxiliary, 2401 S. 31st St., Temple, TX 76508

Seasoned with Sun, Junior League of El Paso, Inc., 520 Thunderbird, El Paso, TX 79912

The Second Helping of the Happy Cooker, Tifereth Israel Sisterhood, 403 Moody Ave., New Castle, PA 16101

Second Round, Tea-Time at the Masters®, Junior League of Augusta, Inc., P.O. Box 3232, Augusta, GA 30904

Secret Recipes II, 4450th Tactical Group, Nellis Air Force Base, Las Vegas, NV 89115

Shamrock Specialties, Trinity High School Foundation, 4011 Shelbyville Rd., Louisville, KY 40207

The Share-Cropper, Central Delta Academy Parent-Teacher Organization, Rt. 1, Box 4, Inverness, MS 38753

Simply Sensational, TWIGS, Auxiliary of the Children's Medical Center, One Children's Plaza, Dayton, OH 45404

Sinfully Good, Catholic Library Association, 461 W. Lancaster Ave., Haverford, PA 19041

A Slice of Nantucket, St. Mary's Guild, St. Mary-Our Lady of the Isle Church, Federal St., Nantucket, MA 02554

Sooner Sampler, Junior League of Norman, Inc., 300 W. Main, Norman, OK 73069

Southern Elegance, Junior League of Gaston County, P.O. Box 3684, Gastonia, NC 28053

Southern Secrets, SouthTrust Corporation, P.O. Box 2554, Birmingham, AL 35290

South of the Fork, Junior League of Dallas, 8003 Inwood Rd., Dallas, TX 75209

The Spence Collection, The Spence School, 22 E. 91st St., New York, NY 10128

Spokane Cooks!, Spokane Community Centers Foundation, E. 2500 Sprague, Spokane, WA 99202

Stanford University Medical Center Auxiliary Cookbook, Stanford University Medical Center Auxiliary, 300 Pasteur Dr., Palo Alto, CA 94305

State Hospital Cooks, Patient/Staff Advocacy Committee, Vermont State Hospital, 103 S. Main St., Waterbury, VT 05676

Steeped in Tradition, Junior Service League of DeLand, P.O. Box 1372, DeLand, FL 32721

Stir Crazy!, The Junior Welfare League of Florence, P.O. Box 3715, Florence, SC 29502

Symphony of Tastes, Anchorage Youth Symphony, P.O. Box 240541, Anchorage, AK 99524

A Taste of Almost Heaven, Monongalia Arts Center, P.O. Box 239, Morgantown, WV 26505

A Taste of Salt Air and Island Kitchens, Ladies Auxiliary of the Block Island Volunteer Fire Department, Beach Ave., Block Island, RI 02807

Taste of the Town—Second Serving, Charity League of Lexington, P.O. Box 722, Lexington, NC 27292

Thou Preparest a Table Before Me, East Avenue United Methodist Church Women, 800 East Ave., York, NE 68467

The Thresher Table, Bethel College Women's Association, P.O. Box 178, North Newton, KS 67117

Thymes Remembered, Junior League of Tallahassee, Inc., 259-B John Knox Rd., Tallahassee, FL 32303

Treasured Recipes from Camargo to Indian Hill, Indian Hill Historical Society, 8100 Given Rd., Cincinnati, OH 45243

The True Essentials of a Feast, Library of Congress/LC Cooking Club, 101 Independence Ave., S.E., Washington, DC 20540

Two and Company, St. Thomas' Church, Garrison Forest, 232 St. Thomas Ln., Owings Mills, MD 21117

Very Innovative Parties, Loma Linda University School of Dentistry Auxiliary, P.O. Box 382, Loma Linda, CA 92354

VIP Cookbook, Volume VI, American Cancer Society, Virginia Division, 124 Park St. S.E., Vienna, VA 22180

West Central Vegetarian Cookbook, West Central Seventh Day Adventist Church, 1154 Wisconsin, Oak Park, IL 60302

We, The Women of Hawaii Cookbook, We, The Women of Hawaii, 67-230 Kupahu St., Waialua, Oahu 96791

What's Cooking?, Sisterhood of Temple Shalom, 215 S. Hillside Ave., Succasunna, NJ 07876

What's Cooking in Philadelphia, Rotary Club of Philadelphia, 1422 Chestnut St., Suite 402, Philadelphia, PA 19102

Woman to Woman Cookbook, Zonta Club of the Black Hills, P.O. Box 8163, Rapid City, SD 57709

You Can't Be Too Rich or Too Thin, Southampton Hospital, 240 Meeting House Ln., Southampton, NY 11968

Index